Guide to Postproduction *for* TV *and* Film

Guide to Postproduction
for TV *and* Film

Managing the Process

Second Edition

Barbara Clark
Susan J. Spohr

Focal Press

An Imprint of Elsevier Science
Amsterdam   Boston   London   New York   Oxford   Paris
San Diego   San Francisco   Singapore   Sydney   Tokyo

Focal Press is an imprint of Elsevier Science.

 Recognizing the importance of preserving what has been written, Elsevier Science prints its books on acid-free paper whenever possible.

Library of Congress Cataloging-in-Publication Data
A catalog record for this book is available from the Library of Congress.
Clark, Barbara, 1959–
    Guide to postproduction for TV and film : managing the process / Barbara Clark and Susan J. Spohr.—2nd ed.
        p.   cm.
    Includes index.
    ISBN 0-240-80506-2 (pbk.)
    1. Motion pictures—Editing.   2. Video tapes—Editing.   I. Spohr, Susan J., 1955–
II. Title.
TR899 .C58 2002
778.5′235—dc21

2002072053

British Library Cataloguing-in-Publication Data
A catalog record for this book is available from the British Library.

The publisher offers special discounts on bulk orders of this book.
For information, please contact:

Manager of Special Sales
Elsevier Science
200 Wheeler Road
Burlington, MA 01803
Tel: 781-221-2212
Fax: 781-221-1615

For information on all Focal Press publications available, contact our World Wide Web home page at: http://www.focalpress.com

10 9 8 7 6 5 4 3 2 1

Printed in the United States of America

Contents

Acknowledgments

As with the first edition of our book, this edition has been a collaborative effort in the truest sense. We again relied heavily on the unselfish contributions of many friends and colleagues to augment our own knowledge and research. We hope they are pleased with the way we incorporated their information into this effort.

We would like to include in this edition the special thanks extended to those who read the first book and provided feedback: Jacqui Adler, Jeanne Beveridge, Selma Brown, John Caper, Leo Chaloukian, Mike Dahruty, Robert Dennis, Rich Garibaldi, the late Suzanne Gervay, Barbara Good, Rick Greenhead, Doug Lackey, Jay Melzer, Les Morford, Golda Savage, Merle Sharpe, Paul Stambaugh, Ioanna Vassiliadas, and Eric Weissler. They had the most time-consuming job of any of those who helped us.

The Second Edition was made possible with help again from many of our friends and colleagues. Most notably we would like to thank Richard Greenberg, Schawn Belston, Revis Scott Call, Jean-Luc Moullet, Ken Quain, Dan McLellan, and Jeff DeWolde.

As always, the most special thanks and appreciation goes to our husbands and child: Fred Spohr, Gary P. Clark, and Bailey Clark. Thanks for all your support.

Introduction

Welcome to the second edition of our book, where we introduce you to the wonderful, wacky, unpredictable, fun, funny, and stressful world of film and television. You'll love it and you'll curse it. But, ultimately we hope to help you enjoy it as much as we do.

In this book we focus on the *postproduction* aspects of making movies and television programs. Postproduction encompasses all steps that take place between production and final delivery. The person who manages this process is called a postproduction supervisor or associate producer. While geared toward these positions, producers, line producers, and those just learning the business will also find this book essential.

Postproduction is a job that, if done well can be both personally and financially rewarding. If done badly, can be miserable (although you may still be rewarded financially—it's a funny business that way).

We have organized this book with the hope of making it nearly idiot proof. Making it completely idiot proof seemed silly because then any old idiot could do it and pandemonium would surely erupt. You'd have idiots running around playing associate producers and producers, moving upward to becoming executives. . . . Wait! This is a little to much like art imitating life. Let's just say that we tried to write a book that will help those who use it.

In this, the second edition of our book, we have made some changes and added some very useful new information. It's been four years since the first edition hit the stands and a lot has changed. Advances have been made in our business of postproduction that you need to know.

You'll find the following changes and updates as you read through this edition.

Chapter 1, Scheduling:

This chapter has been expanded to include more information on feature postproduction for those responsible for completing and delivering movies for theatrical distribution, be it delivery of conventional film or for the new digital cinema.

Chapter 2, Budgeting:

The budget chapter is full of good tips and guides outlining what to include in a postproduction budget and how to direct costs and avoid common mistakes. Our readers have told us they are looking for even more guidance to help with actually gathering vendor bids and plugging in the numbers. Even though we still can't provide exact figures (it is impossible to make generalizations about how much things cost), we have provided more specific guidelines to help anyone putting together a postproduction budget.

Chapter 3, Digital TV & High Definition:

Digital Transmission of television signals and the amazing resolution of high definition videotape are two items that have become integral parts of postproduction. This chapter explains the differences between digital television and high definition television, along with their benefits and drawbacks. It also gives the Federal Communications Commission's (FCC) plan for implementing the rollout of this technology.

Chapter 4, The Film Laboratory:

Next we move onto the film laboratory. A very complete chapter in its own right, you might wonder what else we could include.

Even though some may decry that the end of film is coming, the laboratory business just does not bear that out—at least not yet. Sure, we're seeing more material shot with high definition cameras and effects created digitally, instead of optically in the lab. For the most part, most major motion pictures are still shot on old, dependable film. But, to keep up with the changing expectations of moviegoers and the advances in film processes, many filmmakers (even independents) are incorporating some pretty creative "film processes" into their moviemaking. Steps that call for special baths, silver washes, etc. are referred to as "special handling" in the lab. We'll discuss these lab options so you will understand what to order and budget for when the cinematographer or director requests them as part of your dailies film processing.

We've also added a more detailed section on film damages—how to recognize and understand different types of damage, causes, cures, and preventions. Your film negative is your most precious asset and when the unthinkable happens, often the only thing that saves you is quick thinking and a thorough understanding of your options.

YCMs (yellow/cyan/magenta): We've added a section in this chapter explaining what color separations are and how and when to generate them. YCMs or color separations are the most trusted and proven elements for film preservation and archive. Many years ago, movie studios were more apt to create YCMs for their movies as a means of preservation. These were stored in climate-controlled vaults or the various salt mines around the country used for this purpose. Then sometime 20 or 30 years ago, studios stopped spending the extra money to create these film elements for every film and many films have been lost or severely damaged without any backup materials with which to recreate the negatives.

Fortunately, YCMs are coming back into style as studios and producers realize what a valuable and long-term marketable commodity they have in their motion picture assets. Also, the loss of many films considered "classics" has helped reinforce the fact that special care must be taken to preserve these cultural records of our history for generations to come.

As film stocks change and improve, handling procedures for film (especially exposed, unprocessed negative) must change. This is further enhanced by the tragic events of September 11, 2001, which resulted in increases in airport security and the use of more and more powerful x-ray equipment.

We provide information on the best ways to ship your exposed and unexposed film stock.

Chapter 5, Dailies:

Several years ago, many nontheatrical shows started shooting their images protected for possible projection in the 16 × 9 aspect ratio. This was a preemptive strike against the inevitable beginning of digital and high definition broadcast TV, which adopted 16 × 9 as its aspect ratio. The change was made even though broadcast was still in 4 × 3 (the shape of almost all consumer TVs and monitors sold, even today).

High definition (HD) has finally found a slightly more stable and promising place in the consumer marketplace. With the FCC edict that all networks broadcast at least some primetime programming in HD, productions have been forced to deal with delivering material appropriate for high definition, 16 × 9 and digital broadcasting.

In the previous edition of this book, we did sprinkle 16 × 9 wherever appropriate but didn't include HD because there wasn't anything very definitive to write about. Now there is. So it's here in this edition. We start in Chapter 3 and then continue here, in the Dailies chapter, explaining about HD dailies and then bring it up again wherever it applies throughout the book. This is designed to both educate you, the reader, and help you make efficient and informed decisions throughout the postproduction of your show.

Another area of the dailies process that has evolved is the concept of "tapeless" dailies. Transferring your daily footage from either film or videotape to a hard drive or disk storage system. As computer hard drive and disk storage space costs decrease, the use of this process will increase. We'll walk you through some of the more popular scenarios.

New distribution systems for dailies and other postproduction elements have surfaced and become more economically and logistically viable. We'll discuss some of those systems and information distribution options for you.

Chapter 6, Editorial (Film Editorial and Video Off-Line Editing):

We still find there is sometimes confusion between what constitutes "off-line" and how it differs from the "on-line" process. We are often asked to explain these two steps in the postproduction process. Therefore, we added a more detailed definition of these two processes in hopes of further unraveling the mystery that continues to surround them.

Changes in the way some dailies are handled (for example, high definition or tapeless systems), are impacting the editorial process and how your editors will handle, log, and use the dailies materials. We have expanded this section to explain these changes and their impact on the postproduction of your project.

There is also a new section on desktop editing and some of the new methods and equipment that are being employed.

Chapter 7, On-Line Editing:

As with off-line, we have provided a more detailed explanation of the on-line process and what its role really is in the completion of your project.

In addition, high definition posting has brought about high definition on-line. So, read on as we walk you through what is available now and how that is changing the way some productions are posted.

Chapter 8, Sound:

As the foreign sales market continues to explode on all fronts, creating and delivering materials to service that market have become a standard place for the postproduction manager. To aid in this new challenge, we have added in-depth sections in this chapter to help you with such items as what is a *foreign laugh pass* and how you make one. Also, we tell you how to make materials for *foreign language dubbing* and what to do if you have to create foreign language tracks.

As with video, new sound recording formats have come on the scene. Some of them are an improvement; some bring with them added costs and concerns for the postproduction team. We cover some of the more popular elements that may be offered to you by your sound facility.

In addition to new physical sound formats, there are also additional sound formats such as 5.1 and DolbyE for which we provide definitions and instructions on mixing.

Chapter 9, Completion:

This has always been a big chapter that includes many important steps necessary to complete your project—whether it be film or video. However, we think we can be even more helpful by providing additional information on such items as film opticals (the hows and whens), AB printing, formatted dupes, etc. Film-out is also a reality for some projects that create all, or some, of their picture elements using computers or video and then need to generate film elements of these pieces. If this applies to you, you can now turn to the this chapter and find the answers you need.

This is a chapter where we have also included high definition information, where needed.

Theatrically, e-cinema or digital cinema is becoming more prevalent—especially in larger markets. The steps taken to complete your movie for a digital cinema release differ from the traditional film laboratory processes. We provide a step-by-step guide to help you create materials for digital cinema distribution.

Chapter 10, Delivery:

At this point in your project, you have too much invested to drop the ball at the eleventh hour. Follow the guidelines in this chapter to ensure your materials reach the right person at the right place and at the right time. In this edition, we've expanded the existing checklists, paper trail tips, sample formats, and letters to include new elements and distribution outlets.

Chapter 11, Legal:

How do you know when you need to consult an attorney? Well, we give you guidelines, tips, and even specific situations to help you make this decision. So, even though this chapter appears at the end of the book, you may want to peruse it at the beginning of your project.

Chapter 12, Acquisition:

Acquisitions are products which are "acquired"—stuff that, whether you made it or not—you are now responsible for either delivering or distributing. Several factors such as budgets, experience, and multiple distributors make this type of product very unique in both the completion and distribution areas. Read this chapter and learn the pitfalls before they trip you up; and avoid some very common mistakes that mean less money for the producers and even a cancelled schedule.

Chapter 13, The Future:

Without the aid of a crystal ball, we've pulled together our thoughts of what is ahead for postproduction. Then we coupled that with the opinions of others in our business who we work closely with. This chapter is the culmination of all of the opinions, plus some facts about technology that is currently being worked with in both R&D and in limited application in the real world. Time will tell how closely we've called it.

In the first chapter, Scheduling, we've laid out the steps necessary to post a show and the order in which to complete those steps. The subsequent chapters then explain each of the steps in detail.

In each chapter, we cover the three possible scenarios of postproduction: shooting and finishing on film, shooting on film and finishing on videotape, and shooting and finishing on videotape. We also provide all of the steps you will be required to complete to deliver your product both domestically (in the United States) and internationally. As you read, you will learn about budgets and how costs are calculated, what happens to film when it disappears into the chemical bowels of the film laboratory, how to set-up and manage a cutting room, how to plan and carry-out cost-effective on-lines, color correction, and titling sessions. There are numerous anecdotes throughout to help illustrate points and aid you in avoiding expensive and embarrassing mistakes. And, sometimes just to entertain.

Figures I.1 to I.4 are a series of flowcharts to help illustrate the paths that each method of postproduction will travel.

Shows that use the process in Figure I.1 are feature films, high profile, large budget TV and cable movies, and a few large budget TV series.

Figure I.1 Film Shoot to Film Finish

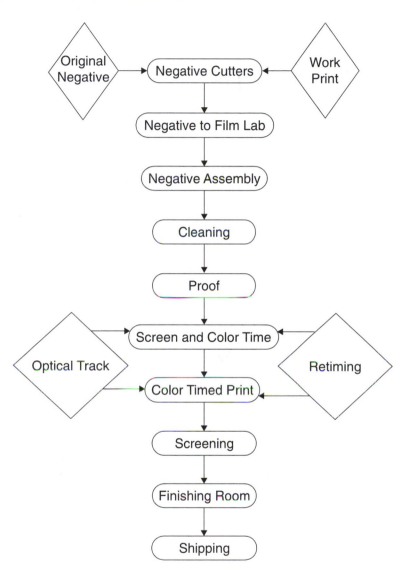

Shows that use the process in Figure I.2 are shot on film and posted on video-tape, for commercials, student projects, TV series, straight-to-video movies, and documentaries.

Figure I.2 Film Shoot and Videotape Finish

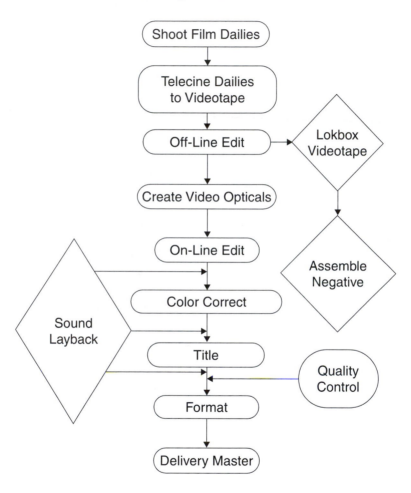

Shows that use the process in Figure I.3 are shot on vide and posted on video-tape, for commercials, student projects, TV series, straight-to-video movies, and documentaries.

Figure I.3 Videotape Shoot to Videotape Finish

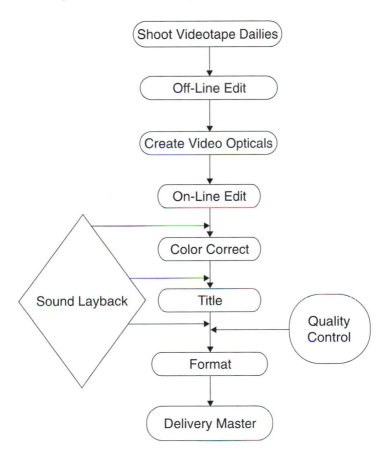

Figure I.4 Creating an Electronic Negative Flowchart

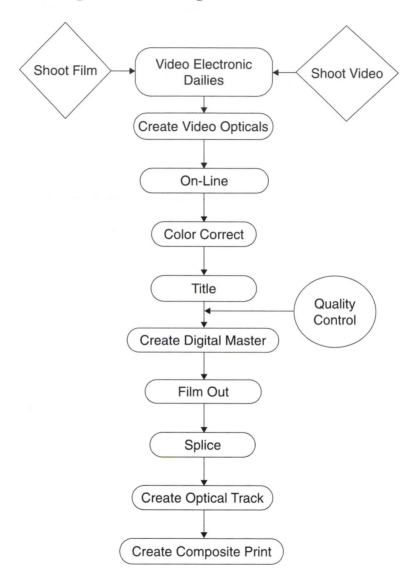

Who Does What and for Whom?

Something else we've added is organizational charts of the various postproduction and show managers and crew. Figures I.5 and I.6 illustrate the reporting structure for these jobs. Bullet point lists highlighting the responsibilities of each position follow these. There may be other jobs assigned to these positions, depending on the size of the project and the budget. But, this should give you a fair idea of what you can expect to be assigned to should you take one of these jobs.

Figure I.5 Management and Crew Flowchart

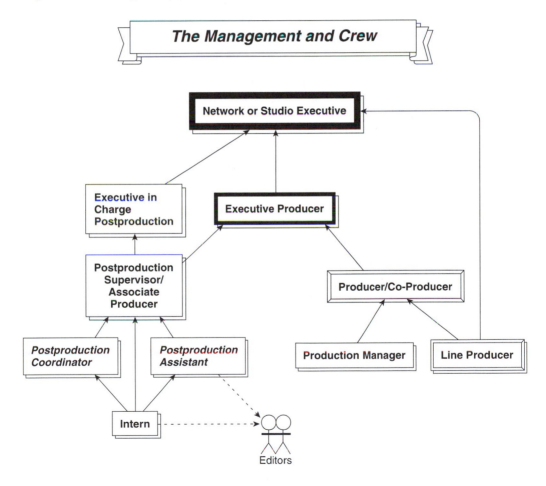

The Management Team

Executive Producer/Co-Executive Producer

- Answers to the Network or Studio Executive
- Ultimately responsible for completion of the project
- Concentrates on the business end of the project and assumes the financial responsibility
- Usually has little time to offer input into technical issues
- May be the owner or head of the production company
- May have multiple shows in production simultaneously
- A show may have more than one executive producer

Producer/Co-Producer

- Answers to the Executive Producer
- Works with attorneys to determine distribution license fees and contract details with distributors
- Has creative input
- Has budgetary authority
- A member of the project team from pre-production through delivery
- Works on one show at a time

Line Producer

- Answers to the Executive Producer and/or the Producer
- Works closely with the Production Manager during principal photography
- Works on the budget and production schedule for principal photography and probably second unit
- On smaller projects the Production Manager may assume this role and be listed as Line Producer in the credits
- Works on one show at a time

Production Manager

- Answers to the Producer
- Responsible for budgeting
- Responsible for scheduling
- Supervises all day-to-day production-related activities
- Is on a project from pre-production through the end of principal photography
- Usually works on one series or movie at a time
- This is often a union position

Executive in Charge of Postproduction

- A studio or network executive
- Provides list of studio or network delivery requirements
- Oversees creation of delivery materials
- Has little creative authority

Postproduction Supervisor/Associate Producer

- Answers to the Producer and Executive in Charge of Postproduction
- Manages all aspects of postproduction, including budgeting, scheduling, editing, sound, mixing, and color-correction
- Creates and delivers final elements to the distributor(s)
- May have some creative input

Postproduction Coordinator

- Answers to the Post Production Supervisor and the Producer
- Works closely with the editors
- Coordinates mountains of paperwork and all film/tape/audio materials
- Keeps track of stock footage and its paperwork
- A key source of communication during postproduction
- Record keeper for the postproduction department
- Manages materials movement

Postproduction Assistant

- Answers to the Postproduction Supervisor
- General assistant to the Postproduction Supervisor
- Assists editorial crew by filling in when editorial assistant or production assistant is not available
- Helps to track down, and coordinates movement, of stock footage, special effects elements, and other materials
- May be responsible for the boxing and inventory of delivery elements

Intern

- Answers to the Postproduction Supervisor and editorial staff
- Helps the postproduction staff wherever needed
- May be paid a token salary or work for college credits
- This is an entry-level position

Figure I.6 Postproduction Staff Flowchart

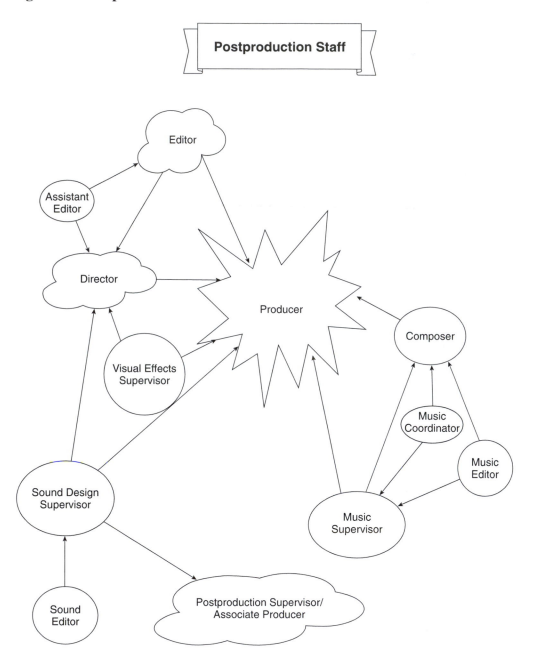

The Postproduction Staff

Editor

- Answers to the Producer and the Director
- Responsible for editing the dailies together, creating the *Editor's Cut*
- Has extensive creative input
- This may be a union position

Assistant Editor

- Answers to the Editor and the Director
- Synchronizes, digitizes (enters sound and picture information into the hard drive of the computer), and logs the dailies materials (picture and track)
- Catalogues and tracks all elements for the editor (i.e., negative, dailies videotapes, sound, print dailies, stock footage, script notes, and any other necessary materials)
- Stays on payroll through delivery to help box and catalogue delivery materials
- There may be one or more assistants on a project
- This may be a union position

Sound Design Supervisor

- Answers to the Producer, the Director, and the Post Supervisor
- Works closely with the Editor
- Responsible for supervising creation of the final sound elements that make the finished sound track

Sound Editor

- Works for the Sound Design Supervisor
- Cuts the audio track to match picture utilizing all the sound elements including effects, production audio, and ADR
- Prepares the audio materials for the sound mix

Music Supervisor

- Answers to the Producer, the Composer, and the Post Supervisor
- Coordinates creation of the musical score
- Prepares the visual materials and cue timings for the Composer
- Supervises music mixdown for dub
- Coordinates materials for the sound mix

- Recommends and purchases prerecorded musical material
- May also act as Music Editor
- May be a union position

Music Editor

- Works for the Composer and with the Music Supervisor
- Prepares and cuts the musical score and purchased musical cues
- Attends music mixdown

Music Coordinator

- Works for the Composer and Music Supervisor
- Coordinates purchase of prerecorded music cues
- Assists composer with duplication of sheet music and other administrative duties
- May also be the Music Supervisor

Visual Effects Supervisor

- Answers to the Producer and the Director
- Works with the Picture Editor and Postproduction Supervisor
- Keeps detailed records of all components used in building visual effects
- Creates visual effects budget
- Supervises the entire effects

How to Use This Book

You can utilize this book in two ways. You can sit down and read it cover to cover. When you are done, you will know postproduction. You can also use this book as a reference to guide you through each phase of your job as needed.

We hope this literary effort gives you aid and comfort on your journey through the postproduction maze. The twists and turns can seem confusing but with our help, you can make it through to the end.

We have guided many TV movies, dramas, situation comedies, and specials through these steps. Along the way, we made mistakes, some expensive, some just embarrassing. The information in this book is necessary for successful film and video postproduction. There is humor in this book because we believe that to do this job, it is essential to keep the job in perspective. And, keeping a sense of humor helps.

We recommend hard work and **above all, have fun!** This job demands hard work, so remembering to have fun can be the hard part.

1 Scheduling

In *Webster's Dictionary*, schedule is defined as:

1. list of details
2. a list of times of recurring events; timetable
3. a timed plan for a project

All three of these definitions apply to postproduction scheduling. This type of scheduling is an art form. Primarily, you are expected to commit to paper a plan encompassing every single step of postproduction, from dailies to delivery. Each phase is dependent on the successful completion of the previous phase. Translation: your schedule needs to be flexible and you need to be very organized and possess a lot of patience.

Once you have mapped out your postproduction schedule and committed it to paper, it is distributed to the show's executive producers and producers, the studio, network executives, and countless others. And, at any given moment, anything can (and usually will) happen to change your schedule. These interruptions can be caused by, but not limited to, bad weather, an ill actor, or the whim of a studio or network executive. Any of these interruptions may cause a ripple effect through your entire schedule.

Creating a Postproduction Schedule

What will be your timetable? Ultimately, your airdate or release date will determine your delivery date (or the delivery date the network has established). If you don't deliver, your show doesn't air. It's that simple.

The areas that the postproduction supervisor or associate producer (possibly even the producer in a videotape shoot/finish show) is responsible for scheduling are listed below. The time allotted for each phase depends, mainly on whether your show is on film or tape and whether it's a half-hour sitcom, an hour-long episodic, a movie of the week (MOW), or a TV or theatrical "feature."

For shows working with videotape dailies, some studios and production companies believe that the use of electronic off-line (nonlinear) editing systems (editing by computer) allows schedules to be accelerated. Others budget more time into their TV projects and call them "features," —a word that traditionally has been reserved for theatrical releases. This is typical of the competitive cable networks. TV and theatrical features have longer schedules to allow for more automatic dialogue replacement (ADR), music, and special effects. More time is required to complete the final audio mix because more audio tracks are involved. In the end, the production executives hope they have a richer, bigger show that will guarantee better ratings than your average MOW.

When posting an MOW, one-hour episodic, half-hour (sitcom), or other special programming, many of the steps are the same and are completed in the same order. The time it takes to complete each step may vary. Some steps may not be necessary for every show.

Here is a list of the basic postproduction steps that you will go through to complete your project and the general order in which these steps will happen. At the end of the chapter are samples of various postproduction schedules.

Always keep the distributor's delivery date foremost in your mind. It is usually tied to an airdate and therefore unchangeable.

Elements of the Postproduction Schedule

1. Principal photography
2. Dailies
3. Second unit photography
4. Editor's cut
5. Director's cut
6. Producer's cut
7. Temporary on-line/temporary dub
8. Network/studio view
9. Picture lock
10. Opticals and film titles
11. Test theatrical screenings
12. Negative cut
13. On-line/assembly edit
14. Answer print (film)
15. Spotting music and sound effects

16. ADR/looping
17. Scoring
18. Color correction (videotape)
19. Prelay/predub
20. Titling (videotape)
21. The print before first trial
22. Mix/dub
23. Fully-formatted answer print
24. Interpositive/duplicate negative
25. Composite answer print
26. Theatrical release prints
27. Delivery duplication/air masters
28. Delivery
29. Air date/release date
30. Overnight ratings

Principal Photography

The principal photography stage is when your primary footage is shot. There is a beginning date and an ending date. When scheduling postproduction for a TV project or feature, you must know the first and last days of principal photography, whether a second-unit shoot is planned, and the delivery date. Knowing the first day of principal photography and the date you must deliver your final master provides the parameters necessary to fill in the rest of the schedule.

For example, a half-hour sitcom will shoot 1 to 2 days per episode. An hour-long episodic will shoot 4 to 8 days per episode. A MOW will shoot 13 to 22 days, and a four-hour mini-series will shoot 25 to 40 days. These are rough estimates. The complexity of the show and the budget determine the exact number of shooting days per program. Situation comedies shoot more than one day when preshoots are scheduled. These are usually scenes that are shot, ahead of time and then transferred and edited together to show to the live audience on the day of principal photography. This material could be used for playback on the set (on a TV monitor) or to show the audience key story points that are shot at another location.

You must be aware of the days of the week you are shooting and whether any Friday night or weekend laboratory processing and telecine transfers are planned. There will be extra charges for weekend work, and it is necessary to alert the lab and telecine house as early as possible so they can staff accordingly. These additional charges may also affect your budget.

Dailies

"Dailies" is the footage that is shot each day, when you are shooting film for either a film-finish or tape-finish show, you rush the footage to the lab each day to have it processed and printed or transferred to videotape for viewing the next day. By shooting on tape, you eliminate the laboratory and telecine processes. But the material you shoot still constitutes "dailies."

When plotting dailies transfer time on your calendar for an episodic or MOW, remember that the actual transfer time will run at least one day behind the day the footage is shot. Film shot on Tuesday gets processed Tuesday night and transferred overnight in the early hours of Wednesday. For multicamera sitcoms, 1 to 2 days of production will take 2 to 3 days to transfer, depending on the number of cameras shooting, the amount of film shot, production values, and the number of shifts per day dedicated to the transfers.

Be sure to read the "Dailies" chapter carefully. If you are planning to transfer your film dailies to videotape, there are many details you will need to provide to your telecine house before they can begin. This is in addition to scheduling the laboratory that will be processing your film.

Second Unit Photography

The entire production unit that shoots the bulk of the footage does not shoot these dailies. They are shot by a small skeleton crew called the second unit, which is made up of either fewer members of the original crew or an entirely different group. Sometimes second unit material is shot simultaneously with the principal dailies while other times it is shot after principal photography has ended. Some shows even start shooting second unit material and establishing shots at the beginning of their shooting schedule.

A second unit crew may shoot establishing shots, inserts, pickup shots, and effects back plates, among other things. Second unit shoots are often shot MOS (without sound) or with wild sound (sound not meant to be matched to picture during the dailies transfer). Once shot, second unit material is handled just like the normal dailies in terms of processing, transfer, and editing.

Editor's Cut

On print daily shows, the editor responsible for creating the "editor's cut" is called the film editor. When cutting electronically, the first version of the project is cut together by the off-line editor. This version is the foundation for the final show assembly. Very often the editor's cut closely resembles the final cut of a show. Shots are assembled from dailies according to the blueprint provided by the script—often with a little help from the director. Being familiar with all of the varying takes, the editor chooses the better takes of each scene. Once all the dailies are shot and delivered to the cutting room, the editor has 1 to 2 days for assembly of episodics and sitcoms, and no more than 6 days, per the Director's Guild of America (DGA), for MOWs and TV movies or projects that have a running time of more than an hour.

Always refer to your guild contracts, as these guidelines may change at any time and can vary depending on the circumstances of your program.

Director's Cut

Once the editor's cut is complete, the director screens the cut. All changes made by the director, become part of the director's cut. Now the director sets the pace of the show, shortening (tightening) and lengthening scenes as the director deems necessary. This cut shows the producers how the director envisioned the movie when it was shot. The director's cut goes to the production company and sometimes to the network executives to view.

Unless the director invites them, it is illegal (per the DGA) for anyone other than the editorial staff to be in the cutting room before the director has finished. Breaking this rule can result in costly fines to the production company. Current Guild rules governing the number of days for the creation of the director's cut allow 1 day with an additional day for changes for 30-minute shows, 15 days for 90-minute MOWs, 20 days for 120-minute programs, and longer for features. If in doubt about the rules, call the DGA. Some directors are very strict about these rules, so exercise caution. Don't second-guess when making the schedule. Stick to the rules.

In TV, the director's job is officially done when shooting is completed and the director's cut has been delivered. Because of TV's fast pace, a new job is often waiting and the director often leaves before the picture is locked. However, the director may supervise the automatic dialogue replacement (ADR), or looping session and the second unit shoot, as well as being present at the final audio mix. The director must be informed when each step is scheduled to take place and where the sessions will be held. It is not incumbent upon the director to participate, but it is an option depending on the director's availability.

Producer's Cut

Following the director, the producer creates a version of the program. This version may or may not incorporate part or all of the director's cut and any other production footage. Producers usually take 2 to 5 days to screen the director's cut and complete their version. The producer's cut will then go to the production company executives and usually the network to be screened. Even in a half-hour sitcom, several versions (called producer's cuts and labeled PC #1, 2, 3, etc.) may be created for executives and the network to view. We have seen seven and eight producer's cuts go out for a single show before everyone was satisfied. In one instance, four copies of each version were sent to the production company and seven VHS copies were sent to the network executives. These costs can really add up.

Temporary music and effects may be incorporated into the producer's cut. With film, special effects not created during production are often too expensive to make for the screening of a producer's cut, since they might not be used in the final version. With electronic off-line editing, simple special effects can be created quite easily by your off-line or on-line editor. Simple titles can be added to help round out the effect. These extras are traditionally saved for use on MOWs, pilots, and theatrical test screenings, as are temporary on-lines and temporary dubs.

Temporary On-Line/Temporary Dub

The producers may decide to create a more completed version of the producer's cut, rather than simply making dubs of the off-line cassette or sending out the work print as is. They spruce up the cut a bit with a temporary on-line and temporary music. These added steps are the exception to the rule and are often saved for use on pilots, MOWs, and cable shows with anticipated foreign theatrical releases. This is an added expense that may not have been included in the budget at the start of the process. The money to do this may have to come from somewhere else in your budget.

Network/Studio View

Once the producer is satisfied with the "producer's cut" videotapes of this version are delivered (on VHS or three quarter-inch [3/4"]) and everyone waits (and waits and waits) for the network notes—usually 2 or more days later.

Picture Lock

Once all the network notes have been addressed, your picture is considered "locked," meaning all of the changes to the cut have been done and approved. This stage is often referred to simply as "picture lock." At this point in a show that has been shot on film, you order the negative cut to begin. For electronic shows, you are ready for on-line. Sound and music editors will need to receive their materials as soon as possible.

Opticals/Simple Visual Effects

You will create film opticals for your cut negative at a laboratory or optical house. It can take a week or longer for the laboratory or optical house to create your optical elements. The more complicated the effect, the longer the process.

For a tape finish, simple opticals can sometimes be incorporated into the on-line session. Be aware that the postproduction facility (or postproduction house) may separate out the time spent in the bay creating opticals and visual effects and charge that time at a higher rate. Double-check the breakdown of your charges before the session begins.

When the electronic opticals are too complicated to be done during an assembly, you can build your electronic opticals or effects before or after your on-line.

This optical master is now part of your on-line source material. These more complicated effects may require several sessions to complete.

Theatrical Test Screenings

Theatrical test screenings are also known as:

> Test Screenings
> Test Audiences
> Sneak Previews
> Advanced Presentations

Test screenings are held for the purpose of measuring audience reactions to a story and its characters. They are also used to gauge the target market for a film. In other words, does the audience laugh and cry where they are supposed to and which age/gender group enjoyed the movie most? The goal is to give the producers and marketing department ideas about how to best market the film, and if story changes need to be made. If changes are made, the film may be tested again to see if the changes were effective. Blockbuster high budget studio backed features test often to give their films the best possible chance.

Negative Cut

All film-finish shows must complete a negative cut. The editor will provide the negative cutter with a completed work print. If you have done an electronic off-line, the negative cutter will ask for a cassette (called a LokBox cassette) and a paper list called a negative cut list or negative conform list. Depending on the number of edits and the amount of time it takes to create all of your opticals and cut them into your cut negative, this process can take a week for an MOW or several weeks for a feature.

On-Line/Assembly Edit

As soon as the picture is locked you can go into on-line editing. In the on-line session, the picture is assembled from the master source elements. You schedule an on-line or assembly session only if you are creating a videotape master.

Simple effects and opticals can also be part of the on-line process. In the on-line or auto-assembly session your show is assembled from your dailies master tapes using the edit decision list (EDL) provided by your off-line editor. Briefly, an EDL is a list made up of all the edits and the corresponding source material that make up a show. An EDL created for a negative cut will include film edge numbers that tell the negative cutter where to cut. An EDL for an electronic on-line includes the "in" and "out" timecode numbers off the videotape master source reels. More information on EDLs is provided in the "Editorial (Film Editorial and Video Off-Line Editing)" chapter.

The ideal situation is to wait to do the on-line until the picture is locked. But, with TV schedules being what they can be, you rarely find yourself in an "ideal" situation. Assembling your show before the picture is locked is rarely an issue with sitcoms and episodics because the format is so short you don't buy much time by rushing the on-line before the cut is completed. But MOWs and mini-series may fall prey to this piecemeal form of assembly. Often the on-line for these 2- to 4-hour shows gets rushed so that work tapes can be made for the sound and music editors, the special effects and graphics creators, and the composer. These folks can then have the maximum amount of time to create their magic.

Answer Print

A film-finish requires that you approve either the first trial/answer print or a proof print, depending on time and budget. A proof print, made from the color timings, is a slide show or filmstrip made up of one to three frames from each scene in the show. A Hazeltine is one machine on which the color-corrections are made. The first trial is the first full print viewed for corrections. Often the director or cinematographer attends. Whether you view a full answer print or a proof print, there will probably be adjustments to the color. If so, a second check print is struck and the process is repeated for the corrected areas until you, the client, are satisfied. What you end up with is either a scene-to-scene color-corrected print or a batch-timed print, depending on your budget and the purpose of making the print. Batch-timing is achieved by grouping many scenes together on one "light" or "color-correction" setting. The answer print is the final print.

Spotting Music and Sound Effects

During music and sound effects spotting, decisions are made regarding the placement of music cues and sound effects. The director, producer, editor, and associate producer view the picture with the composer and special effects supervisor to discuss the various music and effects cues and where they should be placed.

On film-finish shows, this is done either on the flatbed in the cutting room or on a rock-and-roll projector either in a rented room or at a studio. A rock-and-roll projector has the ability to play film backwards and forwards so you can view sections of your film over and over. On videotape projects, cassettes are created for the group to view. This is often done in someone's office or in the off-line edit room.

The addition of sound effects is necessary for two reasons. First, sound effects are added for creative composition. Second, many sound effects, called ambient sound effects, may originally have been recorded as part of the dialogue track. If this original dialogue recording is replaced by looping or dubbing into a foreign language (rather than subtitling), any ambient sound effects recorded as part of the dialogue track will be lost. These effects will have to be recreated as part of a separate audio track called the effects track.

Your sound, music, and effects editors, along with the composer, will all require work elements as soon as possible. For film this will be black and whites and one-to-ones. When cutting electronically, call your music supervisor and effects supervisor and find out the technical requirements for their videotape copies. These will be their working copies of the show. Make sure the music supervisor and effects people know whether you are finishing on film or videotape, as their preparation and tape specifications will be determined by the format you are working with. If at all possible, have these working elements available at the time of the spotting session.

ADR/Looping

ADR (automatic dialogue replacement) is also referred to as "looping." Here dialogue is rerecorded after shooting is complete to replace unusable original production sound. A MOW looping session will usually take 1 day for the "loop group," 2 days for supporting actors, and 1 to 2 days for leading actors. A loop group, sometimes called a Walla group or an ADR group, is a collection of people hired to rerecord dialogue and background voices. (See the "ADR/Looping" section in the "Sound" chapter for more details on what you will need and when to start scheduling this step.) For a special or episodic, 1 day should cover all participants. Looping is not normally done for a sitcom.

Scoring

The score is all the music used in your television show. Any original music is written by a composer. Some composers score using electronic instrumentation. This is known as electronic scoring. They usually work out of their homes or in small studios. The director and producers sit with the composer several times during the postproduction process to evaluate and provide direction for the scoring. If the score is not produced electronically, you will need to book a scoring stage.

Some composers hire a group of musicians and record on actual sound stages (see the "Music/Scoring" section in the "Sound" chapter). This type of scoring is seldom seen in television anymore and is reserved almost exclusively for movies (and even many movie scores are done electronically). If you are using this method for a pilot or MOW, allow 1 day to record the music. Then allow 1 day between the recording and the dubbing stage for the music editor to cut the music.

Your music supervisor will know how many sessions you will need to book. The musicians' union governs the length of time a musician can work without a break. Your music supervisor will help you be sure you don't incur penalties.

Color Correction

Color corrections are done either film-to-tape or tape-to-tape. This is the final time you alter your picture before the credits are added. In color-correction, the picture is evened out on a cut-by-cut basis so the shots flow together with a planned consistency of hue and balance.

The details of a film-to-tape color-correction session will depend on a couple of factors. A MOW being color-corrected from negative or interpositive (IP) may take 2 1/2 to 3 days. A theatrical movie can take from several days, if unsupervised, to many weeks depending on the complexity of the project and who supervises the transfer. From a low-contrast (locon) print, you should finish in 2 days. If the original negative was shot unevenly or the cinematographer is supervising the color-correction, the process may take a little longer. A tape-to-tape correction will take about as long as it takes to correct from a locon.

Color correcting a one-hour episodic from negative or IP may take 1 1/2 to 2 days. From a locon print you should finish in an 8- to 10-hour day. Again, the condition of the original negative, and the original dailies film transfer, as well as the session supervisor, will affect the actual time needed.

A half-hour sitcom should take half the time of an episodic. If you elected to color correct your sitcom dailies, a color-correction session should not be necessary. Again, all the factors listed above will affect your final session time.

Prelay/Predub

If your show includes a lot of sound effects, then your sound effects supervisor may recommend a prelay/predub. This is intended to make the actual dub go more smoothly and easily by reducing the number of individual effects cues and pots the mixer has to control simultaneously. When working on an MOW, your sound effects supervisor and one mixer should be able to complete this in 1 day. More involved projects, such as a feature, will usually take longer.

Titling

In the case of film, this is the point at which you order your title opticals, or credits, and have them spliced into your cut negative. Find out who needs to sign off on the titles prior to ordering the opticals from the optical house or laboratory. Then determine who needs to approve them visually prior to having them spliced into your cut negative. Unlike video, creation of film titles requires a much longer lead time and any changes will have to be shot again by the optical department. It will take several days or longer for the creation of your credits, and changes can take just as long.

Providing credits for the titling of your program is a long, ongoing task. If you are working for a large studio, the credits will usually be provided to you. If you are working for an independent, you often are left to figure them out for yourself.

When creating electronic titles, you can sometimes deliver a computer disk formatted from the original credit list that was typed at the production office. This copy will already have been approved by all and spelling will have been checked. You can simply save your credit data file to a text file on a 3.5″ floppy disk, or CD-ROM, and deliver that to your titling facility. This can eliminate the need for the credits to be retyped at the facility, thus eliminating mistakes due to human error.

It is best to begin the process of compiling and finalizing credits as early into the project as possible. You don't want this to hold up completion and delivery. The producer and other executives often take for themselves the fun job of picking the type style (font), color, and layout (flips, pushes, or wipes) of the credits you so painstakingly compile.

The chapter on "Completion" provides additional information and helpful hints.

Print Before First Trial

This is a film print made from an original negative prior to completion of the color correction process. This print may contain slugs (placeholders) for the main and end titles and any unfinished opticals. With any luck the negative can be submitted to the laboratory early enough so the timer can make some of the color adjustment before this print is stuck. This gives the filmmaker an opportunity to see how the color correction is going. This print is run with the sound mix prior to making an optical sound track negative. This insures that your picture and track are in sync. This print is also used for test screenings.

Mix/Dub

This is one of the most time-consuming and creative events in the entire postproduction process. The producers, director, composer, music supervisor, editor, sound effects supervisor, and sound mixer go through the show scene by scene, making decisions about the placement of music and effects cues and adjusting audio levels.

When all the separate dialogue, music, and effects tracks are completed, they are mixed down onto an unused track (or tracks) of the multitrack element. These tracks become the master sound track or final mix, which is then laid back or dubbed onto the sound track of the videotape master. This master sound track is also the element used to create an optical track in the case of a film-finish project.

The sound dub for an MOW will take up to 3 days and 2 or 3 mixers. Schedule an entire day for an episodic and a half-day for a sitcom. In Canada and on some stages in the United States, dubbing involves one mixer, who mixes the sound sources one at a time. This method can take up to 5 days for a MOW. Whichever method you use, the show opening will traditionally take the longest to dub. When doing an MOW, try to complete 20 to 30 minutes of program each day. This will help keep you on schedule.

If during the session you see that you are going to go over the time allotted, quietly notify the producer. If you need more time than originally budgeted, someone will need to determine if it is more cost-effective to rack up some overtime or add another day to the dub. These additional costs are probably outside of any package deal.

If your show is going to have a laugh track, be sure to schedule the time for your laugh session as early as possible. There are only a handful of laugh guys around. They book up quickly during the TV season, and they don't come cheap.

Fully–Formatted Dupe and Answer Print

If your film is shot with an academy aperture, you've exposed the whole film frame except a strip along one edge where the sound track will be placed. If your film is shot full frame, also known as Super 35, you have exposed the entire film frame leaving no room for a sound track. This aspect ratio is a creative choice giving the film a widescreen or CinemaScope size.

In order to add a sound track to this aspect ratio, there is an extra step you must go through in the film laboratory. First, an interpositive (IP) is made. Then, when the internegative (IN) is struck from the IP the original image is made slightly smaller and moved to the right. This is called formatting. Sound can then be added to the print made from this IN. The result is a check print made from a formatted dupe or a composite answer print.

Interpositive (IP)

This is a print of the original negative on special stock. This stock is made as an intermediate element to serve several purposes. It is a protection element, in case your original negative is damaged. It is an intermediate step to making an interneg- ative or opticals. It can also be used as the transfer medium to master to video. Both Kodak and Fuji make IP stock.

Internegative (IN)

This is a copy of your original negative, made from a positive element. In the case of release printing you may make several of these from which to print. This will help protect your original negative from damage due to over handling. If you use a scene twice in your film, you will need to make an IP of that section. From the IP you'll strike a color corrected acetate dupe (referred to as a dupe neg) to cut into your original negative.

Be sure when making IN elements to cut into your original negative so that the IN segments are made on acetate stock. This is very important because nonacetate stock will not splice properly to your original negative stock. Also, they are different thicknesses so the splice will cause a bump and focus problems at that point. Ultimately the splice will come apart.

Composite Answer Print

This is the first time you see the picture and track together on a big screen. This print is struck only when the color correction process is complete and you have delivered the optical sound track negative to the lab. This is an exciting screening.

A word of caution: Do not invite guests, i.e., actors, agents, etc. to this first screening. View this with the film lab personnel and your post crew to make sure it's in sync and the picture looks good.

Release Prints

These are prints made from dupe negatives. They will be made dry (no wetgate) and will begin to show a small amount of dirt printed in it, as the negatives continue to be used. The prints will be shipped on cores, with trailers and ratings tags added to the heads and tails to theatres around the world. If this is your first film, go to the lab's shipping department where they stack the finished prints and have your picture taken with all the reels of your film.

Delivery Duplication/Air Masters

Delivery dubs are the final tapes delivered to the network, the production company, and the distributor. Some of these tapes are closed-captioned and require special formatting. The networks always require their tapes be delivered with drop-frame timecode. International delivery requirements will vary from network requirements.

If delivery tapes are closed-captioned, you will do this in either a separate formatting session or at the time the dubs are made. See the section on "Closed Captioning" in the "Completion" chapter for more details.

Included in the delivery dubs are the air master and probably an air-protection copy. The full complement of tapes required varies widely from network to network and from production company to production company.

Delivery

At this point the distributor (network, foreign, cable, etc.) actually accepts delivery of your show, meaning all of the delivery requirements have been met. Be sure you know whom you are expected to deliver to, their address, and the exact delivery date and time specified. We cannot stress enough how important it is that you know and understand your delivery requirements from the start of the project.

Air Date

This is when your friends and family sit down in their living rooms and watch for your name to appear on their TV sets. This moment is why we do what we do. Well . . . this and the money. It's a nerve-racking time because if something airs incorrectly, there is no way to take it back.

Overnight Ratings

Regional overnight ratings (called overnights) are available the morning after your show has aired. Nationals become available a couple of days later. To get these numbers, call the network contact for your project. Knowing ratings numbers is not required, but everyone will want them.

Summary

Successful delivery of your show depends on how organized you are and the order in which the steps in your postproduction process are completed. You may very well spend more time updating, reorganizing, and agonizing over your postproduction schedule than you spend on any other part of your job. Any change in that schedule will cause a domino effect that will ripple throughout the entire process—including your budget. Good project management will help ensure that your ripple doesn't become a tidal wave.

It is important that each change to your schedule be incorporated, and the affected steps be adjusted, and everyone involved in your postproduction process be issued an updated schedule in a timely manner. When you are distributing updated schedules, be sure that you deliver them to all your contacts at your various postproduction facilities. It is also a good idea to point out, at least to the postproduction houses, what parts of your schedule have changed. Be sure to date each version of the postproduction schedule that you distribute.

Scheduling Samples

Figures 1.1 to 1.4 are excerpts from sample postproduction schedules. Feel free to pick a postproduction schedule that most closely approximates what your schedule will entail. Use it to help you organize and plan your show's postproduction schedule. There are no extra points for reinventing the wheel.

Figure 1.1 Feature Postproduction Schedule

Last Day of Principal Photography	Insert Date
Re-shoots/Pick Ups	Insert Date
Begin Visual Effects	Insert Date
Editor's Cut	Governed by the DGA. 6 days—Begins promptly after the completion of principal photography.
Director's Cut	Governed by the DGA. Feature: 10 weeks or 1 day in editorial for every 2 days in production, or whichever is longer.
	Low Budget Feature: 6 weeks or 1 day in editorial for every 2 days in production, or whichever is longer.
Producer's Cut	Allow at least 1 week from completion of director's cut.
Test Audience Screening & Previews (may be several)	The number of screenings will be dependent upon the show and its executives. A large budget studio feature, this may take several months. For an independent low budget feature this testing and re-cutting process may take a week or less, if tests are done at all. (The director must be notified at least 24 hours in advance of test screenings.)
Recut (may be several)	This may take 1–3 days.
Studio View	Insert date
Recut	Insert date (if applicable)
Visual Effects Completed & Cut into Work Print	Effects may take two weeks to two months depending upon the work required.
Picture Lock	Insert Date
Begin Ordering Opticals	Allow 2 weeks depending upon the effects
Spotting	2 days, 1 day for sound 1 day for music
Negative Cut	Allow 2 weeks depending upon when the opticals are complete. Insert date that negative cutter gets cut list.
ADR/Looping	Allow 1–2 weeks.
Scoring	Allow 1–3 days (1 day for approximately 20 minutes of music)
Color Correction	10 days
Final Sound Mix	7–10 days or more.
Answer Print	Allow 7 to 10 days after the final roll of complete negative has been delivered to the laboratory.
Interpositive	Allow 2–3 days
Optical Track to Film Laboratory	Processed 1 day prior to final print
Dupe(s)	Allow 2 to 3 days (if a formatted dupe is required, allow 5 days).
Check Print(s) (composite)	1 day after the dupe is completed
Delivery/Access to Distributors	1 day after approval of the final composite print from the dupe or original depending upon the delivery requirements
Release Printing	Allow 2 days for 150–500 prints depending upon the laboratory.
Cast & Crew Screening	Insert Date
Premier/Film Festival	Insert Date

Figure 1.2 Average MOW Film-Finish Sample Schedule*

Principal Photography	20 days
Editor's Cut	2 days
Director's Cut	varies (per DGA)
Producer's Cut	varies
Temp Dub	1 to 2 days
Network View	1 day
Lock Date	3 to 4 days
Negative Cut	3 to 5 days
Spotting	1 day
Spot Music and Effects	1 day
Sound Effects Cutting	7 days
ADR	1 to 2 days
Foley	3 days
Scoring	2 days
Dubbing	3 days
Answer Print	1 day
Delivery Requirements	1 day
Deliver to Network	1 day
Storage of Trims and Work Prints	varies

*The timetables given are approximates and may represent the maximum.

Figure 1.3 One-Hour Episodic Sample Schedule

Show No.	Title	Dir.	Shoot Dates	Editor Cut	Dir. Cut	Studio/ Net. View	Lock	On-Line	ADR	MX FX	Color Correct	TITLE	MIX	Del. Dubs	Avail. for Air	Air-date
101	RED PLANE	COKER	16-Nov to 28-Nov	1-Dec	8-Dec	20-Dec	21-Dec	21-Dec	8-Jan	22-Dec	29-Dec	10-Jan	15-Jan & 16-Jan	18-Jan	18-Jan	22-Jan
102	SOFT GAME	HARD	29-Nov to 7-Dec	12-Dec	14-Dec	22-Dec	28-Dec	28-Dec	4-Jan	29-Dec	8-Jan	8-Jan	11-Jan & 12-Jan	13-Jan	13-Jan	15-Jan
103	HELLO YOU	VAN	8-Dec to 18-Dec	20-Dec	22-Dec	8-Jan	16-Jan	15-Jan	24-Jan	16-Jan	22-Jan	24-Jan	26-Jan & 28-Jan	1-Feb	1-Feb	5-Feb
104	TOAD SONG	HADLE	8-Jan to 18-Jan	18-Jan	22-Jan	29-Jan	31-Jan	31-Jan	6-Feb	1-Feb	6-Feb	7-Feb	6-Feb & 9-Feb	10-Feb	10-Feb	12-Feb
105	HACK	LEE	17-Jan to 25-Jan	29-Jan	31-Jan	6-Feb	7-Feb	7-Feb	12-Feb	8-Feb	8-Feb	13-Feb	14-Feb & 15-Feb	16-Feb	16-Feb	19-Feb
106	JUST US	HARD	28-Jan to 6-Feb	8-Feb	9-Feb	12-Feb	14-Feb	14-Feb	20-Feb	16-Feb	16-Feb	22-Feb	21-Feb & 22-Feb	23-Feb	23-Feb	26-Feb
107	DO IT RIGHT	COKER	7-Feb to 15-Feb	21-Feb	21-Feb	1-Feb	4-Mar	4-Mar	11-Mar	5-Mar	6-Mar	11-Mar	12-Mar & 13-Mar	15-Mar	15-Mar	18-Mar

Figure 1.4 Half-Hour Sitcom Sample Schedule

EPISODE NUMBER	101	102	103	104	105	106
FILM TRANSFER	2-Oct & 3-Oct	11-Oct & 12-Oct	18-Oct & 19-Oct	1-Nov & 2-Nov	8-Nov & 9-Nov	15-Nov & 16-Oct
EDITOR'S CUT	4-Jan	16-Oct	24-Oct	6-Nov	14-Nov	20-Nov
DIRECTOR'S CUT	5-Oct	17-Oct	25-Oct	7-Nov	15-Nov	21-Nov
PRODUCER'S CUT #1	6-Oct	18-Oct	26-Oct	8-Nov	16-Nov	21-Nov
PRODUCER'S CUT #2	9-Oct	19-Oct	27-Oct	9-Nov	N/A	N/A
STUDIO CUT	10-Oct	20-Oct	30-Oct	10-Nov	17-Nov	22-Nov
TEMP ON-LINE	11-Oct	20-Oct	30-Oct	N/A	N/A	N/A
TEMP SWEETEN	12-Oct	23-Oct	1-Nov	N/A	N/A	N/A
NETWORK CUT	13-Oct	24-Oct	2-Nov	13-Nov	20-Nov	27-Nov
ON-LINE	13-Oct	24-Oct	2-Nov	13-Nov	20-Nov	27-Nov
COLOR TIMING	16-Oct	25-Oct	3-Nov	15-Nov	21-Nov	28-Nov
PRELAY	17-Oct	26-Oct	3-Nov	14-Nov	21-Nov	28-Nov
TITLES	17-Oct	26-Oct	6-Nov	15-Nov & 16-Nov	21-Nov	28-Nov
MIX	18-Oct	27-Oct	8-Nov	16-Nov	22-Nov	29-Nov
DELIVER	19-Oct	30-Oct	9-Nov	17-Nov	22-Nov	30-Nov
AIRDATE	TBA	TBA	TBA	TBA	TBA	TBA

Television vs. Theatrical Features

Let's go over the differences between the delivery of TV shows and theatrical release prints and briefly touch on the differences between a TV broadcast and a theatrical release.

When making a theatrical feature, an original negative is cut and an original optical sound track is struck. Once cut, the negative is copied. This is called an interpositive (IP). An IP is a print made on special film stock. From the IP, an internegative (IN) is struck. Usually several internegatives are made and the release prints are made from these. This eliminates the need to go back and reuse the original negative again and again for printing, thus helping to preserve the condition of the original negative. An easy way to remember this process is that film goes negative to positive to negative to positive. When your 35 mm still shots go in for processing, they take the exposed negative from your camera and make prints. If you want reprints and no longer have your original negatives, the lab makes a new negative from your prints and then makes additional prints from that new negative.

In the land of television, it's increasingly rare that negative is ever cut before the final delivery for broadcast is made. The original negative is processed and the selected takes are transferred to videotape for the dailies transfer masters. These masters are used later to assemble your final videotape product. Once your show is assembled and the audio mix is completed, the mix gets laid back to the audio tracks on your videotape in the required configuration and all of your tape copies are made from this original. Well, this is all fine if you are working digitally, because you don't lose any generations in picture quality or sound. However, it doesn't stop here.

You deliver your hit TV show to the network on the specified format. Some networks and cable stations are still taking one-inch (1″), D2, or D3 video format, but many have gone to digital Betacam. Traditionally, the show is copied by the network's video department, formatted (if it was not delivered by you already formatted) and satellited; this transmission is recorded and satellited at airtime in crisp, clean precision, with commercials slugged in the appropriate places.

By the time your gem is broadcast to millions of living rooms across our great land, it has had a long journey. If you are lucky, your program is only three or four generations from the original you delivered. This is one reason why some cinematographers have a love/hate relationship with color-correction. They know that no matter how much they labor over each color-correction, color may change a point or two in transmission. No matter how much work these guys put into the shows, some quality will still be lost (somehow that doesn't stop them from racking up the hours in trying).

The same applies to sound effects and music levels. Shows that are heavy with sound effects and music will require careful attention to audio levels. Widespread digital transmission is still years away. It is amazing, however, that TV quality is as good as it is. Or maybe we should say, as good as it is—sometimes.

2 Budgeting

Only an accountant or a line producer knows budgets well enough to attach human emotions like love and hate to them. They love the feelings of organization and confidence that come with having all your ducks in a row. Yet they hate the fact that no matter how good everything looks on paper, the first little hiccup can toss their budget right out the window unless moneys are factored in to cover the expected unexpected. Knowing all this, these same people will expect you to create a budget before postproduction has started and then expect you to stick to it.

When you are brought in to prepare for postproduction, your first job may be the creation of the budget.

Keep in mind that if your job includes creating a budget, the producers may not give you an exact bottom-line figure, yet they will expect your budget to meet their expectations. You will be held to and benchmarked against this budget throughout the entire postproduction process.

It's helpful to ascertain whether the producer you're working with is more concerned with the product or with cost. In television if a choice has to be made between product quality and product cost, cost often wins out.

We want to be perfectly clear (did we really say that?) that we will not address exact dollar amounts. It would be impossible, and therefore wrong, for us to quote specific figures. Costs to do business vary from year to year. They depend on changing technology, labor, materials costs, stock prices (that's tape and film stock, not your producer's NASDAQ or DOW portfolios), etc. They also vary depending upon the type of project. For example, a facility may be more willing to help out a student or industrial film by giving them special discounts. A large studio that brings a lot of business to a few facilities can usually negotiate a better all around deal than a company or independent film that is only around for one or two projects with no guarantee of long term business. Commercial companies traditionally paid the highest rates—even rate card. In return, they were very demanding, high pressure clients who required a lot of attention and high level of service. The economic down-turns of the past years and lowered advertising dollars have changed the way commercial clients negotiate their rates with postproduction facilities.

So, we know that being a student can bring lower rates. And, we know that being a high volume client can bring lower rates. There are also varying degrees of *lower rates*. Even if you don't have the neediness of a student or the power to bring with you lots of business, you can still negotiate. For example, you could offer all, or much, of your business on a particular project to one or two facilities. That's something.

Negotiating like this is called creating a "package." Package rates should always be lower than the sum of all of its parts. In other words, if you add up the costs for each item separately, that total needs to be more than your package rate. Now, whether that savings is 10%, 15%, or more will depend largely on the scope of your project and the anticipated billing by the facility and your relationship to that facility. Are you a new client or are you someone that is coming back as repeat business? If you have brought multiple shows into a facility, your rates will most likely reflect that relationship. Vendors have to be able to count on a certain amount of repeat business. If you are a new client, be sure to bid your job with several facilities. It is the only way to know if your package is a good deal and it gives you real negotiating power and confidence.

Facilities never want to loose clients and will usually work with you, within reason, on rates and special deals.

The real secret of creating a budget is working through a budget step-by-step, instead of trying to tackle it as one large single task. Show after show, year after year, you will do this and you'll become a master almost without realizing it. The other secret is in the word *math*. Math isn't your strong point, you say? No problem, get a calculator, it's the 21st century, for Pete's sake. After that it's really all just common sense and doing your homework.

It can be daunting to realize that you have to come up with a bottom line number for a postproduction budget *and* be expected to stick with it, especially if this is your first budget. Where do you even start? To help, we've provided a list of necessary tools and handy hints to get you started.

Getting Started on Your Budget

The following are some initial steps you need to take to gather the necessary information for making a budget:

- *Make sure you have an accurate list of all of your delivery requirements*. It is imperative that every area of postproduction is covered in your budget.

Later in this chapter you will find a sample cost of accounting form (Figure 2.1) and a blank sample budget form (Figure 2.2) to help provide you with a checklist of the areas that must be covered. The sample budget form can be adapted for half-hour sitcoms, episodics, MOWs, or longer formats.

- *Know the shoot dates, when the picture must lock, and the delivery date.* Try to determine if these dates are "drop dead" or if there is some flexibility built in that you can use when negotiating with vendors. Armed with this information, and combined with the list of all areas you need to cover in your budget, you are ready to start soliciting realistic bids.

- *Call all your vendor friends.* Being able to call in a favor or two and get a break here or there due to personal relationships may help you negotiate your budget. Many larger production companies have deals and special rates already set up with various postproduction facilities around town. Be sure to check with your executives and producers before approaching houses to make deals on your own.

- *Meet with the vendors to discuss your project.* Discuss with them any special needs or circumstances. These may include, but are not limited to, special effects and opticals, differing film formats, framing issues, special title treatments and graphics needs, delivery schedules and any time constraints, and special voice-overs or narration.

- *Choose your facilities.* Some people like to do each step at a different facility that specializes in a particular area. Many larger facilities offer one-stop shopping. They can handle several or even all phases of your postproduction schedule. Usually you end up with one or two vendors doing all the postproduction on a project.

There are a variety of factors to consider in this step. Sometimes price is the determining factor. Sometimes scheduling conflicts prohibit one facility from doing all of your work. And sometimes producers have promised certain parts or all of your project to a particular facility. A postproduction house is going to want as much of your business as they can get, and it is certainly easier on the entire postproduction process to limit the number of facilities to which you move elements back and forth. The facility may be able to make changes or certain cost incentives to lure you into giving them a larger portion of your business. It's important to consider all of your options.

A Carefully Planned Nightmare

There once was an associate producer who did her dailies and on-line at one facility, sound at another facility, color-correction at a third facility, and duplication at yet another house. Tracking the elements and making sure that everything had been moved from one facility to another for each session was almost a full-time job. And, in tracking any problems that cropped up along the way, it was very time-consuming, and nearly impossible, to accurately determine where a problem had started and decide who should be fiscally responsible for any fixes. Schlepping from house to house at each stage and trying to schedule work around the availability of several facilities and still make deadlines was extremely taxing. Plus, a facility is going to be less inclined to work with you on costs or to bail you out in an emergency if they are getting only a small portion of the entire job.

The following is a list of the postproduction areas you may need to budget to complete your project. Remember that sometimes all of these areas can be handled in one or two facilities.

Areas to Budget

1. Film process and prep for dailies
2. Edit room equipment
3. Postproduction staff (post supervisor, editors, assistants, etc.)
4. Telecine transfer and editorial
5. Titles and opticals
6. Stock shots
7. Sound mix, looping, effects, and layback
8. Postproduction film and lab—interpositive/locon/internegative/check print
9. Test screenings
10. Visual effects
11. Music composition, scoring, editing, purchasing
12. Negative cut
13. Duplication
14. Delivery elements

Understanding Costs and Bids

The vendor will usually give you cost estimates over the phone and follow-up with a hard copy of their proposed package a day or so later. A verbal estimate allows you to start on your budget right away. If you have never done a budget, ask your auditor for a blank postproduction budget. You can then break down the costs as you get them and negotiate your rates.

On the sample cost of accounting form (Figure 2.1), the account numbers 3700, 3800, 4000, 4400, 4500, 4600, 4700, 4800, 4900, 5000, 5100, and 5200 all apply to postproduction. These are the areas highlighted. Some of these areas are broken down further on the sample budget form (Figure 2.2). For the purposes of this discussion we will refer to these sample forms and their account numbers to detail each area your budget will cover. These are the budget line items you must concentrate on when you create your postproduction budget. Please note that each company you work with will provide a budget form for you to use. Each variety of budget form will have its own system of line-item numbers. The ones we use here are for reference and explanation in this book only. Also there are a number of computer budgeting software programs available that can be purchased off the shelf. These come as generic budget spreadsheets and cost-accounting ledgers. Some are industry-specific.

As your bids come back (or as they are provided to you by your company), it will be easier for you to fill in the blank budget. There are several ways to fill in a budget (but we recommend pencil . . . just kidding). Costs can be broken down in a number of ways. It may not be easy at first glance to know whether you have been offered a good deal. Be sure you understand the bids and can translate the dollar amounts to the budget form. Don't be afraid to ask questions!

Not understanding will catch up with you. Someone, usually an executive, will want you to explain a cost and you'll look inept and unqualified if you cannot. Or, someone will explain something to you and you will feel stupid as it dawns on you that you've been had with double-talk.

We don't say things like this to ruffle your feathers or put you on the defensive. We've both been that incapable, unqualified, and stupid person once or twice in our careers and we're hoping to make your way a little easier by pointing out some of the simple traps we can get ourselves into.

When the vendor's bid comes back to you, first break it down into the individual components. Facilities like to give package deals. They should represent a better rate for the client and more profit for the facility by locking in a guaranteed amount of work. However, these bids can be harder to dissect.

Many package deals will not give a specific rate for individual items like tape stock or a per hour rate for say on-line editorial or laybacks. Without an idea of what you will be paying per tape or per hour it's very difficult to compare bids. In this case we recommend calling the facility that gave you the package deal and ask what would the rate be if you needed one hour of editorial or an additional tape. And what will you pay if you exceed the allotted package estimate. This will give you a better idea of what the rate is outside the package.

Knowing what steps will be necessary to complete the job will also help. Perhaps you need to make a full set of theatrical delivery requirements including a release print. So, talk to the laboratory about what elements you'll need to make release prints. You will need to make an answer print (incorporate the final color corrections) from your original negative. You'll need to create an interpositive, a duplicate negative or internegative, and a check print with sound. The facility will give you a bid on the per foot price on making these elements. Further research will reveal that each of these elements will need to be inspected and leadered. The final check print will need to be mounted on plastic reels and put in shipping cases, called Goldbergs. Make sure these items are included in your original bid. Does your bid include labor charges? Those will need to be factored in, so make sure you get these figures.

As you can see, there are a lot of details to some projects. It will benefit you to take the time and learn what is needed to get your job done. You will end up with a more accurate budget that you can stick to.

Purchase Orders

A purchase order (P.O.) is the written record of items purchased or rented and the per-unit cost applied to those items.

If we convince you of nothing else throughout this entire book, we hope to be able to impress upon you how vital purchase orders will be when it is time to reconcile the moneys you authorized to be spent on the postproduction of your project.

Actual purchase orders will vary widely in design and form. But they will all contain the same facts. There will be a place to record the vendor to whom you are issuing the purchase order, what is being ordered, the quantity, the price per unit, and the total dollar amount. Be sure to date all of your purchase orders. Each purchase order will carry its own number. This is your tracking system. Some vendors will require that you provide a purchase order. So, even if you don't set up a system from the start, you will need to be prepared to issue some purchase orders during the postproduction process.

Create a purchase order book or log to track each purchase order number when it is assigned. It will be helpful to note some general information about who that purchase order number went to and what for.

Often production accounting will want a regular tally of your purchase order totals so they can create their budget-to-date and cost-to-complete reports for the producers. These reports tell the producers how much money has been spent to date and provide an estimate on how much it will cost to complete the project.

Purchase order instructions should also include specific information about the service ordered. For example, if a purchase order is made for work cassettes, make sure it names whom the cassettes are for and how they are to be made.

If you are posting a series, each episode needs to have its own separate purchase order numbering system and set of purchase orders. This allows you to quickly and accurately track work for each episode.

When approving invoices and costs, it is convenient to have a hard copy of each purchase order to attach to the actual paperwork to back up the work that was done.

Sample Budget

Before diving into the "detail" area of postproduction we are going to make an important note about protocol. If you are a postproduction supervisor on a project and have the honor of viewing the complete budget for your show (with the summary top sheet attached) behave accordingly. Do not repeat the figures you have seen or the bottom line to anyone. These numbers are privileged information, and the fact that they have been shown to you means that you are respected and trusted. Do not risk your job or your reputation by sharing this information. We have written this book with some humor and light heartedness that is needed in this crazy business, but this advice is not a joke and given in all seriousness.

If you have seen the budget, you will probably be required to attend the weekly budget meetings. The producer, auditor, production manager, and postproducton supervisor are brought together to review how much has been spent to date and how the estimates are holding up. As the postproduction supervisor you will be asked for details relating to moneys spent and estimates of costs to be incurred going forward. These meetings are not meant to put you in the hot seat but a time when everyone can talk about what's been spent and what is expected in the future. Keep your P.O.'s up-to-date and an eye on the schedule and you will do fine.

A Sample Budget

Figure 2.1 shows what the cover page of a project budget may look like, called *The Top Sheet*. This is an accounting of each area that may be included in the budget. The Top Sheet will contain the final amounts budgeted for the entire project, including pre-production, production, and postproduction. On this sheet the page number for each item refers to the page in the full budget where the line items are located. These items are called the *account and detail areas*. A total budget for a project can include many pages. The highlighted areas on the sheet represent all those costs that fall under the purview of postproduction.

Figure 2.2 is a sample page from the actual budget. This shows the line-item breakdowns of the subaccounts in detail. This is where you list each cost separately, and their account totals go into the "total" column on the cover page under their respective account numbers.

The following is an item-by-item description of each line item in the sample budget. For weekly shows you will have a new budget for each episode. For MOWs you will have one budget for the entire completion process of that show.

Figure 2.1 Sample Budget Form

Acct#	Description	Page#			Total
1100	STORY & RIGHTS	1			0
1200	PRODUCER'S UNIT	1			0
1300	DIRECTION	2			0
1400	CAST	3			0
1500	TRAVEL & EXPENSES	3			0
1900	FRINGE BENEFITS	4			0
	TOTAL ABOVE THE LINE	4			0
2000	PRODUCTION STAFF	4			0
2100	EXTRA TALENT	5			0
2600	SPECIAL EFFECTS	9			0
2700	SET DRESSING	9			0
2800	PROPERTY	10			0
3200	LIGHTING	13			0
3300	CAMERA	14			0
3400	PRODUCTION SOUND	15			0
3500	TRANSPORTATION	16			0
3600	LOCATION EXPENSE	17			0
3700	FILM & LAB PRODUCTION	18			0
3800	VIDEO PRODUCTION	19			0
3900	SPECIAL UNIT	19			0
4000	SECOND UNIT	20			0
4100	TESTS	20			0
4200	STUDIO CHARGES	20			0
4300	FRINGE BENEFITS/PRODUCTION	21			0
	TOTAL PRODUCTION	21			0
4400	PHOTOGRAPHIC EFX & INSERTS	21			0
4500	EDITORIAL & PROJECTION	22			0
4600	MUSIC	23			0
4700	POSTPRODUCTION SOUND	24			0
4800	FILM LAB/POSTPRODUCTION	25			0
4900	TITLES AND OPTICALS	26			0
5000	VIDEO POSTPRODUCTION	26			0
5100	STOCK FOOTAGE	27			0
5200	FRINGE BENEFITS-POSTPRODUCTION	28			0
	TOTAL POST PRODUCTION	28			0
6500	PUBLICITY	28			0
6800	GENERAL EXPENSE	28			0
7400	FRINGE BENEFITS-OTHER	29			0
8200	ANCILLARY COSTS	30			0
8300	SECOND RUN COSTS	30			0
8900	ACCOUNTING USE ONLY	30			0
	TOTAL OTHER	30			0
9000	TOTAL FRINGES				
	GRAND TOTAL				

Figure 2.2 Cost of Accounting Form

Acct#	Description	Page#			Total
4900	TITLES				
4920	MAIN TITLES-ARTWORK				0
4921	END TITLES-ARTWORK				0
4922	SUBTITLES				0
4923	LOCALE TITLES				0
4924	OPTICALS-TITLES				0
4985	OTHER COSTS				0
	TOTAL FOR 4900				0
5000	VIDEO POSTPRODUCTION				0
5001	VIDEO EDITING-LAB & FACILITY				0
	OFF-LINE				0
	ON-LINE				0
5002	VIDEO TRANSFER-TELECINE				0
	NEGATIVE				0
	POSITIVE				0
5003	VIDEO LABOR & MATERIALS				0
	PRODUCER COPIES				0
	DIRECTOR COPIES				0
	COMPOSER COPIES				0
5004	VIDEO-NETWORK REQUIREMENT				0
	CASSETTES				0
	AIR TAPES				0
	PROMO				0
5013	EQUIPMENT PURCHASES				0
5014	VIDEO STOCK PURCHASES				0
5016	EQUIPMENT RENTALS				0
5017	STUDIO FACILITIES				0
5020	SATELLITE TRANS. CHARGES				0
5085	OTHER COSTS				0
	TOTAL FOR 5000				0

Film and Lab Production

3700 Film and Lab Production

This section is where you will put all of your costs for items such as laboratory expenses and raw film materials. Video expenses are found in the 3800 account.

3710 Raw Film Stock

This number is based on either a general daily average or the director's known average. Your production manager usually provides this information. Your laboratory can help you estimate this cost based on the type of project you are budgeting. On an episodic or situation comedy, where the director may change week to week, you will want to allow for a change in shooting styles. Some directors will use more film than others. Young or inexperienced directors may tend to shoot more footage (and choose more circled takes). Also, the more cameras that are rolling, the more film that is shot. A conservative estimate is 5000 feet of 35mm film per day for a single camera shoot.

3712 Develop Dailies

This represents the actual dailies footage developed by the laboratory. This number will always be smaller than the amount of film purchased. This figure is based on an equation of 80% of daily average film shot multiplied by the per-foot-developing rate. We have seen the average vary from 60% to 85% and go as high as 90%. Normally, film print dailies come in around 60% of this total. If you are not ordering print dailies, be aware there is a laboratory charge for prepping and cleaning film for telecine transfer. Any special handling charges will be included here.

Video Production

3800 Video Production

Your production manager will usually be responsible for providing this cost. We have included it here because sometimes in shows that shoot on videotape instead of film, this falls under the associate producer's jurisdiction. If you are shooting on film without any video production, you can plug any playback requirements in here. Monitors and other equipment used for playback on the set, or equipment to watch dailies on location, also qualify to be put here.

3814 Videocassette Dailies

To arrive at this number, calculate shoot days times the number of videocassettes plus the costs of stock and duplications that you will be making. Your transfer house will include these totals in their dailies telecine transfer bid. It is possible to collect these cassette tapes when the picture locks and use them on another show if you do several projects for one production company. Unless you are doubling up dailies footage or shooting several cameras every day, budget for a 4-hour telecine session for each day of dailies. You will master to at least one videotape master per day. One deviation will be if you are going directly to another medium such as CD or hard drive.

Second Unit

4000 Second Unit

Second-unit production operates under the DGA umbrella, so traditionally your production manager handles it. As with video production above, there are some circumstances, such as tape-based programs, in which the associate producer will handle this area. Be sure that any playback or additional film and laboratory costs incurred during second-unit production are accounted for. You can add these costs to production's existing film and lab budgets and totals, or break them out separately. Find out how your company prefers to see these costs.

Photographic Effects and Inserts

4400 Photographic Effects and Inserts

Keep a separate accounting for any special effects, animation, or insert shots you shoot or have created. Visual effects budgets have a way of growing exponentially at the blink of an eye. Go to the experts, show them a script, and get their best bids. Unless you have a lot of experience in this area, do not try to guess these costs on your own. Costs may include pin-registered film transfers and videotape-to-film transform. Pinpoint these costs as specifically as you can.

Editorial and Projection

4500 Editorial and Projection

If you are the postproduction supervisor and there is not a separate line item in the budget for your salary, put one in here. Add a couple of extra zeros just to see who's keeping track . . . just kidding!

4501 Editor/4502 Assistant Editor

The editor and assistant editor will have a standard rate and it will be a union-mandated wage or higher—whether or not you are crewing a union show. If yours is a nonunion show, the editor and assistant editor may not insist on strict adherence to the union-mandated hours, but expect to pay extra for weekends and sixth and seventh days. Either you or the production manager may be responsible for negotiating the editor's and assistant editor's rates.

How long the editor stays with a project depends on the project and on the producer. Sometimes for a movie of the week, the editor is let go once the picture locks. The lower-paid assistant editor is often kept on the payroll until the picture is delivered. Some producers will bring the editor back for the audio dub. Check with your producer before committing the editor's schedule to paper.

4503 Apprentice Editors

On a union shoot, there is a set rate for this position. Otherwise, this position is usually paid the same rate as a runner or production assistant (PA). Apprentice editors are brought on staff when the project has a very tight schedule and there is a large volume of film or videotape (or if the producer has committed to hiring someone's kid and there's nowhere else to put them). In TV, they are usually kept on staff until the director has viewed the editor's cut. In features, they work through delivery. It is rare that apprentice editors are employed on episodics or sitcoms. Sometimes when an episodic has a tight postproduction schedule and employs two editors and one assistant editor, an apprentice editor will be brought on to assist the assistant. They still may be required to perform some PA duties, such as pickups and deliveries.

4505 Sound Effects Editor and Assistant

These folks normally come as a package deal with the sound effects company. The sound effects company employs people and their services on behalf of their clients. The salaries for these two positions are usually covered in the package price. Our sample budget discussion has a separate line item for these two positions, as well as the sound effects costs (item 4711). If you are doing the postproduction in a foreign country, you may have to pay a separate rate to the effects editor and assistant effects editor, plus any additional costs for using effects that are not contained in their existing library. In this instance, these positions are on your payroll and you must pay pension, health and welfare, and all applicable taxes.

4506 Music Editor and Assistant

Occasionally this shows up as a line item under the music section of your budget. The music editor and assistant will charge a standard rate for the number of weeks involved. Find out what additional rate will apply should you go beyond the initial contracted time. The price you pay for the music editor will usually include an assistant, but not always, so check. The editor and assistant will be responsible for their own union costs. You will still need to budget for all applicable taxes, such as payroll taxes and pension. There should be no unexpected expenses here unless you have large delays or a rush situation that requires the editor to hire an additional assistant to meet the accelerated deadline.

4511 Film Coding

When dailies are on film instead of videotape, the film is coded with a number that is stamped onto the edge of the film. A corresponding number is stamped in the same spot on the magnetic tape, or mag, so they can be sunk and edited. The film can be sent out to be coded, but more commonly a coding machine is rented as part of the equipment in the cutting room. This is a very necessary expense. Don't let the person approving the budget cut this item. They may not understand how important this is. (Sometimes in this job you have to find a way to play advocate and teacher.)

4512 Script Continuity

Check your foreign delivery requirements. Usually they will call for a continuity script. The continuity person will require a 3/4″ videotape with visible timecode and a final script. The continuity person usually charges a standard fee for a two-hour MOW. They charge by the reel for film shows—even though they receive a videotape and not film. Add the script duplication and videotape dubbing costs to get your total.

4513 Foreign Delivery Requirements

These numbers are often included with the film and lab postproduction costs. For this sample budget, this area covers all foreign videotape masters, standards conversions, interpositives and internegatives, extra film prints, and foreign audio tracks. Refer to your delivery requirements. It is good to keep these foreign costs separate. Then, if the network calls for an audit of your budget (not an uncommon occurrence), these costs won't get mixed in with the domestic expenses. Don't forget to ask about line-up charges for the IP and IN and syncing charges for the sound track. You'll have to allot additional moneys for both.

4514 Screen Dailies/Projection

This covers screening room rental for film shows. All labs provide free screening of your film dailies during regular business hours. If you are running 16mm films, the lab may have only one room available to screen 16mm. So be advised of potential scheduling conflicts at the lab.

Most tape dailies are screened in someone's office or on the set. If you have to rent monitors or VCRs (usually purchasing them is less expensive), put that cost here. If you have to rent a theatre on location, put that cost here, also.

4516 Purchases and Supplies

Put expenses here for film or videotape cutting-room supplies. These will include tape, gloves, grease pencils, film cleaner, office supplies, and telephones. For a tape show this includes primarily office supplies, tape stock, and a phone. Prior to the start of production, get a list of supplies from your assistant editor.

4517 Cutting Room and Equipment Rental

For a film MOW this will include two rooms, chairs, desks, bookcases, film editing benches, sound heads, and rewinds. For a tape show, you will usually rent one large room and a desk and chair per editor, bookcases, extra chairs, and phones. For either scenario, your assistant editor will provide you with a list of necessary supplies prior to the start of production. These numbers also need to include moneys for the Moviola/flatbed and off-line equipment.

4550 Film Shipment

If your film has to be shipped daily from location to the lab and then cassettes shipped back to the set, add these costs in here. If the film lab does not provide a pickup service, you will need to either have a runner available daily to pickup film or hire a messenger service. Even if the lab offers to arrange for the daily pickup and delivery to the airport, they will charge these costs back to the production. Factor in any messenger costs for transporting film to the airport and lab and cassettes back to the airport, and put those costs here. If you are shooting out of the country, you'll also need a customs broker to send film and/or videotape back and forth. Include those costs here.

4585 Miscellaneous Expenses

This is a really good place to include some extra moneys. Expenses such as parking, mileage, the coffee machine, bottled water, and food will go in this area.

Music

4600 Music

This section will include all costs associated with creating the music for your movie or television show. Often a lump sum will be set aside for creation of the music in your show, though sometimes the costs will be more finely itemized—it depends on the composer. A music license (for nonpublic domain scores) is an additional cost. Be sure to itemize each expense. Check the script for any music references and discuss these costs with your producer. The costs for music transfers to prepare for audio-dubbing prep will also go here.

4601 Composer

Often the composer will charge a package price. If not, break down the fees in the sections that follow. Your music supervisor can help you with these costs.

4602 Orchestrators

In some instances your composer will hand off the completion of smaller pieces of the score to a less expensive music writer or orchestrator. The composer writes the first part, or the underlying theme, and the orchestrator will complete the piece. Some composer packages include these costs. If not, they need to be listed separately in this area. Your music supervisor can advise you in this area should you have questions. This may be a union position with set union wages.

4603 Copyists

A copyist transcribes to paper the musical score, sometimes by hand, for each instrument. Today, this is often done on a computer. Your music supervisor can help you estimate any costs here.

4604 Musicians—Score or Prescore

If your composer needs to hire musicians, these costs will be outside his original package deal. You will have to pay these musicians, their union benefits, and any applicable payroll taxes. If the composition is complicated, there is usually a prescore or rehearsal session prior to recording. This would be rare for television.

4608 Singers

The Screen Actor's Guild (SAG) monitors these people and you will be charged for all applicable union benefits and payroll taxes.

4609 Orchestra Contractor

This person is a union orchestra member who watches after the union rules and tracks the musicians' hours and breaks. This individual will handle all of the union paperwork and provide packets of signed W2s, I9s, and contracts for the session.

4628 Studio Time

If you are going to have an orchestral score, a scoring stage will be in your future. Make sure it is also in your budget. Don't forget to add in the mix-down time after the scoring session if your mix-down is being done at the same location as you are scoring. Remember to add in tape stock costs to the session fees.

4646 Music Rights and Licenses

Some shows budget money to purchase already existing music. You can purchase the rights for the lyrics and hire an actor/singer to sing or play the tune. Or, you may purchase the right to use the original recording. You may incur additional costs for uses in foreign markets. Put all related costs here—and they can be costly.

4647 Rental Instruments/Cartage

If your composer writes an orchestral score, the musicians hired may need to rent their musical instruments, if they do not own them, or pay to have them moved from storage to the session (cartage), put those charges here. You may not know these numbers until you are closer to the actual scoring session. The music supervisor can help you with this estimate.

Postproduction Sound

4700 Postproduction Sound

These budget items will include any effects, sweetening, looping, or mixing. Sometimes this number comes as a package flat rate. The company doing your sound transfer can help you estimate these costs to arrive at a reasonable figure. We have provided line items to help you list these costs separately should that be required. This will become necessary especially if you are posting in a foreign country.

4711 Sound Transfer

When posting on film, you will have daily costs for transferring your production audio to a magnetic tape format for use in the cutting room. When your sound is transferred to magnetic tape, the cost will be about 80% of the film developing average. (On many TV shows you don't transfer sound to mag, so this does not always apply.) Studios still get picture film and track deliveries, which they use for audience previews. So you may have to include this in your budget. These costs can be hard to estimate. An MOW will usually average 2500 to 3500 feet per day, so be sure to err on the high side.

The sound-effects company may need to make sound prints or reprints of the original production sound either for use in cutting or if there has been damage from use or mishandling during the postproduction process. If you are recording production audio on DIVA disk, you will need to transfer this sound to another medium (probably DAT or DA88) with timecode for dailies transfer.

4712 Magnetic Film

When posting on film, put your sound transfers used for looping and effects here. If you are posting on videotape, you may still have to order audiotape transfers, so add those numbers here. It is sometimes difficult to accurately estimate these numbers early in the postproduction process. Your sound editor may be able to help with early estimates.

4713 Looping and Narration

Put sound-facility (looping stage or narration booth) costs here. Usually the facility and the sound effects company are separate. Sometimes you get lucky and can work a package deal. The suggested looping schedule in the "Scheduling" chapter should help you here with your estimates. Add Screen Actor's Guild fees here if applicable.

4714 Foley

The sound effects company will include foley artists in your foley package, so don't add that payroll here. This area holds your sound or stage facility package costs. Your package should include 3 days of foley for a low budget feature or MOW.

4715 Sound Effects Recording

Projects that require the sound effects editors to record unusual or special sounds will incur additional costs above any negotiated package rate. The editor will need to go out into the field or onto a stage to get the right sound. The sound editor will include these costs in the sound effects bid when made aware of them ahead of time. If your sound effects editor feels that a rented Porsche driven up the coast will be necessary to record the perfect sports car road trip sounds, be skeptical. Unless, of course, it is determined that you need to go along to supervise, in which case you may find that this is a perfectly reasonable request.

4717 Optical Sound Track

This is the sound track that is married to a print. It is created by the sound house and applied to your print by the film laboratory. An optical track is typically used only for projection sound. Don't forget to include the laboratory developing charges and labor for the lab to sync the track to your picture.

4722 Dubbing

This area will include any effects, sweetening, looping, or mixing. Sometimes this number comes as a flat rate. But to list costs separately, add 3 days for an MOW (or whatever dubbing time is appropriate for your project), any extra equipment or stock required, the looping stage and the sound effects company's bid, temp dub, predub, and final 24-track mix. Include any mix-downs to 4- or 2-track, DA88, and any music elements for delivery requirements. The company doing your sound transfer can help you estimate these costs and arrive at a reasonable figure.

4724 Foreign Delivery Requirements

Any additional sound tracks, such as foreign-fill music and effects, will cost extra and must be budgeted. Put those costs here.

Film Laboratory and Postproduction

4800 Film Laboratory/Postproduction

For film shows you will have reprints of sound and film, B negative, and stock footage transfers. For the most part, you'll have to estimate these costs. Your lab rep should be able to help you come up with a reasonable figure. For tape shows you will have transfers for stock footage, inserts, and B neg.

When budgeting for videotape duplication and videotape stock, be sure to allow enough dollars that you have some room for extra "unforeseen" copies that come up throughout the process. You'll always end up making many more copies than you originally expected. There are numerous versions of the editor's cut, director's cut, producer's cut, and studio recuts. There will be promotional duplication requirements, delivery tapes, effects-company copies, music dubs, composer dubs, copyright dubs, dubs for editor and director (per their contracts), and on and on. Add any special visual effects to the lab/postproduction section. Also add to this section the fees for purchase of stock footage and costs to transfer or print the stock footage shots. The postproduction supervisor's salary also goes in this section.

4824 Negative Cutter

Your negative cutter will charge by the reel and be competitive in price. If your budget form does not include a separate line item for on-line costs and you are not planning to cut negative, you can break out your on-line costs here.

4828 Answer Print

If this is a film show you may need an answer print. The lab will provide a cost estimate. The lab can also help with budgeting any film element you create for your final telecine transfer. An interpositive (IP) may also be required for either your film-to-tape telecine transfer or for a foreign delivery requirement. An IP is also an excellent protection element against damage to your original negative. These "items" are charged per foot. Add 3% for waste and labor for leadering.

4831 Picture Leader

You will need to purchase the prepicture countdown (academy leader) and picture start leader for a film show. You can list that cost here or include it in the editorial supplies.

Titles and Opticals

4900 Titles and Opticals

For film shows, opticals are created independently from the rest of the film process. A special title and optical department (or separate company should you choose to go outside your film lab) will create these elements. Look to your laboratory contact for guidance. Based on the number of opticals in your project, it may be more cost effective to cut your negative into A & B rolls. There will be a laboratory premium for A/B printing, and additional costs for opaque leader, but the costs are worth comparing. See more about A/B printing in the "Completion" chapter. Remember to determine as early as possible if your titles will require special treatment, because those additional costs should be included here. You will usually need to keep your textless backgrounds after the titles and opticals are created to fulfill your foreign delivery requirements.

For videotape-finish shows, your titles and opticals (or picture effects) will be done either as part of your editorial package or at a separate house that specializes in electronic graphics. Try to pin down your executives early so you can factor those costs in. Titles and opticals that will require work at a graphics house are going to cost a lot more than ones you build in your on-line session. New shows will require that a main title be created, this can be expensive. MOWs often have the graphics department at their on-line facility create the main titles. This should be included in your titling hourly rate and will be much less costly.

Video Postproduction

5000 Video Postproduction

Most movie and television shows include some video postproduction steps in their completion process. These steps can include video dailies, electronic off-line, computer-generated opticals, effects, and titles. Ancillary costs include editorial personnel, materials, videotape stock, and viewing cassettes.

5001 Video Editing (Off-Line/On-Line)

The bid for your on-line will go here. You can list your off-line costs here or include them under cutting room and equipment rental (item 4517 in this discussion). If you combine both into this area, be sure to itemize the costs.

5002 Color Correction/Telecine Video Transfer

Color correction for an MOW will vary depending on the source and condition of the film or videotape. When transferring to videotape from a low-contrast print, budget at least 2 8-hour days. When transferring from a negative or interpositive, allow 3 8-hour days. For a tape to tape color-correction budget 1 to 2 days. If the cinematographer and director expect to supervise the entire color-correction process, this could add additional time. Make sure mastering stock costs are included in the color-correction bid. Do not put dailies transfer costs here. Those belong under video production (item 3814 in this discussion).

Posting in high definition does cost more money in this area. However, depending on your delivery requirements, you may find it more cost effective, and better quality, if you are being asked to deliver multiple versions/standards. The same holds true for mastering in PAL. PAL is a higher resolution than NTSC, so you can do all of your final work in this standard and then do a down conversion to NTSC, which should be acceptable to any of your distributors.

5003 Video Labor and Material

List final delivery cassette duplication here, as well as rough-cut and locked-picture cassette copies. Use purchase orders to track the number of cassettes you make, as this section will balloon very quickly and you will need to be able to trace where the money has gone.

5004 Video-Network Requirements

This figure is obtained by adding all the costs necessary to make all of the materials in your network delivery requirements.

5014 Video Stock Purchases

If you provide the facility with videotape blank stock, put the cost of purchasing that stock here. You can save a lot of money this way, but it is also hard to keep track of your stock and keep it replenished at the facility. For shows cutting electronically, you will also need to purchase stock to output the various cuts to from your off-line system. It is best to output to black and coded stock, which is more expensive than raw videotape stock.

5020 Satellite Transmission Charges

Sometimes you will know at the start that you will need to satellite your program for broadcast. For example, airing in Canada requires a satellite transmission, as do syndicated shows. Other times this becomes necessary just to make it on the air due to late schedules and completion problems. If you have any inkling that you will need to satellite your program, get a bid and put those figures here.

5100 Stock Footage

This section covers the purchase of stock footage, transfer fees, messenger costs, and any lab fees for optical preparation. Itemize these costs as specifically as you can so you can justify them later should there be an audit. If you have already listed these costs in the film lab/postproduction section, do not duplicate them here.

Fringe Benefits—Postproduction

5200 Fringe Benefits—Postproduction

Get these figures from your accounting department or auditor. Items in this section will include payroll taxes, pension costs, health and welfare insurance, and any rental fees paid to crew members who are authorized to use their own supplies.

The Rules of Thumb

Everything costs more and takes longer than expected. Unfortunately, there is no formula to accurately estimate these costs. If this is your first budget, you will rely heavily on your postproduction facilities and department supervisors to help guide you. Budgeting gets easier and more accurate with experience. Knowing your producer, doing several of the same type of project, and knowing the director will get you a long ways toward getting your budget in the ballpark.

The information in this chapter is meant to be used as a guide. Equations, when noted, are tools with which to estimate your "best guess." Many variables affect the bottom line. Keep a detailed log of purchase orders and amounts and reasons why extra things are needed or become necessary. Always be able to back yourself up when the producers or auditors start questioning costs. You are spending someone else's money, and your purchases should all be backed up with authorization, paperwork, purchase orders, and memos. The more paper flying around, the less explaining you'll have to do.

If you've come to the last page of this chapter and still have some areas in which you are unclear, pick up the phone and call someone. Get references from your auditor or the post facility for people working on projects similar to yours. Your auditor may be a good accountant, but postproduction is a specialty. And, unless the auditor concentrates on film or television as their sole business, they may not know all of the intricacies of postproduction. Just remember to do your homework, go with your gut and question things that don't seem right.

3 Digital TV and High Definition

While often referred to interchangeably, digital television (DTV) and high definition television (HDTV) are not one in the same. Digital television refers to the method of *transmission* of a television signal. High Definition television describes the *resolution*, or picture quality, of the program being transmitted. And, while high definition television is broadcast digitally, digital television need not be high definition.

The FCC's Plan

In December 1996, the Federal Communications Commission (FCC) adopted a new digital television system for use in the United States, generally referred to as DTV. And while there are some very real hurdles to overcome, and costs to cover, before widespread DTV can become a reality for the consumer worldwide, there are some very compelling reasons to switch to DTV. As most who read this are aware, the FCC gave the networks free broadcast channels with the caveat that they use this new space to broadcast digital television—and that they do it within a specified period of time. The extra channel allows for the new digital channel to be simulcast while still transmitting their current analog programming. One of the many times in life when something turned out to be much easier said than done.

In any case, the FCC's schedule to rollout this digital broadcasting mandate goes something like this:

Today: Network affiliates in the 30 largest markets must broadcast some digital television.

May 2002: All commercial stations in the United States must begin digital broadcasts.

> May 2003: All noncommercial stations in the United States must begin digital broadcasts.
>
> May 2006: Analog television broadcasts will cease in the United States.

In order to maintain viewership, the broadcasters are allowed to simulcast analog television along with their digital transmissions until analog is completely phased out.

Failure to comply with these FCC mandates will result in loss of the digital channel. As you might suspect, the FCC has built into this schedule a series of checkpoints to avoid leaving viewers out in the cold.

Digital Television Highlights

Some of the highlights of DTV include:

- *A wider picture area.* The shape of the new high definition TVs more closely resembles a motion picture screen. The new aspect ratio is 16:9, as opposed to today's ratio of 4:3 (a rectangle instead of a square).
- *A sharper picture if transmitting high definition images.* More channel bandwidth when transmitting standard definition DTV. This increase can mean more channels or the ability to transmit other data along with the television program.
- *Better sound quality with Dolby Digital 5.1 surround sound.*

The hurdles include:

- Many cities will need to build new broadcast antennas to transmit DTV. Who will bear these costs and where these new towers will be located are going to be difficult questions to answer for many communities.
- Our existing analog NTSC televisions and monitors will need to be replaced or upgraded to receive this new digital signal. Therefore, if the majority of consumers are not set up to receive digital television by the year 2006 cutoff date, the FCC is going to have to make some revisions to their schedule or many American's will no longer be able to watch television. Certainly, not what anyone wants.
- The new TV sets are currently very expensive. Part of the reason is that the FCC did not set one DTV/HDTV standard so, of course, there are several. Because they currently vary from network to network, the new receivers must be able to accommodate whatever signal is coming in. This is a pretty tall order for current technology. How affordable televisions will be in the future, only the future knows.

Even with all of these issues to solve, there is widespread agreement that going to digital television is a good thing for consumers, broadcasters, advertisers, and any others that can benefit or profit from this venture. DTV allows for a lot more data to be transmitted, these transmissions won't breakdown or succumb to interference over long distances as NTSC does now. In the same amount of bandwidth you can cram a lot more information into a digital signal than you can an analog signal. Better sound, better pictures, and truly interactive television will be ours with DTV.

Our NTSC Broadcast System

To really understand the potential benefits of DTV and HDTV, it might be helpful to briefly review our current television broadcast system.

Motion picture film has the highest resolution of any format in common use in media today. Many of the programs shot for television are still shot on film. That film is then converted to video. As film is usually projected at 24 frames per second (fps) in the United States, and video runs at 30 frames per second, converting the film to video involves a rather complex and cumbersome process of frame doubling to make 24 fps into 30 fps. So, our current NTSC system requires a less-than-perfect manipulation of film-originated programming for viewing.

As we said, film resolution is very high, approximately six times that of NTSC 525 or PAL 625 images today. So, even though film records images at a very high resolution, we're only able to capture a measly 525 of those lines onto videotape. The image is further reduced when one learns that only 483 of those lines are dedicated to the actual picture image. That seems unacceptable, yet this is the broadcast system we've known and learned to live with for more than 50 years of television. It's amazing what we're missing out on and most people don't even know it. People might be more upset to find this out if they weren't learning at the same time that they're probably going to need a new, really expensive TV to view better images. And, to date only one manufacturer has built the digital decoders into TV sets. So, you may also have to invest in a set top box to decode these beautiful images. Okay, back to our story.

So, these 525 lines of video are broken down into frames and fields. As stated, NTSC video runs at approximately 30 frames per second. Each of these frames is made up of 2 parts (called fields). These are known as the odd and even fields with each field shown for 1/60 of a second. Together they equal one video frame at 1/30 of a second, which is called interlace. We'll come back to this later.

The current television picture's 525 lines are scanned horizontally. The odd lines are scanned from the top of the screen to the bottom, and then back to the top to fill in the even lines. Once all of the odd and even lines are filled-in, a complete picture frame has been created. This happens about every 1/30th of a second.

In the United States, television's aspect ratio was 4:3. FCC regulations governing vertical and horizontal blanking made it mandatory that the entire screen be filled with picture. To comply, features shown on television were always panned and scanned so that the TV screen was filled top to bottom and side to side with picture information. In the 1980's, the FCC removed the blanking regulations, thus, paving the way for broadcast of letterbox images.

MPEG2 Compression

Due to the way the image forms on the screen, analog TV is not a candidate for the high quality digital MPEG (Motion Picture Experts Group)2 compression, while DTV is perfect for this.

Digital transmission uses MPEG2 compression. Essentially, with MPEG2 compression an image is broken down into information bits (ones and zeros) and compressed, transmitted, then reassembled exactly as they were. Because the information is digital, there is no loss of information or picture degradation. For example, the fact the signal can be so compressed while maintaining broadcast quality means less bandwidth is now needed to transmit a TV show. This potentially leaves room in the channel to compress and send other data simultaneously. You can see why this can be a good and profitable format for broadcasters.

High Definition TV

HDTV is digital TV and digital video at their best. With HDTV, those 525 lines of picture information we have with NTSC now become 1125 scanned lines, where 1080 of those make up the active picture area. This increase in the lines multiplies the number of pixels (the small dots that make up the picture detail). The current analog 4:3 sets have about 300,000 pixels. In contrast, the wider 16:9 HDTV screen is made up of over 2 million pixels. The enhanced picture detail in HDTV is quite remarkable—almost 3-D like.

This increased picture detail is a huge problem for analog TV. It would take the equivalent of five TV channels to broadcast one HDTV image. Enter DTV with its powerful compression that can fit six standard definition TV channels where there is currently one. Or, one digital HDTV channel where one analog channel would be.

Basically, the Advanced Television Systems Committee (ATSC) considers any number of scan lines above 480 high definition. The ATSC provides guidelines for broadcasters on how to transmit digital television signals. They also dictate MPEG2 as the compression format for all digital broadcast signals. MPEG2 was developed to compress the huge amount of information needed for the HD program.

Interlace

NTSC is 30 fps *interlace* (i) and PAL is 25 fps *interlace* (i). The electron gun scans top to bottom, working left to right across the screen until the 525 lines are scanned. First, all of the odd lines are scanned and then the even lines are scanned. Each full scan of either even or odd numbered lines equals a "field." Two fields make a frame.

Interlace scanning creates artifacts. These artifacts are introduced because each of the two fields that make up a frame is scanned at different moments in time. So, a snapshot of the two parts that are put together to make a whole are taken of the image at a slightly different point. This is because by the time the first field is completed and the second field starts, the image has moved. When put together they aren't going to match perfectly. This is most apparent in shots with a lot of movement. The edges become serrated along with flicker on horizontal edges and misaligned frames. The artifacts are only going to be found in images that originated on film, as film runs at 24 fps and is progressive (see below). Images shot on video are already shot 30i, so there is no interpolation.

Interlace doesn't just affect standard definition film-originated images, until recently, 1080 images have been interlaced also. Only 720p HD images were recorded progressively. This is due mostly to the fact that the 1080 HD format came along before the ability to transfer and record that format in the progressive mode. Therefore, there is a lot of HD product that is 1080i. The image benefits greatly from the increased number of scan lines, but is still plagued by artifacts inherent in the interlace method.

Progressive

Motion pictures are projected theatrically at 24 fps, progressive (24p) in the United States. On video, progressive images scan from top to bottom in one sequence. All lines that make up a frame are filled-in in one pass. Computer monitors display progressively.

There are numerous advantages to adopting the progressive format for all film-to-video programs. The key benefit of progressive scanning is the elimination of the motion artifacts inherent in the interlace formats, such as serrated edges on moving objects. In addition, to the introduction of progressive video display, the frame rate is also changed from 30 fps to 24 fps. Thus, 24p (1080 lines progressively scanned at 24 frames per second) is born.

24p

One obvious advantage to 24p is that the need for frame doubling (3:2 pulldown) to accommodate 24 fps into video's 30 fps is eliminated. This allows 24p for one video frame for each film frame. Many of the motion artifacts inherent in interlaced formats are a thing of the past. Couple this with 1080 lines of resolution and you've got one heck of a clear, detailed picture. This is known as 1080/24p. One thousand eighty lines of resolution run at 24fps progressively.

Digital Broadcast

All networks require delivery of some material that is appropriate for broadcast via digital television. Eliminating the 3:2 pulldown issue and all the problems that can bring (broken 3:2 sequences caused in video editing is the biggest problem), makes the material much easier to prepare for digital broadcast. As we learned earlier, digital broadcasts are compressed to fit more information into a bandwidth. The NTSC standard was a durable means of transmitting information analog signals to consumers for more than 50 years. However, this method does not lend itself to bandwidth compression. It is an inefficient system. It is also not a very high quality method due to the resolution constrictions in the 525 line format and artifacts inherent in an interlace format.

Digital television broadcasting answers all of the efficiency and quality issues in one fell swoop. This would have also been a good time for some consensus among broadcasters regarding which digital/HD formats they would choose. Unfortunately, this has not been the case. There are three different standards being required by the broadcasters and at the moment, no one seems willing to budge. The three standards are 480p (which is not considered HD), 720p, and 1080i. This has caused a big dilemma for postproduction facilities when deciding how to equip their facilities and how to future proof themselves in this business. Basically, they've found themselves in a position of having to have the capability to provide materials in all three formats (plus you have to add in 1080/24p as a mastering format). If they don't, then they might 1) be left out of a portion of the available business and 2) possibly make a wrong choice of formats and be completely left out should some make it and some not (think VHS and Beta).

The only bright star in this whole confusing debate about formats is 24p. The attraction for 24p (aside from the purely technical stuff) is it will make it much easier for postproduction facilities to meet the different format demands being made by the different broadcasters. From a 24p originated master, any of the three formats can be down converted without introduction of artifacting (except possibly 1080i to some extent).

Digital television has also brought us a new aspect ratio. In addition to our standard 4:3 (shown either in letterbox or full frame), we now have 16:9. This is the native aspect ratio of all HDTV formats and has become established as a standard definition aspect ratio as well. The difficulty really arises with how your TV will 1) know what aspect ratio is being received and 2) know how you want that aspect ratio displayed. Think about it. When a 16:9 image is displayed on a 4:3 screen, some aspect ratio conversion is going to be necessary. The rectangle 16:9 image just does not fit into the 4:3 square. So, does your TV lop off the sides? Squeeze in the sides, creating a top and bottom letterbox? Hmmm. It's a brainteaser and a real source of headache for the manufacturers trying to design set top boxes to do this.

In turn, what will happen to a 4:3 image when it is upconverted to HDTV or shown on a 16:9 monitor? Will there just be black bars on the sides where there is no image? Will the image be blown up to fill in the rectangle and then tilted so the hangover on either the top or the bottom (caused by enlarging the overall image so much) is just arbitrarily lopped off? Again, hmmm.

And the Answer Is . . .

The discussions, arguments, debates (and probably barroom brawls—you know how emotional engineers can get about their technology) are far from over. Even the answer to the question, "Are DTV and HDTV here to stay?" will bring more than one response, depending on who you are asking. The only things we know for sure are the ones based in pure science. Analog broadcasts are an inefficient use of available bandwidth; digital broadcasts are more efficient. HD pictures have a higher resolution, offering more picture detail than current NTSC pictures. The progressive format does not contain the motion artifacts found in interlace pictures. Aside from these few absolutes, at the time of this book's publication, just about everything else about DTV and HDTV seems up in the air.

4 The Film Laboratory

The film laboratory is one of the few remaining technical areas in moving pictures that has changed very little and still manages to thrive.

Film is processed pretty much the same as it was in the silent-movie days. Film itself has improved, but film processing has remained relatively unchanged. (There are issues causing change in film labs, such as EPA regulations regarding harmful chemicals in the air and water. But, for our purposes, we'll let those issues remain the headaches of the lab-guys themselves.) One improvement in the labs is the increased speed at which large amounts of film can be pushed through the development process with almost guaranteed safety to your negative. If you are interested, it is well worth the time to take a tour of your film laboratory. The laboratory supervisor is usually willing to extend this courtesy so you can better understand the process.

Motion Picture Film Formats

Motion picture film is available in 8 mm, 16 mm, 35 mm, and 70 mm formats and is shot either normal academy aperture or super (except for 70 mm, which is handled completely differently from the others). The difference is the part of the film frame that is exposed. In the super format, super 8 mm and super 16 mm are their own film formats and have perforations (sprocket holes) down one side only. With super 35 mm the entire film frame is exposed from perforation to perforation. When normal academy framing is used, one edge of the frame is left unexposed. This area is reserved for the sound track if you are making a composite print and is otherwise left blank.

saves $

Three- and Four-Perf Film

Thirty-five millimeter film can be shot as three-perf or four-perf. This refers to the number of perforations or sprocket holes per frame of picture along the sides of the film. Three-perf has three sprocket holes on each side of each film frame, while four-perf has four sprocket holes on each side of each film frame. Some sitcoms are choosing to shoot three-perf. This gives a 25% smaller image area, but allows 25% more frames of picture out of the same amount of film. This equals a 25% saving in raw-film stock costs. The technology is finally here which allows three-perf film edgecode information to be encoded and decoded accurately for ease in negative cutting. A new and confusing way to save money! The slightly reduced image size results from shooting a new frame every third perf instead of every fourth perf.

Aspect Ratio

The aspect ratio refers to the ratio of width to height of your pictures. Either the camera used for shooting or the projector the film is shown on determines it. The aspect ratio of television is 1.33:1. You will also see this referred to as 4:3 (pronounced four by three) or full frame. Features are most often 1.85:1, although they are also shot 1.66:1 and 2.35:1. Features shot in 2.35:1 are also called scope or anamorphic pictures.

The photographed aperture and aspect ratio can be different from the projected aperture. The aspect ratio represents how you want the exposed area of the film framed when it is projected or transferred. The key to framing is to find the proper center of the frame. Be sure you know at what aspect ratio your film is being shot so you can inform the transfer house. Some companies shoot 16:9 protected for HDTV so the negative can be retransferred and used for HDTV without reshooting. This changes the image "centerline." Because they expose different areas of the film frame, different apertures use different centerlines. The super 35 mm image exposes the film frame from perforation to perforation. Therefore, the center of the image is the center of the film frame. Normal academy aperture leaves an edge for a sound track, so the center is offset from the center of the film frame. The transfer house must be informed of this so they can compensate for this offset when setting up the film for transfer, otherwise the center of your picture may be off. It sounds confusing because it is. Just make sure your transfer house is clear on the intended projection aperture and image center. Often it is not possible to tell just by looking at the image on the telecine.

Figure 4.1 shows size and relationship of various aspect ratios to one another.

Figure 4.1 Common Aspect Ratios

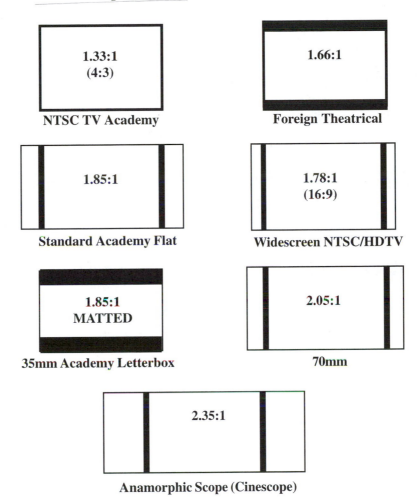

1.33:1 (4:3) — NTSC TV Academy	1.66:1 — Foreign Theatrical
1.85:1 — Standard Academy Flat	1.78:1 (16:9) — Widescreen NTSC/HDTV
1.85:1 MATTED — 35mm Academy Letterbox	2.05:1 — 70mm

2.35:1 — Anamorphic Scope (Cinescope)

Negative Processing Path

When your film is dropped at the laboratory, it is logged and scheduled for processing. The purchase order, any written instructions, and camera reports are reviewed
for any special processing or prep instructions. Special instructions are included in
the processing write-up. Once the film is developed it goes to negative assembly
where the camera rolls are spliced into lab rolls. Thirty-five-millimeter film is built
into approximately 1000-foot or 2000-foot rolls. Sixteen-millimeter film is built into
approximately 1200-foot rolls. The film is spliced in camera roll order. Leader is
added to the film rolls. If any punching is required, it is done in negative assembly.
The film is then cleaned, placed in plastic bags, and put into boxes or cans. Camera
reports

reports either go into each individual box or are gathered and taped as a group to the inside of the top of the first box.

The cost for developing and preparing your film for transfer is always calculated per foot. The lab keeps an accurate daily count of the amount of film for each project they process. If you need a daily footage count for budget purposes, the lab will have that information each morning.

When receiving film print dailies, a negative report is available daily from the lab. If you are doing electronic dailies, negative reports from the lab will not exist (unless you're having the dailies printed). The lab will note anything they can easily see during the develop-and-prep process. Obvious damage such as perf damage, torn film, edge fogging, or severe scratches will be reported in the morning to the client. More subtle damage will not be noticed until the film is looked at, and that doesn't happen until the telecine transfer.

Figure 4.2 shows these steps in a flowchart form.

Figure 4.2 Processing Negative and Film Dailies

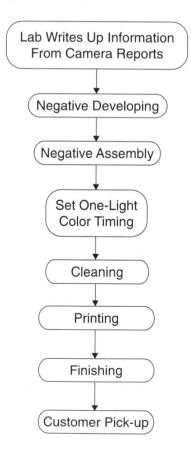

Processing Dailies

When shooting film there are some important issues to set up with the laboratory before you deliver them film to process after that first day of shooting.

Laboratory Processing Schedule

Know what time the lab starts processing film for overnight dailies. Know the weekday, weekend, and holiday processing schedules. Be aware that most labs do not process film Saturday night or Sundays. Labs that process color and black-and-white film usually process color film overnight and black-and-white film during the day. But, for a premium fee, most labs will open for a client that needs special off-hour services. Labs also offer daylight developing services. Film can be developed in a few hours during the day for an extra charge. This charge is usually a flat fee plus your normal costs of developing on a per-foot basis.

Scheduling Film Processing

Let the laboratory supervisor know when you will be delivering film and when you need to have it processed (and printed, in the case of film dailies). Make sure your timetable is realistic. It may be that you will have to "break off" film before shooting is completed each day to give the laboratory enough time to negative for your telecine transfer session or make prints for screening or cutting.

Traditionally, the turnaround for developing, cleaning, and prepping for telecine transfer is 3 to 6 hours, depending on the amount of film you are turning in and the lab's workload. This estimation is based on approximately 5000 to 6000 feet of 35 mm film that does not require special handling by the lab. If you have a 1 A.M. transfer scheduled, you may need to take a portion of your film in for processing by 7 or 8 P.M. to assure on-time delivery of your film to the transfer house. Any special processing needs, such as push-stop developing, will slow down the film-developing process.

Push processing (sometimes called "force" processing) requires special handling. When the cinematographer asks that film be "pushed" or "forced" the lab must slow down the transport speed of the negative through the developer, increasing the negative exposure. Because this process requires an equipment speed change in the lab, this film is generally developed at the end of the night or the processing run. Push processing is one example of special handling that may be requested by the cinematographer that will slow down the turnaround of your dailies from the laboratory.

Inform the Laboratory

Tell the lab what the processed film will be used for, such as film dailies or telecine dailies. When processing negative for telecine transfer, make sure the lab supervisor understands that you are doing a telecine dailies transfer and that you will need the film cleaned and prepped before it is picked up from the lab. Prepping film for transfer means putting it on a core, adding leader, and splicing camera rolls together to make 1000-foot rolls (or as close to 1000 feet as possible). Some shows still require that their film be punched either at the head of each camera roll or at each circled take. The punch is usually made just before the close of the clapper in the slate well before useable action. The punch identifies the 00 frame and is forced as the A frame during transfer. Punching puts a hole punch in your film at head, head and tail, or circled takes, depending on your instructions. This is a guide for the telecine colorist and negative cutter. The punch becomes your film reference. This also serves as a double check for the electronic off-line editor to calculate which frame is the A frame of video. The A frame is the first two-field frame of video in a 3:2 pulldown sequence in 24-frame NTSC video. A video sequence is made up of four video frames: A, B, C, and D. The A frame is made up of two video fields, the B frame is made up of three fields, the C frame is made up of two fields, and the D frame is made up of three fields. Then it starts over with a two-field A frame. This is all due to the fact that 24-frame NTSC film runs at 24 frames per second and video runs at 30 frames per second, and 24 does not divide into 30 evenly.

Some labs are limiting the service of punching film—or at least offering this service as a step in overnight dailies prep for telecine. Today's electronic off-line systems have rendered the practice of punching each take unnecessary as an A-frame double check. A punch at the head of each camera roll allows the telecine colorist and the editor to verify the 3:2 sequencing on the very first edit. If the first edit is right, the sequencing should remain constant for the remainder of the roll. Punching at the lab is very labor-intensive for the lab. It slows down the prep process, affects how quickly your dailies get out of the lab, and can add additional costs.

Special Handling

A special laboratory process is classified as any process that is not within the normal instruction of "develop negative normal and make a daily print." Special processes require special handling and personal attention to get them right. *Therefore, if you are going to order a special treatment in the film laboratory when your film is processed or printed, read this section.*

Directors of photography (DPs) are very special people, the world is framed slightly differently for them than for most people. They are creative and express themselves in a visual medium. This is the very reason they are hired to "shoot" a project. To achieve this visual perfection they must search out *all* the ways possible to manipulate film, through lighting, diffusion, gels, cameras, film stocks, and film processing. Once a "look" is decided upon for a project, the way to achieve that look is their responsibility, and it takes a team effort and participation to create it. Often it is the laboratory that will counsel a DP through the technical maze of special processes available to arrive at a systematic approach to achieving the look they want for their film. Included in the approach, or not, the film laboratory must be informed of every special film stock and special process necessary to the final result.

Not all laboratories do all things. Before you embark upon the biggest, most expensive, creative process you have ever dreamed of accomplishing, talk to the people who can help you, the film laboratory and the raw stock supplier. Just because you have a deal at a "big" laboratory doesn't mean they process all types of film, or process all types of film everyday.

For example, 16 mm is not always processed every day of the week, and neither is black-and-white film stock. Both of these negative stocks were once staples of Hollywood. Most TV shows and documentaries were shot in 16 mm and at one time black and white was the color of the day. But today these stocks are not as popular as they once were. Color film took the world by storm and 16 mm has been elbowed over by high definition and the superior quality of grain and aspect ratio of 35 mm. Although most of the major laboratories still process both, the quantities in which they are used are low and the processing baths are limited to certain days or specific hours.

Smaller laboratories may specialize in these film stocks and therefore the processing is more frequent. You also need to know if you are going to cut negative. If you plan to shoot both black-and-white and color stocks you need to ask the experts how to achieve the look you want, because black-and-white stock does not splice or cut together with color negative stock.

Color reversal stock was once used in the news business. A news crew could go into the field, shoot live footage for a story, return to the office, process the film, and project it in time for the 5 o'clock news, creating a print was not necessary. Today the news crews use videotape. Reversal stock has certain visual properties that have become popular with cinematographers trying to obtain the cutting edge look, but not every laboratory processes the old reversal stocks. If you have a lab agreement with a large motion picture laboratory talk to them about your needs and stock choices. What they can do is create a package deal to include processes that they do not cover, but will subcontract out for your situation. The agreement will be custom tailored to your project.

Other special needs include a process called bleach bypass, skip bleach, or silver #12 retention. Most laboratories will do this for the DP with the signed consent that it does not have a guaranteed result. The process involves the negative skipping a chemical bath, thereby achieving a high amount of contrast. The negative from multiple projects usually travels with other projects in the film chain but because this is irregular and involves skipping baths, this film will have to travel alone at the end of the day's film run. So heads up that this roll of dailies will be running a little later than usual. Sometimes producers don't want to chance their negative stock being processed in an unusual and possibly unstable method. They will then suggest to bleach bypass the prints instead, depending upon the creative use of the look. There may be other ways to achieve the same end result, by digitally enhancing the negative and re-outputting this to film. Another method could be to create interpositives and internegatives from bypass negatives or reversal stocks and cut these new stable negatives into the rest of regular action negative.

The list of special treatments does not end here. There are many more tricks a DP can employ to dazzle the audience. However, all of these processes take time, planning, and often more money. Anything that takes special attention will cost a little more and must be scheduled well in advance. Don't confuse the laboratory with verbal or spur of the moment instructions. You take a chance that the negative will either be processed incorrectly or not processed at all, until you are contacted by a supervisor sometime at their convenience. Talk to the laboratory and raw stock supplier, they will suggest testing and methods that are best for your project. Most of all take the time to research it before you shoot.

Flashing—It's Not What You Might Think

This is a term used to describe another one of the many artistic treatments you can apply to film. Just as the name implies the stock is flashed or exposed to light, with or without a filter. It can be flashed either before or after exposure through the camera and prior to processing. Again the laboratory will flash for you, however they must have specific instructions and you must give them ample time to arrange for this "no guarantee of results" treatment.

Camera and Makeup Tests

Schedule camera and makeup tests in advance. If you are shooting camera or makeup tests before initial photography begins, make sure the lab supervisor is aware of this and knows when your film is being shot and delivered to the laboratory. The operations manager at the laboratory will need to know if you are testing different film stocks so they can be assembled and marked in a usable fashion for review later. Often, a camera test involves such a small amount of film that (in lab terms) the lab may process your camera test at no charge, especially if they are scheduled to process all of your daily footage. Similarly, the transfer house may agree to schedule a viewing of your camera test in a telecine bay or screening room if they will be transferring your dailies. Freebies vary on a situation-by-situation basis; often depending on the amount of business a client does at a facility, how much the facility wants to woo the client, or the facility's relationship with the client.

Film Cans, Bags, Cores, and Blank Camera Reports

Film cans, bags, and cores come from the laboratory. The laboratory that is processing your film will provide you, free of charge, with cores, film cans, film bags, and blank camera reports for your shoot. These can normally be provided by the lab the same day they are requested. The lab will need to know how many you need, whether you'll shoot 400-feet, 1000-feet, or 2000-feet loads, and if you're shooting 16 mm or 35 mm film. Some labs preprint the camera reports with the production company name and project title.

Film Damage

To learn to effectively handle film damage problems, you must first learn to recognize when a problem is really a problem, be able to ascertain how serious the problem (if there is one) really is, and the best approach to solving that problem and moving on with your project.

To aid you in this process, the following 13 film damage scenarios will be discussed in detail, followed by our advice on how to recover and move forward. Unfortunately, the news will not be all good. However, it should give you enough confidence to help you find answers and provide solutions to those who need them.

1. Perforation/Edge tears
2. Camera scratches—both from the gate and foreign bodies
3. Fogging/Light leaks
4. Film loaded in reverse
5. Double exposure
6. Camera running off-speed
7. Skiving
8. Water damage
9. Density shifts/Breathing and HMIs
10. X-ray
11. Laboratory errors
12. Stock damage
13. Film weave

Production is a race, the shooting schedule must be finished, money, time, limited locations, and actors schedules are all delicately balanced on these two little details, time and money. The last thing a filmmaker wants to hear is that the film, which represents the days work, has been damaged.

Film damage ranges from minor and inconsequential to absolutely devastating. This section was written to inform the filmmaker of common types of damage, possible causes, terms used to describe them, and some suggestions of how to correct a problem, if it can be corrected at all.

Film manufactures and laboratories have extensive knowledge and experience with film damage, they even employ experts to assess film problems. When you encounter film damage it is best to discuss questions or repair suggestions to these experts. First, the exact location of the damage must be identified (i.e., edgecode and foot and frames on the negative). Then the negative may have to be printed to obtain a proper visual assessment. During dailies processing and printing the laboratory will make note of any fogging, tears, scratches, or other problems they encounter. The lab representative will then call the producer, DP, or other production representative with a brief report and suggestions to help determine your next step.

A word of caution: Insurance. In pre-production and while creating your budget it might be tempting to bypass this expense, however, it could be the most costly decision you ever make.

Perforation/Edge Tears

The little square holes on the edges of the film are called perforations, or perfs for short. Most often the perfs are torn due to stress from improper threading of the camera. As the camera gears begin to drive the film through the gate and onto the take up roll, pressure is put on the film to unwind and rewind onto the take up roll. If the perfs are off, just a little, or the thread is not correct, or the edge of the film has a little nick the perfs become stressed and eventually break. This might also be referred to as edge tears. If the camera really jams, then the film becomes creased, torn, and unusable in that area. To avoid a negative film jam in the developing and printing areas of the lab, minor perf /edge tears are usually taped or patched at the lab. Sometimes the patch is inadvertently left on the negative prior to printing or residue might be left from this patch and it will be visible on the print. Both the residue and the patch can be removed, usually with no further damage. It is not advisable to cut the perf damaged negative into your final cut negative.

Scratches

This is the biggest everyday occurrence. Every project will have some type of film scratch. They can range from barely visible to unusable footage.

Camera scratches: These are the most common type of negative scratches. The gate area has a claw mechanism that may get out of alignment and cause the claw to drag or pull against the negative scratching it. The magazine that holds the film may not be loaded correctly or there might be a little rough edge rubbing against the negative causing a negative scratch.

Dirt is also a very large factor here. While shooting in the desert or at the beach sand and debris may get into the camera or magazine while loading or cleaning the gate. The dirt rubs against the film causing a scratch. This type of scratch is easy to identify; it's usually straight with a build up of emulsion at the end of the scratch where the film was scraped up.

Gate clean outs are good because, even though they sometimes initiate debris which causes a scratch, it usually disperses the offending matter and ends the problem. While the gate is open the camera operator feels around to make sure there is no build up of film shavings or emulsion, blows air into the crevices, and resets the negative. But a scratched film is not usable right?

Before you panic, first determine that the negative is actually scratched and not just the daily print you ran with your crew. The laboratory will help you determine the damage and offer suggestions on repairs. Now that you have scratched film and it's a take you absolutely have to use in your project what do you do?

First thing is get the lab involved and ask for advice. If it's a cell scratch, damage to the base side of the film not the emulsion side with all the layers, then it's possible that it can be printed on a wetgate printer and the wet solution will fill in the scratch and hide it on the prints. If it's on the emulsion side there isn't any solution that will help. The options left are to blow up the shot to reposition the scratch out of frame, reshoot, recut, or digitally fix.

Handling scratches occur as the term implies, through *handling*. The negative is handled in negative cutting and in the making of opticals. They are identified and treated in the same way that camera scratches are. Usually the negative is inspected, and if determined that a wet gate solution will help, a wet print is made. If it looks good cut the negative into your project. All release prints that are made from your original are made wet so the scratches will be filled in each time your negative is printed.

Fogging/Light Leaks

Film is a light sensitive material and must be loaded, unloaded, and processed in the dark. If the camera door is left open, even just the smallest crack, or the thread up/re-can to or from the camera is not done in darkness, darkroom, or changing bag, it is possible that your film will become "fogged."

Negative fog: It will be apparent in both your telecine and on your prints. The light will leave a "fog," or flash of light, on the negative that is nearest to the light exposure, usually one edge of the roll. The fog may disappear at a camera clean out, which means the camera door was minutely ajar and then closed tightly after the clean out. The fogged film cannot be fixed. Reshooting is recommended if you cannot work around the fogged shots. Any digital fixes will be very costly.

Print fog: Thousands of feet of film are printed in the film laboratory each night. With this amount of material being processed it is possible that during the printing process the print will be accidentally fogged. It's usually at the tail of the roll and sometimes the tail is not completely printed, or "printed short." This is just a printing error and no harm has been done to your negative. The lab will reprint this roll at no charge.

Film Loaded in Reverse

Usually film loaded improperly is an error but on a rare occasion it is done to achieve a particular look. The most common reason film is exposed "backwards" is that it was left tails out, the camera loader not knowing the roll is this way, reloads the film into the camera. The film now has the backing side up and the Keykode on the opposite side as it runs through the gate. This may happen with short ends.

Another reason film may be loaded in reverse is with film left over that is resold after a show has finished shooting. Whether they are short ends from your shoot or you have purchased short ends, there is a chance that the end of unexposed portion of a roll was in haste rolled onto another core for future use, leaving it tails out. This might not sound like an issue, but consider the exposure might be slightly off and the impossible issue of capturing Keykode. In telecine a bar code reader on the right side edge of the film captures the Keykode, if the Keykode is now reversed, the reader won't be able to read it; additionally it is now in descending order rather than the numerical ascending order. This means someone has to make note of the Keykode by hand when it comes time for cutting. If you are exposing the film for look or reverse action be advised that everything comes with a price.

Double Exposure

Once in a lifetime a camera loader will forget to label an exposed roll and accidentally reload it into the camera and re-expose it again. This is unfixable. What you will see on a print made from the double exposed negative will be both scenes shot on top of one another. If this is what you intended the better way to achieve a double exposure would be to shoot both scenes separately and have them optically put together by an optical house.

Camera Running Off-Speed

If you are trying to shoot a certain effect you might run the camera at high or slow speed. If you are shooting for normal action and the camera is running at other than 24 fps, you will have sync sound problems. Strange things do happen, although they may be rare. There has been only one time we have had the crystal in the camera off calibration and the camera ran at an off-speed. This was only apparent after trying to sync dailies. It took all morning to figure out the problem before we changed the camera. The sound editor altered the audio in post and we were back in sync, we were lucky. Should this happen to you, you have two choices, alter your sound or reshoot.

Skiving

The first AC, or the DP, will several times throughout the day, open the camera gate, take a look inside, blow out the gate with canned air, and sometimes feel the gate area. They then rethread the negative and close the camera. They are checking for dirt, lint, and skiving. Skiving are little hair-like strands of film that are being shaved off the edge of the negative as it goes through the camera. This is due to improper threading or something wrong with the gate. Upon observation the camera operator will clean out the gate, rethread, and check again later. If the skiving continues the little shavings will wind into the film and thus become stuck. Some of the skiving will come off in the developing bath; however, much of it will remain embedded in the film. It will be evident in telecine and on the prints. If you pay to have the negative rewashed it may come lose; you might also have a film technician take the main offending pieces off by hand. This hand cleaning could be costly, and you still might have a little mark left behind where the skiving was embedded. If you are going to master to video a little electronic dirt removal should hide or remove the worst of the problem. Printing for a theatrical release and can't live with it? Do a digital fix and film out from electronic media to fix the problem, otherwise reshoot.

Water Damage

If you are shooting near water there is a danger of the camera and/or your negative taking a swim. Film labs see this on occasion, and yes they do snicker and roll their eyes. Just remember it wasn't them on that leaky boat, they have no idea what happened. If your camera or exposed negative does go in the drink keep the negative wet. Let's be perfectly clear—keep it submerged in water, in a bucket, or in a plastic bag or in an ice chest, just keep it from drying out. If the wet film begins to dry it will stick to itself and when it is unwound will pull apart, removing some of the layers. Deliver the fully submerged roll(s) to the lab in water and they will process it. Because it is now considered contaminated this will be the last negative they will process that day. It has to go in by itself at the end of the bath. This is to protect the other negatives from any contamination it might leave in the bath. What will it look like? It might warp or curl causing the image to look out of focus near the edges when printed or telecined. It might have water spots, which may be removed by hand with a special solvent. It might look pretty good. If the warping is minimal and there is no further damage it might be useable. We recommend you try your best to save it. Reshooting is always costly.

Use caution and pay the insurance rather than have a fatal accident trying to recover a sinking camera or film. Note: This also applies if the film gets wet from melted snow and ice.

Density Shifts (Light Shifts)/Breathing and HMIs

HMI's are a type of halogen light used to light up sets. Ninety nine percent of the time an HMI won't represent any threat to your film. However, there are a few things that can cause the gas in the bulb of the HMI to pulse at a slower/faster than the normal rate of 60 Hz. Electricity has a normal pulse, which causes all electrical machines to have a natural rhythm. This rhythm is so slight that the human eye does not perceive it. The electrical rhythm of the HMI has been timed to sync with the camera's shutter opening and closing.

If however, the rhythm is interrupted, or changed such as the gas tube of the HMI failing or a change of electrical frequency, the ballast (the bulbs' electrical regulator) fails, the pulse or rhythm will change. The pulse of the electricity surging and ebbing will be very evident as it is photographed in sequence on the motion picture negative. Negative exposed with this light pulse is not usable. Telecine or print from this type of damaged negative will seem to be lighter and gradually darker, and then lighter again, hence, the term breathing.

What to do? Well, it really depends on the shot you intend to use. If it's an entire scene with coverage and it all contains breathing you won't be able to cut it together, because you can never smooth out the breathing to look even. No color correction, special printing, or telecine can fix it. If, however, you have a shot that is a single, stand-alone shot, and the breathing is very slight and it cuts away to another scene you might get away with it. We recommend you reshoot or cut around the material.

X-Ray Damage

Yikes!!!! This is possibly the worst news, next to your camera falling into the ocean or the lead actor leaving your movie before it's finished. It's an awful sinking feeling and unfortunately many filmmakers have experienced this fate. The reason this news is **so** bad is that it effects not just one shot, location, or roll, or even one day, but an entire shipment of film and the effected film is unusable. It could happen to unexposed film (raw stock) or exposed unprocessed film (prior to sending it to the lab). If the negative has been processed there is no further threat of damage by x-ray.

What does x-ray/radioactive damage look like and how does it differ from the breathing of HMIs? It looks similar to fog, there is a point of contact, and the film will have a lighter/brighter looking exposure toward the side of the film that has had the greatest contact.

HMIs have a breathing rhythm that effects the entire frame, not a visual point of contact. X-ray damage is distinct and usually one side of the frame that has a foggy or bright area fanning out across the frame. The lab will be able to determine whether the damage occurred before or after exposure by evaluating the wind of the film. As the film is wound around a core the wind is small and as the film takes up the wind gradually becomes larger and larger. If the film was damaged prior to exposure in the camera the breathing, or rhythm, of the damage will be less or longer between the point of contact on the first scenes shot, because the first part of the raw stock was on the largest part of the wind. If the damage was after exposure it will be less evident or longer between points of contact on the last scenes shot because the film is left tails out from the camera and the tail is the largest part of the wind. This would only be true if the film was not rewound, after x-ray damage and prior to camera exposure, which may happen on a rare occasion when using short ends.

You will not know that you have radioactive or x-ray damage until the film is processed and either projected or transferred to tape. The laboratory will advise you to print part of a roll and view the negative in a telecine bay to evaluate the damage. Any damage that is there is not reversible. This becomes an insurance claim.

Laboratory Errors

Once in a great while the film laboratory will create accidental damage—sometimes it's inconsequential and then on rare occasions it's an insurance claim. Because damaged prints can be replaced and reprinted we will only explore damage to the original camera negative.

Torn or ripped negative: There is more than one type of physical negative damage. Sometimes a perf will have a weakened edge and rip or tear as in the **Perforation Tear** explanation above. Another type of negative tear that can be very costly can happen once a negative is conformed. When the negative is conformed it is physically cut. Hot splicing then reinforces these cuts. This fuses the pieces of negative together permanently without being evident to the viewing audience.

Hot splices are durable, strong, and made to withstand the tension of printing. However, occasionally Murphy's Law takes effect and one of these splices comes apart on a printing machine and your negative is in trouble. The damage can range from a corner of the spliced frame folding back upon itself to the negative ripping in half.

A folded frame can be removed and the show can be pulled up one frame without a sync problem. But, if you're on the other edge of the damage spectrum and your film has ripped in half, one solution is to replace the damaged film with alternate takes. Using alternative takes can make up for additional loss of frames on each side of the splice.

The other alternative is digital repairs. This entails hours/days of artistry by a film restoration specialist. First the damaged negative is scanned into a computer and then digitally hand painted frame by frame to replace the missing picture information, and then output back to film. The new negative is cut into the show, spliced, re-timed, and printed. This makes a beautiful fix and, if done properly, no one will be able to easily tell the difference between the fix and the original. Digital fixes impact not only your budget but your schedule as well.

If neither of these fixes is an option another alternative might be to either output film from a video master made before the damage occurred—such as a dailies transfer master. One last suggestion would be to make a duplicate negative from an existing interpositive or a dupe from a print. The latter is a last resort as the inserted piece will be difficult to time and the grain will be evident, but your project will be fixed.

Chemical Issues: *Soup Stop* or developing stop are not lab-friendly words. In the lab film runs through the laboratory processing in a long chain spliced together end to end, project to project, traveling together through many processing chemical baths and dryers. If this chain of film must be stopped during processing, the negative may remain in the chemical baths too long causing irreversible damage. Perforation tears, splices breaking apart, machine malfunctions, or human error could cause the "stop." Most of the time film that sits in the developing bath too long is unusable. Even if there is an image it will have processed unevenly with light and dark areas evident where the film was wrapped around rollers in the bath. Your only choices are to use another take, another camera roll, or reshoot the ruined footage.

Streaking is the term for chemical stains. These are usually seen on prints, but on rare occasions you can spot them on the negative. A faulty lab "squeegee," splashing, or chemical problems cause this streaking. Often re-washing the negative will remove the stains. Sometimes film has to be spotted or cleaned by hand.

Debris left on the negative is usually the result of static cling or friction that builds up from running the negative back and forth through the telecine. On very rare occasions debris is left on the negative due to dirty cleaning or processing solution in the lab. Either way, re-cleaning may take care of the problem. If the negative is handled through cutting or telecine, and the dirt will become embedded, it will be very difficult to remove. It will have to be removed by hand and may leave a mark or impression where the debris was stuck to the film. Removing dirt by hand is time consuming and expensive.

Sometimes debris is found to be the result of a stock defect (see Stock Damage below). The only way to correct this problem is to reshoot, correct digitally and re-output to film or use a dirt removal system on your digital masters.

Wet Wrap is a term used to describe what happens when a wet spot is left on the film and it is then wound up around a core. The wet area sticks to the film it is wrapped around. As the film is unwound the wet spot might tear apart or a layer of the film may be removed. This is not repairable. However, sometimes the only damage is a faint watermark, which may be removed by hand cleaning. This type of damage does not happen very often.

Stock Damage

Every couple of years we hear about raw stock damage. This is raw stock purchased from the manufacturer that has built-in damage. This is very rare and sometimes difficult to detect. Most of the time the damage is debris that is manufactured into the base of the film. It looks like lots of black dirt and yet it doesn't clean off. If you have a dirt problem that doesn't go away with the usual cleaning techniques have the lab and the manufacturer inspect the negative. They will give you a diagnosis and suggest how to resolve the problem. If it is a stock problem you are left with the same old suggestions, reshoot, recut, or digitally fix. If the manufacturer is at fault you will probably get free raw stock in an amount equal to the damaged stock. Now you remember why you bought that insurance.

Short ends: Many low budget filmmakers have no choice but to shoot with re-cans or short ends. This is left over raw stock from a production that has sold back excess film to a film broker. The film manufacturers will not buy back excess film or the short ends left over from a larger roll, they sell fresh from the factory only. Short ends or re-cans are usually in good condition and not very old, but the broker can't always guarantee quality. When buying film this way, it would be in your best interest to do what is called a "snip test." The laboratory will test a few rolls either free or at a very nominal cost.

The test will tell you the density of the negative and where it should read according to the manufacturer. This will give you an indication if its quality is worthy of your creative endeavors. The stock will also have a stock number that can be tracked through the manufacturer that will tell you the date it was made, indicating how old the negative is. You will want to do everything possible to ensure that the negative you are using is in good condition and is not damaged (x-ray damage applies here, too) prior to your use. Snip tests are not necessary on purchases of fresh stock from the manufacturer.

Film Weave

Another common film problem is weave. Weave manifests itself as side-to-side movement of the entire film frame. The movement will be readily apparent in the frame area if the matte is removed from the projector while viewing a daily print. Some amount of motion is always present when a film element is played, and a minor amount is acceptable. The severity is going to be the issue. Movement is especially problematic if you are using the shot as a background (backplate) for effects.

Stock problems such as shrinkage can be the culprit. There may also have been a problem inside the camera and the film was weaving as the images were being photographed. There is new equipment being tested in the market that can actually fix, or greatly reduce, the amount of film weave you see. However, this is an electronic fix, which will only help your project if you are delivering on videotape or record the fixes onto tape and then re-output to film.

We Just Meant to Inform, Not Frighten

The above has been a very long and scary list of bad and ugly things that can happen to your negative. Your best course of action is for everything you can, protect yourself from having any damage happen in the first place. That said, should you have film damage, have the damage that does occur professionally diagnosed prior to having a complete mental and financial breakdown. Finally, we recommend that you not consider foregoing production insurance as a way to cut costs and make sure you shoot enough coverage to back yourself up if you do lose shots.

This information is not intended to keep you up at night (that's your producer's job). It's simply meant to educate you about some of the problems that can occur, ways to avoid or minimize the impact to your project, and keep you going to the end of your movie. Keep everything we tell you in perspective. Millions of feet of film are shot and processed daily around the world. Thousands of movies and TV shows are successfully completed each year. Forewarned is forearmed, nothing more. Now, go out and shoot some film!

Creating Other Negatives and Prints

To make a theatrical print (release print to show in theaters), the original negative is cut and an original optical sound track is struck. Release prints are made from an internegative and an optical track.

Once your original negative has been cut, the negative is copied. This copy is called an interpositive (IP). An interpositive is an intermediate positive picture element made on special film stock. From the IP other negatives, called internegatives (IN), can be struck. (Once the initial IN has been struck, a check print is made to check the overall color.) Usually several internegatives are made and the release prints are made from these. This eliminates the need to go back and reuse the original negative again and again for printing; thus preserving the original negative's quality.

Should your original cut negative become damaged, new sections of IN can be created from the IP and spliced into your original cut negative element. The replacement section will be two generations away from your original element.

If your show is going to have a film-finish, the negative is cut once the show has been locked and opticals are complete, regardless of whether or not dailies are transferred to videotape for an electronic off-line edit. What happens next is up to the client's preference and the delivery requirements.

Creation of a color-corrected print is done at the film lab. First you will need to approve a proof print. The proof print is a slide show of one to three frames of each scene from the show. Often, the director or cinematographer attends this screening. You may have adjustments and two or more trial prints may need to be made before you archive your answer print.

After you have approved the color-correction of your negative, a first trial/answer print or an interpositive is struck. Either of these can be the source for the film transfer to videotape. If the first trial is made on locon stock, it is usually referred to as a locon print. Be sure to order these elements with the wetgate process. In wetgate printing, the film, as it travels through the printing gate, is exposed to a liquid solution that works to mask minus density marks and spots. These imperfections manifest as dirt or minor scratches on the negative. If successful, this wetgate process will make it seem that these imperfections have "disappeared." Due to the softer emulsions of the negative stocks, embedded dirt and handling marks are not uncommon in cut negative. The wetgate process, when printing, will temporarily remove these minus density spots that show up white on the screen or video monitor.

Consider the risk each time you use your original cut negative. While the equipment you run your film on in telecine is extremely gentle to your negative, human error or mechanical troubles could result in a scratch to your negative, and once your negative has been damaged that section is rendered useless. Often a wetgate print or other restoration method can be used to create a usable piece of film to replace the damaged area, but there is no way to repair your negative. Should damage occur and you have to replace the show with another piece of negative, make sure your negative cutter has compensated for any frames that may have been lost.

When preparing a film-finish for your project, you will need to make interpositive sections for creating your opticals. In preparation, your editor will instruct your negative cutter to pull and identify appropriate scenes from the original negative for delivery to the laboratory. The negative cutter should leader and splice the segments. If not, the lab will do this for you but they will charge you extra for this service.

Cut Negative

If any of these selected sections have already been cut together by the negative cutter, then the lab will receive that entire roll of cut negative. The negative cutter will not separate those segments from the rest of the roll. As the lab will receive the entire roll, those sections affected will have to be identified by edgecode. The negative cutter will create a list with essentially in and out points by noting the head and tail edgecode numbers. Five to ten feet of extra footage needs to be included in this measurement at both the head and tail of each segment. This is necessary for the machines to have time to come up to speed when shooting the opticals. If the lab feels this additional footage has not been figured into the information you provide, they will add it. In addition to the list of in and out edgecode numbers, the negative cutter will usually mark the sections with small paper tabs that protrude from the reel. These give the lab a visual reference for the beginning and end points of the sections. Because of this method of making the segments, IPs or INs made from cut reels are called *paper-to-paper* sections.

Laboratories make IPs sometime during the daytime once all of their dailies footage have been processed. If an order calls for an IP, an IN (dupe neg), and a check print to be made, don't expect all of these elements to be ready the next day. The IP will be turned around in 1 day and the next day the dupe will be made. Depending upon the traffic in the laboratory, the check print might be ready the same day as the dupe, but most likely the day after.

Acetate vs. Estar

When making a duplicate negative of a shot or scene to cut into your original negative you must order an "acetate" dupe, this is very important. Estar negative stock
and acetate film stock cannot be spliced together. They are two different thicknesses
and the splice will not stay, it will come undone and your negative will break apart.
Most laboratories will make estar dupes unless otherwise requested, so it is up to
you to request the correct film stock.

Adding Sound

From the optical sound track negative (OSTN) an exposure of the sound track is
made on your print. This is done by printing the negative on a continuous-contact
printer (CCP). This printer has two heads, allowing separate picture and sound areas
of the film to be exposed. As the IN and OSTN travel over these heads, the first head
exposes the picture element. The second head exposes the sound area. The exposed
print stock is then put through a print processor to develop the picture. The next step
is to apply a second developing solution (application) to the sound track area of the
print stock. This redevelops the sound track area only, in order to make a higher-
contrast image. When your print is projected, this higher-contrast image is scanned
by the light beam of an optical sound reader and reproduces your sound. The light
source is called the exciter lamp. The light passing through the optical track is translated into an electrical current. This electrical current is an analog reproduction of
the sound track and can be amplified by the playback equipment. This type of sound
track is called an optical track.

Figures 4.3 and 4.4 illustrate the optical track placement on the film frame.

Figure 4.3 Optical Track Placement on 35mm Film

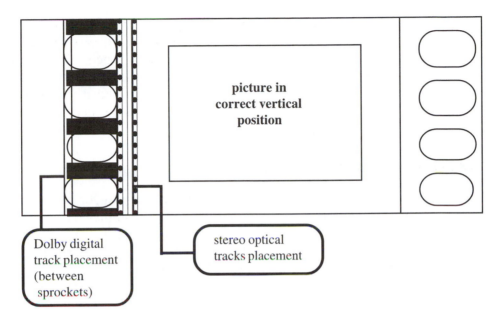

Figure 4.4 SDDS Track Placement on 35mm Film

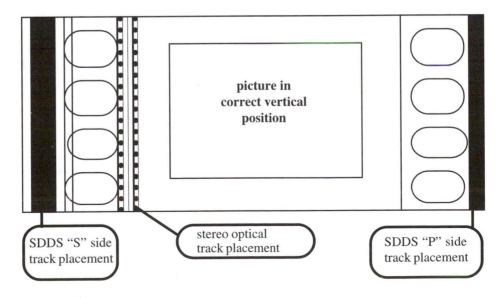

Application Splash

The part of the processing machine used to reapply the developer for the above sound track is called the "applicator." This is essentially a little wheel or sprayer that applies the developer onto the sound track area of the film. When this sprayer becomes clogged or dirty, it can spray droplets of developer onto the picture area. When this happens it adversely affects the silver in the picture and the film is irreparably damaged. A new print will have to be made. This damage is detectable both visually and audibly.

Creating a Telecine Print

Once the trial print has been approved, a locon, answer print, or interpositive is made from which to telecine. A locon is a print made with all the color-corrections from the trial print process printed onto a low-contrast film stock. This stock is designed for use as a film to videotape element. When deciding which type of print to strike, also refer to your domestic and foreign delivery requirements. If one of them requires a particular print type be delivered, you may be able to satisfy that requirement here and still have a print from which to telecine.

There are two degrees of color-corrected prints. One is a batch-timed print and the other is a fully timed print. Because it represents a grouping of scenes with the same overall correction, the batch-timed print will require considerably more time to color correct in telecine. The fully timed print, having been color-corrected scene-to-scene prior to being printed, will require less time. The amount of extra time needed will depend on how evenly the negative was shot in the first place and the degree of variance from scene-to-scene in the picture.

A general rule of thumb is that you will need at least half as much time to complete the color-correction from a batch-timed print as you will need to complete color-correction from a fully timed print. Again, this will depend on how even the original negative is from scene-to-scene and how drastic the changes in picture are that you are trying to match from take to take.

Creating Yellow/Cyan/Magenta (YCM)

In the 1930's, Technicolor Corporation developed a process called the Technicolor process to print color motion pictures.

A light source recording the image was projected through a lens into a *Split Prism Cube*. This cube divided up the image into green and minus green components. These components were refracted into three separation negative film stocks. One stock received the green information, one stock the red information, and one stock (blue sensitive with a red coated emulsion) received the blue information. Then light was emitted through the three layers of exposed negative combined and printed onto a fourth piece of negative, yielding a full color positive element. This three-strip dye transfer process was used for motion pictures throughout the 1930's and 1940's.

Today the YCMs starts at three separate film strips. Each filmstrip represents a black and white interpretation of one of the colors: red, green, or blue. Then dye is applied to the film to bring out the colors. Due to the technical nature of each separation and the thickness of the gelatins where the images are recorded, red dye cannot be used in the dye process for coating the red separations. So, the opposite of red, or cyan, is used. For the same reasons, magenta dye is used for green, and yellow for blue. Thus, we have our three-color separations (yellow/cyan/magenta) that, when combined, makes our color image.

The "clear" filmstrip used to initially create these dye-coated separations is actually a piece of black-and-white negative photographically exposed to a silver positive image. This process adds contrast and richness to the final color negative. Thus, we have our YCM (yellow/cyan/magenta) silver separation master positives.

What Are YCM Masters?

So, what are YCM masters? YCM Silver Separation Master Positives are black-and-white records that represent each of the three color layers present in the emulsion of color negative film.

Why Create YCM Masters?

Because the vegetable dyes used in the emulsion of color film break down (fade) over time. In black-and-white film, the metal silver is used when making the image. As a metal (rather than the organic vegetable dye) silver doesn't fade. It holds the color dye colors.

What Is the Process?

A color negative is printed to YCM Master Positive Stock three times. On each pass, different filters are used representing a different color dye layer. The result is a set of YCM masters. To check the integrity of the YCM masters, they are immediately printed back to a single piece of new color negative stock (run three times, once with each record). The resulting *recombined internegative* is then printed and screened. Anomalies in the masters can be clearly spotted in screening.

Archivally speaking, the YCM masters can be similarly recombined in the future (as many times as necessary) to recreate the original color content of the original negative long after it has faded past the point of being printable. Thus, they preserve the cleanest, most true representation of the images that were originally captured when the movie was shot.

Is the Result Always Positive?

Is the image on YCM masters a negative image or a positive image? Depending on the source material, YCM masters can be either positive or negative. Most commonly, though, YCM masters are created from original cut camera negative. Consequently, they are usually positives.

The newest film for creating YCM Silver Separation provides improved sharpness and grain highlights for more consistent results and better colors.

When Are YCMs Needed?

YCMs are the only known guarantee that the film you shoot today, can be reprinted and shown in its original beauty, long after the original negative has begun to fade with age or suffered damage from handling or misuse.

This is very important to studios and filmmakers around the world who have come to realize what a valuable asset their project can be to them. Even just a few years ago, most people had no idea that the demand for product would be so intense and widespread. With the growth of cable channels, satellite transmission to consumers, the Internet, and DVD and video rental markets virtually around the world, it seems there is a constant need for more and more product.

Aside from the commercial arguments for protecting these assets, there is the social importance of maintaining a record of our cultural heritage. Movies have always represented a window into our past (and sometimes our future). Generations now feel they know and understand generations past simply by watching the movies that were made about them and by them. Many feel we have a moral obligation to preserve this information for generations to come—a sort of moving picture history of mankind.

It is encouraging to us in the industry who share this belief and passion about our moving picture history, that the trend of once again creating YCMs, solely for the purpose of archiving this product, seems to have found a home in our industry.

Shipping Exposed Negative

In response to the September 11, 2001, airline tragedies, new and increased scanning procedures have been put into place by both the U.S. Postal Service and the airline industry. These new procedures put negatives at risk of fogging and exposure.

For safety, all commercial airlines x-ray their cargo. Carry-on luggage and luggage checked in at the gate/curb all go through x-ray inspection. Most overnight couriers however, do not x-ray their cargo.

In the past, airport x-ray equipment had little or no effect on unprocessed film. The new higher intensity scanners have been tested and shown to have the potential to fog both unprocessed color and black-and-white film. Processed film appears unaffected.

The U.S. Postal Service has begun installing new electron beam scanners for use in sterilizing items sent through the mail. This technology will fully expose undeveloped film as if it had been exposed to sunlight. It is rumored that this equipment may even cause damage to exposed film, prints, DVDs, picture CDs, and videotapes. Because it is still unclear to what extent this equipment will be used, it is best to err on the side of caution until more information is available.

Carry-on bags used to be considered safer from damage due to radiation. The x-ray used are lower intensity, however, in some instances airports may be supplementing these checkpoints with higher intensity machines that will fog unprocessed films. In most cases, no additional warnings are being posted.

We have also seen damage due to radioactive isotopes being shipped alongside unprocessed negative. This renders the same result, useless film.

You will not know that you have radioactive or x-ray damage until the film is processed and either projected or transferred to tape. The laboratory will advise you to print part of a roll and view it in a telecine bay to evaluate the damage. Any damage that is there is irreversible. This becomes an insurance claim.

The following tips are offered to help you safeguard your film:

- Make sure there is no unprocessed film in your checked baggage.
- Carry undeveloped film with your carry-on baggage and ask for hand inspection.
- Contact the airport ahead of time if you plan to carry large amounts of unprocessed film so they can arrange a special baggage inspection.
- If you are randomly chosen to step out of the normal security check line into another line, know that your carry-on baggage will probably be scanned as checked baggage. Remove your unprocessed film from your carry-on so it can be hand inspected.
- Send your film via a cargo carrier or expediter that will certify that your film will not be x-rayed. Most airfreight shipping services use their own aircraft and do not employ x-ray scanning of customers' packages on domestic routes. However, you should verify this information before sending your film.
- Goods shipped as freight on passenger airlines are subject to high-intensity x-ray scanning. If you are shipping film as unaccompanied freight, label DO NOT X-RAY/CONTACT SENDER.
- Try to purchase your film locally to your shoot and process locally before shipping.

Summary

Most film laboratories offer a variety of services. They develop your film and prepare it for telecine transfer, create prints, and repair damaged film. Some have optical departments where they can create your film effects and titles, blow-ups, and repositions. To fully understand and appreciate the work that goes on at the film laboratory, take a tour. Your salesperson or laboratory supervisor will be glad to arrange one for you.

Footage Conversions

Someone will always be asking you to convert your film footage into run time. For your convenience, Figure 4.5 is a film footage guide that provides an exact conversion for both 35mm and 16mm film.

Figure 4.5 Footage Conversion Chart

SECONDS	35mm FOOTAGE	16mm FOOTAGE	MINUTES	35mm FOOTAGE	16mm FOOTAGE
1	1.5	3/5	1	90	36
2	3	1 1/5	2	180	72
3	4.5	1 4/5	3	270	108
4	6	2 2/5	4	360	144
5	7.5	3	5	450	180
6	9	3 2/5	6	540	216
7	10.5	4 1/5	7	630	252
8	12	4 4/5	8	720	288
9	13.5	5 2/5	9	810	324
10	15	6	10	900	360
11	16.5	6 2/5	11	990	396
12	18	7 1/5	12	1080	432
13	19.5	7 4/5	13	1170	468
14	21	8 2/5	14	1260	504
15	22.5	9	15	1350	540
16	24	9 2/5	16	1440	576
17	25.5	10 1/5	17	1530	612
18	27	10 4/5	18	1620	648
19	28.5	11 2/5	19	1710	684
20	30	12	20	1800	720
21	31.5	12 3/5	21	1890	756
22	33	13 1/5	22	1980	792
23	34.5	13 4/5	23	2070	828
24	36	14 2/5	24	2160	864
25	37.5	15	25	2250	900
26	39	15 3/5	26	2340	936
27	40.5	16 1/5	27	2430	972
28	42	16 4/5	28	2520	1008
29	43.5	17 2/5	29	2610	1044
30	45	18	30	2700	1080

5 Dailies

"If I'd wanted them at the end of the day, I'd have renamed them nightlies!" *stormed the producer frustrated by the fact that it was nearly 9 A.M. and he* *had yet to see a minute of the previous day's film.*

In a film shoot, "dailies," as the name implies, is the footage that is shot each day and rushed to the lab for processing, then on to telecine or printing so you and your crew can view them, usually the next morning. Heaven help the facility with technical difficulties that delay the completion of "dailies." The dailies from a tape shoot are still the footage that is shot each day; it just does not require processing.

It is good to remember that no amount of preparation and preplanning can guarantee trouble-free dailies every single day of your shoot. To paraphrase a popular saying, "stuff happens." But, by being as prepared as you possibly can on your end, you'll seriously up the odds of a successful dailies experience.

It is a fact of life that your transfer facility will occasionally fall victim to that same "stuff happens" curse. Should trouble visit itself upon your transfer facility, try to keep it all in perspective. Before screaming and yelling and carrying on about how you're pulling your work or not paying your bill, remember that no facility will want an angry client. They want to get your work out smoothly and quickly each day— as quickly as you want to be out. Pick your battles and make sure the reaction is equal to the harm. Remember that this is entertainment after all!

When speaking of dailies, the conversation will eventually have to branch off into one or more of the three types of dailies: 1) film print dailies, 2) standard definition dailies, or 3) high definition dailies. In this chapter, we'll talk about all three.

It is important to remember as you read on that, as with many of the postproduction steps we cover in this book, these three types of dailies need not be mutually exclusive of each other. It is possible, and in some cases probable, that you will utilize more than one type of dailies during your project.

In any case, before we get started on the specifics of the different dailies options, we've got some other items to cover first.

The good news is that regardless which one, or more, of the three types of dailies you employ to post your project, they have many similarities. And, there are many steps that will be the same. Especially, the steps you take to get to that fork in the road.

These similarities will be determined by your answer to one simple question. Are you shooting film or videotape? The answer to this question will let you know if you are going to be dealing with a film laboratory or not. Obviously, if you are shooting film, it has to be at a minimum, developed, before you can do anything else with it. You know this from shooting with your 35 mm still camera. Once the film is exposed and you've used up all of your pictures on a roll, you cannot see those pictures, share them, cut them up, or e-mail them to someone, until you have taken them in for developing.

On the other hand, if you are shooting with your home video camera, you can review, copy, and share the pictures you have shot with your family and friends as soon as you rewind the footage. And, of course, there are the digital cameras which are becoming more and more popular every day.

The same applies for your movie or TV shows. If you are shooting your footage on film, it must be developed at a film lab. If you are shooting your footage on videotape, it is ready to go.

Dropping Film at the Laboratory

Whether you will be creating film dailies or videotape dailies (or both) from your film shoot, someone from the production crew will drop your film at the laboratory each day after shooting.

Episodic dailies (including MOWs, mini-series, and specials) have a starting shoot date and ending shoot date spanning anywhere from 3 weeks to an entire TV season. Film for these projects is shot on consecutive days until the project is completed or the season ends. The lab receives film and sound daily. Motion picture film dailies also have a starting shoot date and ending shoot date. The lab receives film and sound for each day of shooting.

It is important to know ahead of time what time of day the film must be dropped off to the lab in order to have the film processed in time to start your dailies transfer. Therefore, you must also know what time your telecine transfer is scheduled;

Figure 5.1 The importance of having dailies: or a step-by-step guide to unemployment

this is handled in more detail in "The Film Laboratory" chapter of this book. In any case, commit this simple set of facts to memory: no film processed, no film-to-tape transfer, no dailies in the morning, nothing for your assistant editor to do, nothing for the editor to cut, nothing to show the producers, no good for you. For those with questions, see the flowchart above, Figure 5.1.

The sound will be delivered to the transfer house one of two ways: either it will be dropped off at the film lab with the exposed negative and delivered to the transfer house with the processed film, or someone from the production crew will drop off the sound separately to the transfer house each night after shooting. It is important to clear up this detail before shooting begins. In the case of film print dailies, the production sound is usually dropped at the sound-transfer facility.

Camera Reports

If your show is being shot on film, you should know how to read a camera report. One camera report is created for each roll of film that you shoot. The same applies to sound reports. Each production sound reel will also have its own report. Each camera and sound report will have multiple carbonless copies attached. The original always stays with the film or sound element and goes to the postproduction facility.

One copy stays with the production crew and one copy is sent to the production office for the editor's reference.

Knowing how to read camera and sound reports will help you better communicate with both production and your postproduction facility if you have questions or need information about certain takes. We have provided samples of both camera and sound reports with a corresponding explanation regarding each section of the reports. (The information on reading a sound report is found under "Production Sound" in the "Sound" chapter.)

The Camera Report

The camera assistant completes this form as a written record of what is photographed on a particular roll of film and any special circumstances required for processing, printing, and/or transferring the pictures on the roll.

One camera report goes into each can of film. Even if you're shooting short ends (which were discussed in "The Film Laboratory" chapter), every roll of film you turn in to the lab must be accompanied by a *fully completed* camera report.

Camera Report Breakdown

The report's layout may differ slightly from lab to lab (prior to shooting you will get blank camera reports from the laboratory that is processing your film), but all of the information listed in this discussion must be listed on each camera report.

Figure 5.2 Sample Camera Report

A **Laboratory Name**
Laboratory Address
Laboratory Phone#

B **Prod. Co.** Greenville Productions *C* **Date:** 12/19/01

D **Picture Title & Eps#:** The Danes #9278 *E* **Loader:** Andy H.

F **Director:** G. Paul *G* **D.P.:** S. Fred

H **ROLL#** A3 ☐ **BLACK & WHITE** ☒ **COLOR**

I **EMUL** 7245 *J* **MAG#** 6

DEVELOP *K* **FOOTAGE_____**
☒ **NORMAL** ☐ **PUSH____STOP(S)** ☐ **PULL_____STOP**

FILM WORKPRINT *L*
☐ **PRINT ALL** ☐ **PRINT CIRCLED TAKES**

VIDEO TRANSFER *L*
☐ **TRANSFER ALL** ☒ **TRANSFER CIRCLED TAKES**
TRANSFER AT _24___ FPS

M SCENE #	*N* 1 6	2 7	PRINT CIRCLED 3 8	TAKES 4 9	5 10	*O* REMARKS
12A	(20)	(20)	(20)			MOS
12B	10	10	(15)			
	10	10	(10)			Xfr 36fps
12C	10	20	(20)	(20)	(20)	
12D	no roll	15	15	(15)		Transfer warm
	15	(15)				
	13	(20)	(20)	(20)	no roll	Night Ext.
	20	(20)	20	(20)		

		G.	270	*P*
		N.G	150	*Q*
		W.	30	*R*
		T.	450	*S*

Here is a description of each section of the sample camera report (Figure 5.2):

A. *Laboratory name, address, and telephone number* are usually preprinted on the camera report.
B. *Name of production company.*
C. *Shoot date.*
D. *Show title* (if there is not a separate space to write in an episode number, then the episode number should be included here).
E. *Name of loader/assistant cameraperson.*

F. *Name of director.*

G. *Name of director of photography (cinematographer).*

H. *Camera roll number.* Be sure to note if it is A camera, B camera, etc.

I. *Emulsion.* The lab needs this information for processing.

J. *Magazine number.* This is very important if you have to track a film problem that occurred during production. Problems such as scratches and fogging sometimes trace back to a camera magazine problem. It is important to be able to isolate which magazine is causing the problem.

K. *Development instructions.* If this area is left blank, the lab will assume normal process.

L. *Print/transfer instructions.* Instructs whether *all* or *selected takes* are to be printed or transferred.

M. *Scene numbers.*

N. *Take numbers.* It would require too much room to provide spaces for all the possible number of takes a director may shoot for one scene. It is generally understood that, after the take spaces are filled in across the row, the scene number is left blank on the next row and the takes continue in ascending order. This repeats until all the takes are listed. You know you've moved on to the next scene when it is listed in the "scene" column. In the "take" boxes the amount of footage shot for that take is usually listed. For circled takes that are to be transferred or printed, the footage number is circled.

O. *Remarks.* Comments are noted that relate to the takes in that row. This might tell the colorist if it is a night exterior or to color warm or cool, or if it was shot at an off speed. The colorist looks here for all subjective guides for the transfer and any special shooting circumstances.

P. *This is approximately how many feet shot on the roll are usable.*

Q. *This is approximately how many feet on the roll are not usable.*

R. *This is the amount of waste on the camera roll.*

S. *This is approximately how many feet of exposed film (usable or not) are to be processed.*

Any missing information means your camera assistant has done an incomplete job. Any time you find a member of the production crew providing incomplete information, correct the problem immediately. Any information left off these reports affects you directly in the dailies process.

Videotape-Shoot Camera Report

Sometimes in the field video shoots will either create slightly less detailed camera reports than film shoots, and sometimes they don't create any camera reports at all. If there are not any camera reports created by production, then it will fall to the editor or assistant editor to create a log once the dailies have been digitized. Figure 5.3 is an example of what a video camera report (sometimes called a Video Log) might look like.

Figure 5.3 Sample Video Log

Video Dailies Log Sheet	
Tape I.D.	**Project Title:**
Logged by:_____	**Shoot Date:**_____ /____ /_____
Time code:	**Description:**
____:____:____:____	
____:____:____:____	
____:____:____:____	
____:____:____:____	
____:____:____:____	
____:____:____:____	
____:____:____:____	
____:____:____:____	
____:____:____:____	
____:____:____:____	
____:____:____:____	
____:____:____:____	
____:____:____:____	
____:____:____:____	
____:____:____:____	
____:____:____:____	
____:____:____:____	
____:____:____:____	
____:____:____:____	
____:____:____:____	
____:____:____:____	
____:____:____:____	
____:____:____:____	
____:____:____:____	
____:____:____:____	
____:____:____:____	
____:____:____:____	
____:____:____:____	
____:____:____:____	
____:____:____:____	
____:____:____:____	
____:____:____:____	
____:____:____:____	
____:____:____:____	

Video Camera Report/Video Log Breakdown

Tape ID: This should be some identifier that also exists on the videotape label. It could be a number, such as tape 101. It could be more detailed if necessary, such as A Camera Tape 2. Whatever the ID is, it needs to be an easy reference for both the EDL and the on-line assistant so the correct tapes are used in the on-line.

Project Title: If you are creating a movie this will just be the name of the movie. If you are shooting a series for television, this will be the series name plus an episode name and number. It's important to use both the episode name and number wherever possible in your materials. Often when shows go to air, the network changes the episode numbers to reflect either their own internal system or maybe airdate order. Having the episode title also means there will always be a cross-reference should the actual production numbers change during the project. This is very common in TV that is distributed both domestically first-run, internationally, and in syndication. One of these groups may very well need to change episode numbers for their accounting or scheduling purposes.

Logged by: This will be the name or initials of the person who created the log. This could be helpful if there is missing information or if there is trouble reading someone's handwriting.

Shoot Date: This is the date the videotape that is being logged was shot.

Timecode: This is the timecode on the videotape that corresponds to the description provided.

Description: This is information about a particular timecode. It could include scene and take information, a description of the scene, highlight certain dialogue or events, etc.

Television Dailies

Television dailies fall into three categories:

- Film print dailies (with 35 mm or 16 mm magnetic sound or MOS),
- Standard definition or high definition videotape dailies transferred from film to tape (with sound or MOS),
- Standard definition or high definition videotape dailies shot on videotape with sound.

Film Print Dailies

Film print dailies are rare nowadays in television. This is due primarily to the costs and turnaround time required working with cutting film. However, some large scale cable movies or network events may still see at least a few days of film print dailies. In addition, they'll create video dailies for use in nonlinear electronic editing.

When you are working with print dailies, your film that is shot each day is taken to a film laboratory for overnight processing and printing. Simultaneously, the production sound (1/4″, 1/2″, DAT, etc.) is dropped off for transfer to magnetic tape (mag)—usually single-stripe (mono). These are also referred to as one-to-ones (or 1 :1). A double system (film and sound) of the selected or circled takes is usually ready for the assistant editor to start working with the next morning. Do not assume the film lab that is processing and printing your dailies can also do your sound transfers. Be sure to check with them. If you need to go out of house to process your audio and don't already have a sound house in mind, the lab supervisor will suggest a place.

The laboratory creates your print rolls by physically cutting apart the circled take negatives and splicing them together to make roll. This roll of cut negative is then printed. The takes that are circled are generally referred to as A negative, selects, or circled takes. The takes that are not printed are called B negative.

The individual pieces of B negative film are placed as individual small rolls inside a film box or can. These are sent to the negative cutter for storage. Negative is never stored in the editorial room. The negative cutter organizes these out takes so they are easy to access should someone want to order another take to be printed. That is why the printing of nonselected takes is called B negative. This term was carried over from film to videotape with the onset of electronic dailies.

With print dailies, the director and cinematographer (plus any others deemed necessary) will often go to a screening room (usually at the lab) and watch the dailies projected. If you will be screening print dailies in a screening room, make sure you have booked the room with your lab ahead of time. Due to demands on the set, the cinematographer often screens MOS dailies early in the morning prior to call time. The remainder of the executives will usually wait and come in later to screen after the editor syncs the picture and sound together.

Film-to-Tape Dailies

Film-to-tape dailies are dailies that are shot on film, then either a) developed and prepped at the film laboratory for telecine transfer to videotape or b) transferred from film print dailies once they've been synced and screened. Most large budget features use this second method. Instead of the client receiving film print dailies, they receive their dailies on videotape only.

Telecine Film Prep

Before it can be transferred, your film must be properly prepared by the lab (this preparation is referred to as "prep"). Telecine prep is a step normally done by the laboratory that is processing your negative. The lab puts your processed negative in the necessary form for telecine. To do this they build the film into what are called "lab rolls" by tying camera rolls together until they have a roll that is approximately 1000 or 2000 feet for 35 mm film and 1200 feet for 16 mm film. The rolls are tied in order by camera. In other words, all the A camera rolls are tied in ascending order, then the B rolls are tied together in ascending order, and so on. You may have turned in ten 400-foot rolls of exposed 35 mm film to the lab, but the telecine house may receive four 1000-foot rolls for transfer. The original negative is not cut during prep for a film-to-tape transfer.

The laboratory builds these lab rolls onto a small round plastic core that loads easily onto the telecine machine. They also leader the head and tail of each lab roll with at least 12 to 16 feet of leader. More leader at the head of the roll equals a cleaner first frame of picture. The 12 to 16 feet of leader at the head and tail of each roll is necessary to make sure the film threads through the roller system of the telecine machine and keeps proper tension throughout transfer of the entire roll. The lab may also punch a small hole at the head of either each camera roll or each lab roll, depending on the specifications for the transfer and the telecine house requirements.

This hole is made by taking a single-hole hand punch and making a hole in the film frame during the slate prior to usable action. If the lab does not punch at the least the head of each camera roll, the telecine colorist will do this during the transfer. The punch is usually just before the close of the clapper in the slate, well before usable action. The punch identifies the 00 frame and is forced as the A video frame of the edit. (This is a guide for the telecine colorist and negative cutter. The punch becomes a reference and serves as a double check for the electronic off-line editor to calculate which frame is the A frame of video.) When 24-frames-per-second (fps) film is converted to 30-fps video, the method used for this calculation is called the 3:2 pulldown. Every other film frame is held for three video fields, resulting in a sequence of three fields, two fields, three fields, two fields. The A frame is the frame in the 3:2 sequence which is reproduced as a complete video frame. Therefore, the A frame is made up of video fields one and two; the B frame is made up of fields one, and two, and one; the C frame is made up of fields two, and one only; and the D frame is video fields two, and one, and two.

Figure 5.4   3:2 Diagram

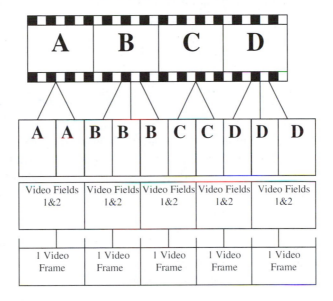

This does not apply during 30 fps transfers in NTSC, 25 fps transfers in PAL, multicamera transfers, or when you are doing an off-speed transfer. An off-speed transfer is when you have your film transferred at other than 24 fps in NTSC or 25 fps in PAL.

See the "Editorial (Film Editorial and Video Off-Line Editing)" chapter for information on how film print dailies are prepped for screening and telecine.

The Dailies Film Transfer

When transferring your dailies from original camera negative, the telecine colorist lays down each roll of film to videotape in order starting with the A camera (unless otherwise instructed) for single-camera shows. Multicamera shows (sitcoms) traditionally start the transfer with the B camera. The B camera (the geography camera) has the widest shot. You will always want to transfer the widest shot first in a multicam show, setting the look and then coloring the close-ups to match the wide shots. To set up the telecine for transfer, the telecine is sized with an SMPTE alignment-and-resolution chart to ensure proper registration. TAF (telecine analysis film) is used to set a standard color balance and exposure. Unless otherwise noted, the film will be transferred with a standard Academy aperture. It is extremely important to inform the transfer house if you shot with an alternative framing setup.

When the telecine has been set up and tested by the colorist, the film to be transferred is put up and threaded through the rollers, across the gate, and onto the take-up reel. Film comes from the lab heads out.

The colorist then begins the transfer according to the transfer specifications you have provided. If you have not specified a film transfer rate, your film will be transferred at 24 frames per second.

It is common with multicamera shows to color correct the dailies during initial transfer. The colorist will stop at each lighting or shot change, and after the color has been corrected, several frames will be saved in a still store. This way, if pickup shots or later takes come back to this setting, the colorist can call up this still store to use as a color reference. This is done so that each shot in each setup matches perfectly and when the editor cuts the shots together they will be timed to one another. When there are multiple episodes or when dailies are transferred over several days, the colorist uses these still-store images to provide continuity.

When doing a best-light or one-light transfer, the colorist will still take time to adjust the look of each new scene, with minor adjustments happening "on the fly" as the take is laid down to videotape. These corrections may also be saved in a still store for use as a reference throughout the dailies run. The dailies will need color-correction after the assembly, but the picture will be laid down within the proper specifications for that tape-to-tape correction. In other words, the whites (video levels) will peak below 100 IRE units (used to measure video units) without clipping and the blacks will remain uncrushed at the legal NTSC level below 7.5 IRE units. This gives the tape-to-tape colorist approximately the same latitude for applying corrections tape-to-tape as coloring from your original cut negative.

The term "crushed blacks" describes video black levels at or below 7.5 IRE in the NTSC world (below 0 in the PAL standard). These levels are characterized by loss of detail in dark areas of the picture. Adherence to these technical parameters provides the tape-to-tape colorist the range and latitude necessary to do the job well.

Too much secondary color-correction on dailies that are scheduled to finish with tape-to-tape color-correction will usually backfire. By color correcting dailies too much you may limit the colorist's flexibility down the road when your show is assembled and you are trying to achieve a fluid look scene-to-scene. It is often hard to convince executives of this concept. Sometimes producers and network executives worry that if the dailies are not color-corrected they won't get the look they want in their finished product. In reality the opposite is true. If it really becomes an issue during the dailies transfer process, you may need to schedule a small tape-to-tape color-correction test to show the executives that down the road they will be better able to get what they want in their final product. It is really important that you stick to the technical-level guidelines set by your transfer house if you are planning to color correct your show tape-to-tape after it is assembled onto videotape.

During this film-to-tape dailies transfer, many other things are going on in the telecine bay while your film is being laid to videotape.

Some postproduction facilities provide a dual record system for dailies film-to-tape transfers. In essence, one color-correction (meeting all of the technical requirements for the tape-to-tape color-correction to be done later) is laid to the telecine master videotape. A slightly richer colored image is recorded onto separate videotape from which all of the viewing cassettes will be made. Cassettes delivered to network and production executives will look closer to the final color-correction without compromising the actual tape-to-tape color-correction session.

Film Print to Tape Dailies

The negative dailies footage has been cut (circle takes separated out) and printed. The sound has been transferred to magnetic tape and synced to picture. If done properly, the Keykode from the original negative has been printed through and exists on the print being transferred. When transferring from daily prints, the transfer is done for the sole purpose of creating videotape work cassettes to enter into an off-line system for electronic editing. This videotape material will never be considered as "master" material. The advantage is that the show can be viewed on a large screen (such as in the screening room at a film lab) and be available to edit electronically. Both are required when posting a theatrical movie.

Transferring 16:9 Dailies

Some studios and production companies began shooting 16:9 in the mid-1990's to protect the image on their negative for use when high-definition and/or digital television became a broadcast standard. Throughout the late 1990's many more studios and production companies jumped on this bandwagon. This means that even though the focus of the action is still current broadcast television 1.33:1 aspect ratio (also referred to as 4:3), there is exposed picture on the negative that can be utilized for wider picture that will be broadcast in high-definition television. This opened up a whole new set of issues that must be worked out in telecine.

Before one frame of dailies footage is transferred, it must be determined if the dailies are going to be laid to videotape in the current television 1.33:1 aspect ratio or in the 16:9 format. It is necessary to provide a framing chart when you are shooting 16:9, regardless of how you plan to proceed with this image through postproduction. The framing chart will be necessary both in telecine and in on-line if your image will need to be unsqueezed at any time. The purpose of the framing chart is to accurately identify the "center" of the image.

Transferring 16:9 as 4:3

In this situation the 4:3 image is "extracted" from the entire exposed 16:9 area and none of the image that falls outside the 4:3 area is transferred to videotape. It is imperative, then, that you provide the telecine house with a framing chart so they are sure to frame the image on the telecine to match up exactly where the cinematographer framed the 4:3 area in the camera.

Film shoot shows that protect their image for 16:9 and transfer their dailies in high definition will not chose this 4:3 method. When the source is available in 16:9 and transferred in HD, the aspect ratio will always be 16:9. If needed, the 4:3 image will be extracted later.

Transferring the 16:9 Image

In this situation, the entire 16:9 exposed area of the negative is transferred. The image that is laid down to the videotape will be "squeezed." When played back through a 16:9 monitor, the image will be "unsqueezed" by the monitor and everything will be normal. However, if you play it back on a regular 4:3 TV set, the images will appear slightly taller and compressed from side to side. Therefore, to deliver a 4:3 image for broadcast, this "squeezed" image must be altered. There are two ways to do this. The first way is to unsqueeze the image into a 4:3 with a letterbox (a space left at the top and bottom of the screen, filled in with black bars); thereby allowing for the entire image at the sides to be included in the 4:3 television picture. This is not an acceptable solution for most broadcast situations. However, the 2001 TV season did see several popular dramas choosing this method for broadcast. Possibly this is the networks way of easing people into the widescreen 16:9 format. Or perhaps just a creative decision to allow for more "theatrical-like" compositions when framing shots. The letterbox in some cases is a compromise between 4:3 full frame and a true 16:9 letterbox (1:77) image. It does allow some additional image space on the picture sides without having such large black bars at the top and the bottom of the picture.

The second option is to extract the image with an aspect-ratio converter or an image converter in an edit bay. This will create a normal-looking 4:3 full frame image. With this solution, you will lose some of the image from the sides of the picture and your image will be slightly softer and the grain slightly enhanced, as the picture will have to be blown up to fill in the top and bottom of the screen.

As you can see, depending on how your producer wants to go and your ultimate delivery requirements, there are several points in postproduction at which you can extract the 4:3 image, if you are shooting initially protected for 16:9. The first opportunity is here at the dailies stage.

You can lay down pictures in 4:3 at the initial dailies transfer. This means the 16:9 image lives only on film. The dailies will have to be re-telecined to utilize that material outside the 4:3 box. Ultimately not a very practical solution unless you're sure you are never going to use that 16:9 aspect ratio (then why shoot that way to begin with?). Or, your dailies are just a work medium and you plan to go back and cut negative. Still, in this case too, why not transfer the extra picture information and give your editors more material to work with?

A HD dailies film to video transfer does not differ drastically from a standard definition transfer, the harder parts really come later. Most TV programs when transferring to HD transfer to HDCam stock. (Unlike feature transfers which in HD usually record to D5 or D6 stock.) The stock is slightly cheaper and the compression rate slightly higher. It is also the same stock you will use if you are shooting with the 1080 HD video camera. The Keykode will still be captured and stored to a file for use in electronic editing. It is the same with the sound timecode.

Work Cassettes

If you shot your dailies framed for 4:3 or you are pulling out the 4:3 image during your dailies transfer, then any cassettes you make from those dailies masters will not have to be altered. If, however, you are transferring your dailies in a squeezed 16:9 format, you have a decision to make regarding editors and viewing cassettes. There are three options: 1) you can deliver cassettes with the squeezed image; 2) you can deliver cassettes with a hard matte or letterbox at the top and bottom; or 3) you can run your dailies image through an aspect-ratio converter and extract the 4:3 image and record onto another videotape.

Should you choose the third option, be sure to discuss all of your visible window information requirements with the transfer house well in advance of the start of your dailies. Depending on how complex your requirements are, the facility may need time to involve engineering in a special setup to handle your footage on a daily basis. You should also expect a delay in receiving your dailies cassettes each day. Fortunately shooting in 16:9 has become more the norm than not, so that a facility handling many TV shows should be able to easily accommodate whichever process you chose. If they cannot, maybe you need to re-evaluate using that facility for your dailies. It is not always wise to be the guinea pig when you're trying to adhere to the nearly impossibly short deliver dates TV imposes—even if the costs are being reduced as an incentive. You may find yourself muttering "penny wise, pound foolish" more than once during the season.

Work Cassettes—High Definition Projects

When transferring your film dailies to HD, you will need to factor in time for a down conversion each day. Your masters will be in HD (probably HDCam for TV) but your producer, executives, etc. will be expecting to watch those dailies each morning on their TVs, which are probably not HD. And, most likely your editors are cutting on a standard definition nonlinear editing system, so they too will need standard definition (SD) tapes to work with.

Depending on your facility's capabilities you may have to go somewhere else for the down conversion. Or, maybe move to another machine within the same facility. Some HD record decks do have an internal down converter built-in. In this case, the facility can create a SD master from which to make all of your dubs as soon as your telecine is done. Just a little something else you have to be sure to arrange ahead of time so you don't find yourself with HD dailies and no way for anyone to view or edit them. Also you'll need this information to factor into your budget.

Again, if you chose a transfer facility that is already doing HD TV dailies, then it should just be a brief conversation and negotiation into your package, instead of a daily stress point.

Film Transfer with Sound

When there is sound to be synched to picture, this can be done during the telecine transfer. The colorist lines up the frame of the clapper closing with the sound of the slate closing recorded on the production audio and lay the picture and sound down together, in sync, onto the videotape master. Because film runs normally at 24 fps and your sound is running at 30 fps there can be up to a three-field discrepancy between the visual of the clapper closing and the corresponding audio. The accepted rule of thumb is that one frame early or late between when you see the clapper close and when you hear the clapper close is acceptable. A two- to three-field (one video frame) discrepancy instead of "hard" sync can happen because of the difference in film and audiotape run speeds. With film running at 24 fps the closest sync for a film-finish is within one twelfth of a second. With a video finish (which runs at 30 fps) the closest sync is one tenth of a second. In multicamera shoots, the cameras are not synchronized to each other, meaning you are now synchronizing several cameras to one audio playback source, all with potential fractional discrepancies.

Dailies can be transferred from film to videotape either with or without sound. Traditionally, they are transferred with sync sound. But there are editors that prefer to load the digital production audio source directly into their nonlinear off-line system. Hey, while we're on the subject of production audio and dailies transfers . . . Oops, here we go sticking our noses into production's business. (But it's for a really good cause—your sanity and your budget.)

Production Audio Recording Tips

We are going to interject some very important advice concerning the production values practiced when recording your production audio in the field. Any of the following can adversely affect postproduction sound throughout the entire process. The care taken when your sound is originally recorded on the set will directly affect how much money and time it will take for your postproduction facility to render usable dailies. Some of the following points are discussed in detail in Chapter 8. But we feel that some stuff is so important that it needs to be said at every opportunity.

1. *Always shoot sync sound dailies using an electronic slate.* This is an electronic slate that along with the traditional camera roll, scene and take information, has a red LED readout that gives a visual reference of the production sound timecode. The timecode displayed on this LED readout needs to match the timecode being laid down to your production audiotape during recording. The telecine colorist uses this timecode to physically find the take on the sound element, and it can also be a secondary reference to the off-line editor when verifying the sound EDL.

2. *Make sure the slate is in focus.* It is very time-consuming for a telecine operator, assistant editor, and editor to try and decipher the slate to determine the scene and take if the information on the slate is illegible. It is also important that the visual timecode reference be in focus so the production sound timecode is readable, and therefore, more synchable (we're not sure that's a word, but it says what we mean).

3. *Make sure the slate is in the camera frame when the clapper closes.* No one will be able to use the clapper to sync your shot if they cannot see the stick when it makes contact with the slate. Don't be offended by this seemingly obvious advice. We see this mistake time and time again by some of the most seasoned professional production crews (that's right, we're not naming names, but you know who you are and you *should* be embarrassed). Everyone is focusing their attention on the shot, but the person marking the scene, and the camera operator(s) must be aware of the position of the clapper in relationship to what the camera is seeing in the frame.

4. *If you are rolling multiple cameras make sure that all the cameras see the slate before it closes so all cameras see the visible timecode reference.* This will also help you ensure that you are giving the 10 seconds of audio preroll so vital to the telecine operator's ability to sync your sound.

5. *Make sure the slate and sticks are readable.* If you are shooting a scene that is taking place at the top of a tall building and you are shooting from the ground, don't put the slate at the top of the building where it will be impossible to read! You may need to shoot the slate, clap the sticks to mark the picture and sound, and then leave the shot rolling while you refocus on the building top.

6. If you are shooting a dark scene, be sure to illuminate the slate so when the stick makes contact with the slate it is visible on the film. The timecode numbers are electronic and readable in the dark; the close of the clapper is the only way to verify sync at the beginning of the take if the audio time-

code fails. Some productions shine a light on the slate and some apply a glow-in-the-dark substance or tape along the bottom of the stick and the top of the slate so the clapper closing is visible.

7. *Make sure the production sound recordist verbally slates each take.* This way, if the timecode on your slate is inaccurate or unreadable, the telecine operator has a back-up source to use to find sync and identify the correct takes on the audiotape. Synching sound to picture is a very time-consuming part of dailies telecine transfer.

8. *If the production audio timecode is to become the linear timecode on your dailies, roll the audiotape on MOS takes.* If you do not, then the telecine operator must assemble the shot by jam-syncing the timecode so it locks and generates, continuing from the previous take. This is time-consuming and will probably mean these takes will need to go at the end of the transfer. There is also the danger of causing a timecode break in the dailies, which will then cause problems when digitizing. The off-line editor can use this sound for room tones/noise in the cut.

Okay, where were we before we took this little detour into production tips? Right . . . dailies. Let the fun continue . . .

Transfer Data

When your dailies film is transferred to videotape, identification information about the film can be logged during the telecine process. This information is usually referred to as the edge numbers or Keykode (this is a Kodak product name) numbers. These edge numbers are read by the telecine, matched up with their corresponding video and audio timecode (if applicable) and incorporated into a database. This combination of information is saved on a floppy disk or CD-ROM, thus enabling a film shoot to be edited in video and all edits matched back to the original negative for release in any format. These edge numbers become references for the negative cutter. Having this information logged in this manner during the transfer can save days of manual data entry and avoids human error during editing and negative cutting. The edge numbers are printed along the film's edge every 16 frames on 35 mm film and every 20 frames on 16 mm film.

Every day, after the telecine transfer, the editor's cassette is available to the client along with a floppy disk containing all of the transfer information. The disk may be called the FLEx File disk, Keylog disk, or Aaton disk, depending on the logging system used. It is a 3.5″ floppy or CD-ROM in a PC format. The electronic off-line editing system then converts the information into a format that it can read. For example: the Avid (nonlinear editing system brand name) has a program called the Avid Log Exchange (.ALE) that performs this conversion function. Your assistant editor runs the disk through this program prior to digitizing the dailies. Along with this disk the editor will receive a paper printout of the transfer information contained on that disk in an easy-to-follow format.

The title of the show, the production company, the date the film was shot, (according to the slate), and the date the material was transferred are listed at the top of the telecine log. The colorist's name, telecine bay, and brief notes are also included there. There is some flexibility in this information so that if you wanted, for example, the file name, shoot day, or other information listed here, that should not be a problem.

Incorporating edge number information into an EDL tells the negative cutter exactly where each shot is located on the original negative camera rolls. The negative cutter is then organized for minimal handling of the original negative. Figure 5.5 shows a few lines from the printout of such a list.

Figure 5.5 Sample Telecine Log

Slate Date:_____   Title:_____   Transfer Date:_____
Bay:_____   Client:_____   Colorist:_____
Notes:_____

(A) Edit	(B) Scene	(C) Take	(D) Camera Roll	(E) Sound Roll	(F) Record TC	(G) Sound TC	(H) Prefix	(I) Key In
1	86	4	A1	1	01:01:05.05.0	09:36:37:25.0	KQ355030	4169+00
(J) Notes:								
2	87	5	A2	1	01:02:12:20.0	10:42:30:05.0	KQ415166	5146+00
Notes: SLATE TC NG								
3	87	6	A2	1	01:04:46:05.0	10:47:50:28.0	KQ415166	5378+00
Notes: SLATE TC NG								
4	GS		A2		01:07:12:10.0		KQ415166	5599+00
Notes: GRAY SCALE								
5	87A	2	A2	1	01:07:15:05.0	11:17:54:02.0	KQ415166	5665+00
Notes: SLATE TC NG								
6	87A	3	A2	1	01:08:28:15.0	11:20:17:18.0	KQ415166	5778+00
Notes: TAIL STICKS								
7	87B	1	A3	1	01:09:46:20.0	11:33:30:05.0	KQ485066	4947+00
Notes: SLATE TC NG REFLECTIONS ON FACE								
8	87B	3	A3	1	01:10:53:15.0	11:36:00:27.0	KQ485066	5065+00
Notes:								
9	701	1	A3		01:15:46:20.0		KQ485066	5664+00
Notes: MOS								

Telecine Report Breakdown

A. *Edit number.* This signifies which edit this is.
B. *Scene number*. This lists the scene number of that edit.
C. *Take number*. This lists the take number for the specified scene.
D. *Camera roll number.* This is the camera roll number that the scene and take are located on.
E. *Sound roll number*. This is the sound roll number that the scene and take are located on.
F. *Tape timecode.* This is the timecode that exists on the videotape master.
G. *Audio timecode.* This is the timecode that was laid onto the production sound when it was recorded in the field.
H. *Edge number or Keykode number prefix.* The eight letters make up the first characters of the edge numbers on the film. This information is specific to a particular camera roll. Each time a new camera roll is put up and transferred, this prefix changes. The letters represent the film manufacturer and where and when the film was made. These aid the film manufacturer in identifying specific information about a particular roll of film when researching possible film stock problems.
I. *Key in/foot and frames.* This counts the number of feet and frames from the head of the camera roll to the point where the take is located. On the telecine log, this number represents the start of the take. The numbers to the left of the plus sign are the footage. The two digits after the plus sign represent the number of frames. When looking at this printout for a transfer that is going to an electronic off-line cut, you should always see "+00" for the frames.
J. *Comment line.* The colorist is provided with several character spaces in which to make any important notations about that particular take. Items such as negative scratch, MOS take, and tail sticks, are put here for the editor's reference.

On the sample log, look at the camera roll column (column D). Notice that when the camera roll number changes, so does the prefix (column H). Also notice that the foot and frame numbers (column I) are in ascending order from edit to edit—until the camera roll changes, and then they start counting over again in the new camera roll. If there is a glitch in the telecine equipment, the prefix of the key number may not update in the database. While the transfer house can fix this for you, it can also be fixed on the client's side directly in the off-line system. The telecine colorist is doing many things during the transfer, including double-checking and keeping track of all the necessary information. Sometimes small errors in your list will go undetected by the colorist. Most are minor and can be corrected on the off-line side as text edits.

Incorporating edge number information into an EDL tells the negative cutter exactly where each shot is located on the original negative camera rolls. The negative cutter is then organized for minimal handling of the original negative.

Naming the Telecine File

The colorist must enter a name for the telecine file database being created for each videotape dailies reel. It is wise to have that database name have an obvious reference back to the dailies information located in that file. The colorist has six characters available. Depending on the database software, there may or may not be the option of mixing alphabetical and numeric characters. In the case of the FLEx File, this is an option. So, if you are shooting an MOW and you are shooting for 13 days, there will be at least 13 dailies transfer masters. Each will have a different timecode, and the timecodes will preferably be in ascending order. Videotape one can be hour code one, videotape two can be hour code two, and so on. The database name should also be logical. A show named "Me and Dad" could use the title initials as the first part of the database and uses the hour-code number as the information that distinguishes one day from the next. Therefore, the file name for day one, hour code 1 would be MAD01; day two, hour code 2 would be MAD02; and so forth.

A word of caution, this file name will carry through the off-line edit and become the identifier in the source column of your on-line EDL. Many on-line systems will allow only a six-character source name. It is wise to keep your telecine database file names to five characters to avoid any characters being dropped by the on-line system. The reason this can become an issue is that the off-line system will sometimes add characters to this source name as a visual reference identifying an edit command. For example, if a source dissolves to itself in an EDL, the system may place a "B" at the end of the source name, thus making a six character name seven characters. When the list is converted for the on-line, the list management program may drop any characters after six, thus altering your reference for what is happening at that edit.

In any case, the telecine colorist will not be present for your on-line. The database name, which in turn becomes the source reel name in your EDL, must provide a logical reference back to the videotape transfer masters so that in the on-line, it will be easy to determine which videotape the list is calling for at each edit. This becomes especially critical when your sources include reels that carry the same hour code. A phenomenon not uncommon for TV shows, specials, and MOWs (and certainly features!).

We suggest as a final safety measure that you make the dailies file name part of the label information on both the editors' dailies cassettes and the dailies master videotapes. This will eliminate any doubt the on-line editor may have when pairing source names with source tapes.

After the initial film-to-tape transfer, the negative and production sound elements are usually vaulted by the transfer house until they are called for by the client for negative cutting, delivery, or to be put into long-term storage.

Another Transfer Method

Another photography/telecine system available is the Aaton motion picture camera with Keykode/timecode reader for use in telecine. This is an in-camera time-coding system, which is designed to automate the picture and sound synchronizing process. The timecode generator in the Aaton cameras print "time of day" timecode information that is both human and machine-readable. Also embedded in this code may be production information such as film reel, date, and camera equipment. If your show is shooting on an Aaton, be sure the transfer house you choose has the necessary equipment to transfer your film and sound.

The Telecine Transfer Specifications

Before your transfer starts, there are some really important details that you need to give to the transfer facility. Figure 5.6 is a sample of a telecine specification sheet that a facility might give to a client to fill in and return to them. This will provide the facility with the bulk of the information needed to transfer the dailies to meet the client's needs.

Figure 5.6   Sample Telecine Specification Sheet

A
PRODUCTION COMPANY:_____
TITLE:_____
CONTACT:_____PHONE:_____
LABORATORY:_____
B   _____Transfer All   _____Transfer Circled Takes Only
    _____Best Light Transfer   _____Color Correct Dailies

C   **D**

FILM FORMAT	**AUDIO FORMAT**	**AUDIO CH CONFIGURATION**	
_____16 mm	_____1/4″ Nagra	_____CH 1	_____Mono
_____35 mm	_____DAT	_____CH 2	_____Stereo
_____Super 35 mm	_____1/2″	_____CH 3	_____NDFTC 30 FPS
_____Other	_____DA88	_____CH 4	_____DFTC 30 FPS

E
Transfer Speed _____24 FPS _____30 FPS _____Other Aspect Ratio_____
              _____NTSC _____PAL _____24P _____Other

F
_____Single Camera Shoot   _____Multiple Camera Shoot (Sitcom)

G   **H**
MASTER   Record To:_____   Audio Configuration: CH1:_____CH2:_____
_____DFTC _____NDFTC _____Standard Definition _____High Definition CH3:_____CH4:_____

I Vertical Interval Information:
Audio Timecode   _____Yes   _____No   _____(Note any line)
   Keykode   _____Yes   _____No   _____(Note any line)
New Continuous Timecode: _____Yes   _____No   _____DFTC_____NDFTC
Audio Timecode as Longitudinal Code: _____Yes   _____No

J Record Stock Length: _____30 Min _____60 Min   _____Client Stock

K
EDIT CASSETTE (Simultaneous Record) _____3/4″ _____Betacam SP   _____Other
_____Aspect Ratio _____Letterbox

L
Visible Timecode Windows: _____Record Timecode Position _____
              _____Keykode Position _____
              _____Audio Timecode Position _____
              _____Foot and Frames Position _____

M
Audio: CH 1:_____   CH 2:_____

N
Vertical Interval Information: _____Audio   _____Keykode   _____Record Timecode

O
Record Stock Length: _____30 Min   _____60 Min   _____Client Stock

P
Off-Line System: _____Avid _____Lightworks _____MultiCam _____Heavyworks _____Other

Q   _____Telecine Floppy Disk and Printout Required

The following is an explanation of the sample telecine transfer specifications form above:

A. *Production company and film lab information.* Production company, show title, show daily contact, phone numbers, the lab that will be processing the film, whether that lab will be doing the telecine prep, the time the film is scheduled to arrive at the transfer facility and who will deliver it, and where and when the sound is arriving. Phew! That's a lot of important information!

B. *Take information.* Specific information about what takes are to be transferred and how much time the colorist is to spend setting the color for each take.

C. *What film size you are shooting.* It is very important to distinguish here between 35 mm, super 35, and 16 mm. Each is framed differently, and the wrong information here can offset the center of your dailies image, changing the director's framing. The overall transfer speed is also indicated here.

D. *Your production sound format.* Make note if a back-up source will also be recorded and indicate which source is to be used as the primary source for your dailies transfer and which is the back-up. Also fill in the channel designations for your production sound—what is on channel one, channel two. Let the facility know if your production audio was shot mono or stereo and whether your production audio timecode is nondrop-frame timecode (NDFTC) or drop-frame timecode (DFTC). They differ in running time. DFTC adds 3 seconds and 18 frames each hour (1 second and 9 frames each half-hour) over NDFTC. It will be assumed you recorded your audio time-code at 30 fps when working in NTSC.

E. *Transfer speed.* Is this going to be a 24-fps transfer or a 30-fps transfer? Or, is this a special circumstance that requires a nonstandard off-speed transfer? If the later is the case, be sure to talk this over with the facility. The transfer speed range will vary from postproduction house to postproduction house. You may have to go elsewhere for your off-speed film transfer. It is best to know this up front. Also know that if you have film shot off-speed, if the facility will not be able to sync any sound shot with these takes or provide accurate edge number information.

F. *Single camera/multicamera shoot.* Single camera means you are not running multiple cameras for each take. All single-camera shows shoot more than one camera during certain times. This is different, however, than having three or more cameras set up to shoot a different angle of each and every shot.

G. *Video format information.* To what videotape format and standard are you transferring? Do you need DFTC or NDFTC on your master?

H. *Audio information.* Do you want the production sound to appear on the videotape? (What is on channel 1, channel 2, and so on?) Be sure you know how many audio channels are on the tape format you choose.

I. *Vertical interval and timecode information.* If you want your production audio timecode information to be on your dailies master, then answer "yes" to audio code in the vertical interval. If you plan (or, if there is even a remote chance) to cut negative down the road, answer "yes" to putting Keykode in the vertical interval. Edge number information can come only from film, and it is your only method of referencing your videotape cut directly back to your original negative. Using edge numbers along with a computer-generated EDL cuts from hours to minutes the time it takes to cross-reference shots from the video edit to the original negative. The information will be completely frame accurate, with virtually no data-entry errors. If you don't capture the information now, you will have to retransfer the film to get this information should you need it later. On multicamera shows, the production audio timecode usually becomes the linear timecode across all cameras. When doing a multicamera show, you will want to mark "yes" for audio timecode becoming the longitudinal timecode. For single-camera shows, new linear or address-track timecode is generated at the time of the film transfer. Your transfer facility or editor can explain this further if there are questions.

J. *Master stock information.* Let the facility know what stock length to pull for your session and whether you want to use facility stock or provide your own client stock. If your dailies are transferred to 30-minute stock, you will double the number of times the telecine operator has to stop down and format a new tape. The reality in using client stock for the master is that the onus is on the client to pay for any replacements due to stock problems.

K. *Editor's cassette.* This is traditionally recorded at the same time the dailies transfer master is recorded. Facilities refer to this as a simultaneous recording (usually called a "simo"). The postproduction house will need to know what videotape format you require for your simo record. Most off-line systems use 3/4" but some bigger-budget projects looking for higher picture and sound quality from the off-line output will use a Betacam SP. They'll also need to know if your editor's cassettes are to be letterboxed.

L. *Timecode windows.* When choosing what timecode windows you want, if any, on your editor's cassette, be sure to tell the facility where you want each window placed. They also need to know if the windows will be in action-safe or in underscan. "Windows" refer to a rectangle in your video picture that has numbers inside it. The window can be solid black with white numbers or transparent with black numbers. Other information, such as the edge numbers, can be placed in these windows, and there is no limit to the number of windows you can request.

M. *Audio configuration for your editor's cassette.* If you are making a 3/4" you have only two channels of audio. With a Betacam SP you can record four channels of audio. Channels 3 and 4 are call AFM channels. They are embedded in the picture, which means they must be recorded when you record picture. If you layback to Channels 3 and 4 on a Betacam SP, you will record over your picture.

N.   *Vertical interval timecode for your editor's cassette.* This is rarely an issue, but double-check before you give the transfer facility your specifications.

O.   *Editor's cassette stock information.* Let the facility know what stock length to pull for your editor's cassette and whether you want to use facility stock or provide your own client stock. If your dailies are transferred to 30-minute stock, you will double the number of times the telecine operator has to stop down and format a new tape.

P.   *Off-line information.* The facility will want to know the type of nonlinear system you are using.

Q.   *Floppy disk/printout information.* Let the postproduction house know whether you require a floppy disk containing the transfer information. This is generally called a FLEx file or Keylog disk. (Some facilities have proprietary systems that go by different names.) A printout of the disk information is also sent along with the editor's cassette and the floppy disk.

Your transfer house will be happy to answer any questions or offer any advice, should you need it. Remember that they do this for a living! Take advantage of their expertise—they'll be happy you asked.

Road Maps and the Multicamera Shoot

Road maps are another tool that is very useful for both the transfer house and the client when shooting and transferring multicamera shows such as sitcoms.

A road map is a spreadsheet that lists what camera rolled for each take. It also lists what camera roll and sound roll each take is on and each take's duration. Finally, there is a place to note any comments that will help the colorist when transferring that take.

Traditionally used for sitcom telecine transfers, a road map could also be useful for any large production. It provides a guide for the telecine colorist to follow to help clarify:

1.   Which cameras rolled per take;
2.   The duration of each shot;
3.   Which sound roll each shot is on; and
4.   Any comments necessary for each shot, such as "sound didn't roll," "take aborted."

A road map provides a diagram for the colorist creating the layout of the multiple-videotape dailies masters to match the multiple cameras.

Figure 5.7 is a sample of a road map. An explanation for each section of the road map follows.

Figure 5.7 Road Map

A

B
EPS#<u>103</u>
EPS TITLE <u>Trouble Again</u>

A
SHOW <u>Paddy's Wagon</u>
C
SHOOT DATE(S) <u>4/23-4/24</u>

D	E	F				G	H	I	J
		A	B	C	X	SOUND	SOUND		
SC.	TK.	CAMERA	CAMERA	CAMERA	CAMERA	ROLL	TIMECODE	LENGTH	COMMENTS
A	1	1	1	1	1	1	12:14:22	2:42	X Cam aborted take
A	2	1	1	1	1	1	12:35:19	2:39	
A	3	1	1			1	13:01:25	2:54	
B	1	1	2	1	1	1	13:14:21	1:19	
B	2	2	2	2	1	1	13:26:05	1:23	Lens flare
B	3	2	2	2		2	14:01:02	1:07	
B	4	2	2	2	2	2	14:13:09	1:17	
D	1	2	3		2	2	14:20:10	:56	No C scene shot
D	2	2	3	3	2	2	14:23:18	:53	
E	1	3	3	3	3	2	14:33:21	3:06	
PA	1	5	4	4		3	16:22:19	:36	
PB	1	5	5	5	5	4	17:03:21	1:09	

The following is a breakdown of the sample road map:

A. *Title*
B. *Episode number and title*
C. *Shoot date(s)*
D. *Scenes*
E. *Takes*
F. *Put an "X" or camera roll number in each camera roll's box if that camera rolled on this take*
G. *Sound roll number*
H. *Audio timecode* (timecode recording when take started)
I. *Duration of each take.* Either time this yourself with a stopwatch if you are on the set or ask the sound recordist, camera department, or script supervisor to keep track. This information becomes critical during the telecine transfer when deciding how many takes will fit on the videotape stock.
J. *Comments.* This column is for comments regarding each take that the colorist will need later, such as "take aborted" or "sound didn't roll."

High Definition Dailies

You've probably been thinking to yourself, hey self, when is the discussion about standard definition dailies vs. high definition dailies going to kick into *high* gear (no pun intended)? Wonder no more, here we go.

Thus far, the information we've given you pretty much holds true for both standard definition and high definition dailies. That's what we were saying before about so many similarities between the two. And, occasionally so far we've peppered in some pertinent information about high definition. That will continue in this chapter and throughout this book. However, for a brief summary on some differences pertinent to our current discussion, here goes.

As explained in the "Digital TV and High Definition" chapter, *high definition* as it applies to film and television postproduction basically means more picture information than is available with standard definition images—more than 525 (NTSC) or 625 (PAL) lines make up each frame of video.

High definition dailies can be created from film via a telecine transfer just as NTSC or PAL dailies. They can also come from shooting with a high definition video camera. They can also be uprezed (upconverted) from standard definition materials, but except for the odd stock shot, this wouldn't really be done at the dailies stage.

High Definition Dailies Telecine Transfer

As with your standard definition dailies transfer, the facility is going to have some technical questions that you are going to have to answer before they can start your project. First, are you going to transfer your dailies in the "interlace" format or the "progressive" format? You're still going to have to answer "DFTC" or "NDFTC," believe it or not. You're going to need to know how your sound was recorded. Was it recorded in the camera? Is there a back up audio source that you need to do something with within the dailies process?

To review, our current NTSC (and PAL) videotape pictures are recorded onto videotape as "interlace" images. Each frame of video is created by every other line of the picture (the odd numbered lines) filling in from the top of the screen to the bottom of the screen and then from top to bottom every other line fills in (the even numbered lines)—making a complete picture. Once the odd lines have finished this is called a field. When the even lines have all filled in, this is also called a field. These two fields make up a full video frame. "Progressive" images fill-in completely with one pass from top to bottom. This is the way computer screens update.

The interlace and progressive are indicated by either an "i" or a "p" noted after the line count. 1080i indicates that 1080 lines make up the picture in the interlace format. 1080p indicates the same number of lines making up the image but displaying in the progressive mode.

Videotape-Shoot Dailies

If your show is a "tape shoot," meaning your dailies are shot on videotape and not on film, then there is no film laboratory processing involved. The "dailies" masters are created during shooting. You need to know whether an editor's off-line cassette is being run simultaneously on the set. If not, you will need to arrange to have the editor's cassette struck from the master videotapes.

With a videotape shoot, no electronic database is created with the camera, scene and take information is there as with a film to tape transfer. The information will have to be input manually by the assistant editor. The visual timecode reference should make this job quicker and more accurate.

This is an area of postproduction that has seen some of the biggest changes and challenges over the past 2 to 3 years. These changes have been caused by the introduction of feasible high definition videotape cameras.

Both Sony and Panasonic now have viable HD video cameras that are being used to shoot everything from TV series to feature films. The introduction of the latest generation of HD video cameras has catapulted video production to a level it has never reached previously in terms of quality and resolution. Video production has gone from the best it could hope for, with digital Betacam at 525i or 625i lines of resolution interlace, to 720p to 1080/24p.

What's more, these cameras are available in the progressive format. Thus, generating a video image devoid of the interlace interpolation problems which have plagued the world since color TV began.

Many agree that the most recent development: availability of the 24p camera, editing systems, and record machines is a huge leap forward for our industry.

Even if HDTV, for example, never comes to fruition as a commercial medium, we now have a method for transferring film to video in which every video frame has a corresponding film frame. This means that we can make NTSC or PAL tapes from one HD master as if they were coming straight off of film, this is huge. For U.S. domestic TV programs posted in 24p, it means no more problem-ridden upconversions to PAL, pulling out the 3:2 and changing frame rates and cycles. Therefore, if your show is either being shot in 24p or transferring from film to 24p, you are getting 1080 lines of resolution, in the progressive format and at 24 fps.

Editing and Nonlinear Off-Line Cassettes

Should you need to strike editor's cassettes from the dailies masters after your standard def tape shoot, you will order work cassettes (normally 3/4" or Betacam SP videotape) made at a facility that does videotape duplication. Be sure to determine ahead of time if the editor requires any visible timecode on the cassette. The visible timecode in the editor's off-line cassettes is a visual reference only, but most editors prefer it. Be sure to order the editor's cassette to be made with address track timecode. The off-line system locks to the address track timecode on the editor's cassette.

When creating standard definition NTSC work cassettes from your HD videotape masters, you will be ordering a down conversion. You will be coming from a higher resolution tape in either the interlace or progressive format to a standard def tape in the interlace format.

In addition to your editor's cassettes you will need viewing cassettes for the production company executives, studio or network executives, and production staff (director, producer, etc.). To avoid making and paying for multiple down conversions (and they ain't cheap) make a down conversion master, probably to digital Betacam, that you can use to fill all of your standing orders and any that may come up unexpectedly down the road.

Whether your off-line cassette is a simultaneous recording made during a film transfer or tape shoot or is struck later, the editor's cassette's address track timecode must match the timecode recorded on your videotape dailies masters. Therefore, if you are having these tapes created after shooting, be sure to tell the postproduction facility to match the timecode on the editor's cassettes to the masters. Usually the editor's work cassettes will be ordered with visible windows (timecode and/or Keykode). But there will be exceptions. Consult with the production office before making these tapes.

Once the dailies work cassettes are delivered to the cutting room, the assistant editor digitizes them into the nonlinear editing system and the editor proceeds with a cut. When the picture is locked and the editor outputs the EDL, the timecode numbers will correlate directly to the timecode on the videotape masters. This is the first step towards a smooth on-line session.

In addition to soliciting the editor's preference regarding visible windows in the off-line cassettes, be sure to let your producers on the shoot know what the editor has requested. Because while it is perfectly reasonable that the editor should be able to choose how the cassettes are made, this is not a perfectly reasonable business. And, although the editor must work with these tapes daily, the off-line output cassette of the various cuts of the show will also include whatever visible windows are in the editor's cassettes. Some producers and network executives are very particular about how many visible windows are in the picture; even the window size can be an issue with them. And ultimately, these are the people you want to make happy.

Size Is Important

An incident occurred in which an editor requested that the visible timecode window be a larger size than the postproduction house traditionally used. This request came because the producer and director liked to look at multiple shots on the off-line system monitors and the editor was having a hard time reading the timecode in the window. The associate producer agreed and the visible windows were enlarged on the dailies transfers of their next episode. The associate producer called back several days later. She ordered new editor's cassettes to be struck from all their dailies masters utilizing the smaller visible window size. It turns out the producer and the network executives felt they "could not see enough of the picture" because of the larger sized timecode windows.

Fortunately, before making the window larger, the dubbing facility had gotten approval for the size change from the production company. Now, in addition to being responsible for the costs incurred in remaking the editor's cassettes, the production company also had to pay someone to redigitize the dailies in the off-line system. The production company and not the editor is really the client, and had the postproduction house changed the window size without checking with the production company, the production company could have made a reasonable argument for not having to cover the costs incurred in remaking the cassettes and redigitizing the tapes.

Of course, there may be a way to make everyone happy. Read on.

Having "Safe" Picture

A video picture has several physical boundaries. The top and bottom of the picture are defined by the vertical blanking. The sides of the picture are defined by the horizontal blanking. Blanking refers to the scan lines that make up the video image. Some monitors can be adjusted to view several image sizes. Figure 5.8 illustrates image areas affected by the size and type of monitor on which you are viewing.

SAFE TITLE

SAFE_ACTION

ENTIRE IMAGE

16×9 (1.78) SAFE ACTION/SAFE TITLE

Figure 5.8a

SAFE TITLE

SAFE ACTION

ENTIRE IMAGE

4×3 (1.33) SAFE ACTION/SAFE TITLE

Figure 5.8b

Title-safe area. This is discussed in detail in the "Credits and Titling" section of the chapter on "Completion." It does not apply to this section.

Action- or picture-safe area. Also referred to as overscan, this represents the image area that you can see on a normal TV or monitor. It is the area the viewer will see on the television set at home—regardless of the size of the set. It is also the area the producer sees on the TV set in the office or on the editor's monitor when it is in the normal or overscan mode.

Underscan or outside-TV-safe area. This represents the area of the image that falls outside the top and bottom of the picture on a consumer television set. Because many edit system monitors are equipped with the ability to choose between underscan and overscan, you can place visible timecode windows in this area. This allows the editor an increased comfort level by having the visual information available as a reference and double-check, but allows the executives and network to view the material without a visible window obscuring part of the picture and causing a general distraction.

Some monitors will have a slightly larger viewing area than others and therefore may expose the very edge of a visible window that has been placed in underscan. This is still usually preferable to seeing the entire set of numbers constantly updating on the screen.

Dailies Cassettes

This section could be subtitled "the area that can send you way over budget really fast!"

When a show starts up, whether it be an MOW or an episodic, the list of people who receive cassettes of the dailies can be quite extensive. And, no matter how long the list seems on day one, it is almost guaranteed to be a little longer by day two. Usually several copies go to the network executives, the various producers, the executive producers, the director, the cinematographer, and sometimes even actors' agents. This usually goes on for the first few days of an MOW and even the first few episodes of an episodic. Sometimes the videotape postproduction facility makes the cassette copies and sometimes the production company takes care of that in-house. A lot of that depends on the production budget and the quality required from the duplication. Obviously, the postproduction facility can make much more pristine dubs from much better master sources than the production company can in their offices. A typical order may include:

Sample Dailies Cassette Order

	First three days of shoot/first few episodes	Remainder of shoot/episodes
Executive Producer	(1) VHS	(1) VHS
Producer	(1) VHS	(1) VHS
Director	(1) 3/4″	(1) VHS
Cinematographer	(1) 3/4″	(1) VHS
Network	(3 to 4) 3/4″	(1 to 4) 3/4″
Set	(1 to 2) VHS or 3/4″	(1 to 2) VHS/3/4″
Production office	(1) 3/4″ or VHS*	(1) 3/4″/VHS*

*Whether the production office receives 3/4″ or VHS may depend on whether they will be making copies in their office for distribution.

If you are working on a sitcom, the facility rarely makes any tapes beyond the transfer master and the editor's cassette.

If the show is not cutting electronically, the cinematographer and director will go to the lab before the call time each day and screen the film dailies. The lab, free of charge, normally provides the screening.

Dailies Completion Timetable Warning

It is worth repeating that, no matter how early you get dailies to the production office, it will never be early enough. So, know going in that this issue will come up on an almost daily basis. And should you ever be responsible for postproduction on a show where you are told that the dailies can be transferred at the facilities' convenience and that the production office is not expecting to see dailies early each day, watch out! Someone is lying or, at the very least, being naive. Everyone may be saying this at the beginning, but someone high up is going to start wondering why shooting is going on and no dailies are forthcoming. Just be prepared for a change in the telecine game plan.

Alterations to Your Normal Sleep Pattern

As we have said before, dailies often transfer through the night so those cassettes can be delivered early in the morning. (This does not always hold true for multi-camera sitcom dailies, because they shoot for 1 to 2 days per episode, but 2 to 4 days are necessary to transfer all the footage.)

For overnight dailies, any calls regarding film problems or production audio problems will come in the middle of the night. Such items as negative scratches, production audio record errors, focus problems, camera flicker, and missing audio reels are common calls. Sometimes nothing can be done until morning. Other times you will have to wake up enough to make an intelligent decision.

Here's a little exercise we've created to help you practice waking up to make these wee-hour-of-the-morning decisions: Set your clock radio to an all-night talk radio station. Then set the alarm to go off every 2 hours nightly for 1 week. Wake up each time the alarm goes off just enough to figure out what the topic on the radio program is and to form an opinion on the subject. Then go back to sleep. After a week you will be really good at this—or become a sleep-crazed lunatic. Either way, you will be more qualified to do your job as postproduction manager. (That was a joke—we think.)

Alternate Dailies Delivery Methods

Ongoing advances in communication technologies, fiber optics, media storage, and video streaming have opened a new chapter in the distribution of dailies to the client.

View Wherever You Are

Some producers and directors are choosing to receive their dailies on CD-ROM or DVD instead of traditional videotape. Now, no matter where they are, as long as they have access to a computer, they can view their dailies. Once a disk has been delivered to them they could be thousands of feet in the air flying to China or in the middle of a desert. They can still view their transferred footage in fairly decent resolution. This eliminates the need for a playback deck and monitor. The catch? This technology still comes with drawbacks. Time is again our enemy. It takes 4 to 6 hours to burn just 1 hour of dailies onto CD-ROM or DVD. This is on top of the time it takes to transfer the dailies footage. Then the dailies master images and sound are loaded into a computer. A menu describing the data, shoot date, show name, production company, list of material, etc. is created. Then the material is compressed and burned. Once the dailies transfer is completed, normal distribution of cassettes can progress as usual. Those receiving disks have to wait.

The current disks suffer from compression artifacts and can not carry enough edge code information to make them accurate editing tools, but this is changing. We are on the edge of a technology breakthrough that will drastically reduce the burn time while retaining frame accuracy.

Long Distance Dailies

Shooting at a distant location and shipping your footage to your telecine facility can be inconvenient. The lag time between sending your exposed negative for processing and transfer and getting viewing cassettes back to look at can be critical to a shoot, especially if there is concern about equipment, exposure, or a number of other variables. Sometimes the crew has to change locations, and going back for a reshoot is usually very costly. Do you have the shots you need from a location before you relocate? Was the exposure right? Is the camera working properly? These are important factors that need to be addressed.

Shipping dailies back and forth between your location and the lab is usually fine. But there may be times in which this method is too slow. In these instances, other methods for receiving your dailies may be necessary. There are several options available to you. What you choose will depend on your budget and your location.

Delivery System Options

Some companies hardwire multiple locations where you can go and get your dailies. These private networks are able to transmit your footage very fast and promise secure transmissions. The advantage is speed and quality. Images can be captured on tape and/or hard drive and rival DVD quality. The disadvantage is that these tend to be subscriber based and dependent on being hard wired. One practical application is delivering dailies from a distant location to, for example, a movie studio.

Information can also be satellite- or fiber-fed over phone lines. Dailies can also be stored at a secure location on the Internet and accessed by desktop computer. The quality available with this method is very poor—less than VHS and suitable for viewing only.

Several of these methods require advanced planning and have substantial costs attached, but it may be worth all of that to see your dailies as soon as they are transferred. The tapes made from the captured data may or may not be accurate enough for editing, depending on the method used.

These alternate methods for delivering dailies are becoming more popular and accessible. Be prepared to spend some time researching and organizing whatever method you choose.

Troubleshooting Dailies Problems

Sometimes the cause of a film or audio problem is not readily apparent. At times the hardest part about troubleshooting is not coming up with a solution, but determining where the problem originated. Hopefully, if there is a film scratch, the lab has already done the research on their end to determine if it is a predevelop problem (in this case, either the camera's magazine or the film loader is usually the culprit) or a laboratory problem that occurred somewhere along the developing or cleaning process. It is critical to determine if the problem occurred on the set as quickly as possible so that you don't have another day of shooting ruined due to a bad magazine, camera leak, dirt in the camera, or inexperienced loader. As stated earlier, damage or mistakes are often first caught during the telecine transfer of dailies. Here again you will be making decisions in the middle of the night.

After determining the cause of the damage, someone needs to determine if that take can be saved. If there are many takes in the scene, you may wait to see if you can cut around the damage by using other takes.

In the case of a negative scratch, the lab may be able to make a wetgate print of the damaged area. This is a process by which the film is coated with a chemical that can fill in the scratch, often making the initial damage less noticeable or even making it seem to disappear altogether. There are also electronic fixes available, such as a paintbox, which can repair anomalies on the videotape. This will not be an option if you must cut negative for delivery.

Troubleshooting film problems can be complicated because there is always the issue of when the problem originated—pre- or postdevelop or in the telecine transfer. Sometimes, videotape problems can be a little more straightforward. There is still the question of "when" the problem originated. Because no laboratory or processing are involved, once the images are shot the question becomes one of 1) did something happen in the camera or 2) did something happen when copying the footage to other tape mediums.

Prior to HD cameras, the biggest problem in video production was usually if the camera was calibrated properly or maybe problems with extreme weather conditions (cold, hot, moisture) interfering with the camera functions.

With HD, the equipment is still quite new and camera nuances are still being tested. Your biggest allies in the quest to avoid HD camera problems in the field are going to be the camera equipment rental house and the video facility you are using (assuming they have some history with this format).

If your show is shooting HD and this is your first experience with this format, speak with both the rental company and the video facility representative and ask them what types of problems you may encounter once the footage starts the post-production process. Production will have already spoken with the camera rental house, but they are going to be more focused on "production" issues. Doing research on your own may give you a heads up before a problem becomes a reality and starts eating into your budget. This may also provide some insights you can share with production so they can watch out for these traps and try to avoid them.

Even though you are shooting videotape and don't have the initial costs of lab services and processing in your budget, reshoots and fixes are still going to be just as expensive in HD.

The second area to be aware of is transferring your footage to another tape medium. Going from HD tapes (whether 720p, 1080i, or 1080/24p) to a standard definition tape will require a down conversion. As with any standard conversion, there are several types and right ways and wrong ways to do conversions. Again, it is only going to help you to chose a facility with HD experience—and not just HD film-to-tape transfer experience; real dailies experience. Also, try and talk with other HD postproduction supervisors about their experiences. There are enough projects now that have shot with HD cameras that you don't need to be out there reinventing the wheel and you don't have to go in blind. The camera manufacturer, camera rental equipment company, and your video facility will be able to provide good people for you to speak with.

In all cases, before approaching the client or producer with a problem, be sure you have gathered as much information about the problem as is available. If at all possible, go and look at the problem yourself. Have all the obvious possible causes double-checked. Determine all possible solutions and present them to the producer. Be sure to seek the opinions of your lab or postproduction facility and the appropriate crewmembers.

It is imperative that any problem be resolved as quickly as possible. Then, if a reshoot is required, the producer may be able to schedule the reshoot before the production crew leaves the location. It is not the most ideal situation, but your producer will be more impressed by this than if you wait several days and *then* determine that a reshoot is necessary and the location must be rescheduled. It happened to one of us that a reshoot was necessary and the second unit crew was able to add in this reshoot while they were at the location. It was one of those "pat on the back" moments that can seem so few and far between.

Image Stabilization

The telecine gate (the plate that the film travels on as it rides over the scanner) is changed according to the film being transferred. There are separate gates for regular 35 mm, super 35 mm, regular 16 mm, super 16 mm, regular 8 mm, and super 8 mm film formats. Beyond that, there are pin registration gates along with special "servo-systems" that scan the film differently to help minimize the appearance of film weave. There are also different brands of telecine that are geared to work better in certain circumstances. There is the new "Y" front and even those telecines used for HD transfers that when used for standard definition can solve or improve some film problems. Ask around if you are having problems.

Weave occurs because the film has a slight vertical movement as it passes through the gate. All standard film transfers have weave; it is just more noticeable in some instances than in others. If the weave is very noticeable or you require a rock-steady image for special effects, there are several options for you to use.

A real time steady system (RTS) works in conjunction with either a 35 mm gate or a super 16 mm gate to reduce noticeable weave. RTS, electronic pin registration (EPR), and jump free (JF) are set up so the scanner tries to follow the film around as the film passes through the gate to minimize weave. These are all effective systems and one works equally as well as the other. They can be teamed with a servo system (Metaspeed is one brand name) that accomplishes the partial weave correction along with greatly increasing the frames-per-second transfer range.

If you are in a situation where the image you are transferring is part of a multi-layering graphic effect, then you really need to transfer using true pin registration. Unlike electronic pin registration, which transfers in real time, a true pin-registered transfer is very tedious. Essentially, the telecine "locks down" each frame it transfers to completely eliminate any movement. That frame is transferred and the transport moves the film to the next frame, locks it down, and transfers it. This ensures that as you build your layers you will not see movement between the background layer and foreground layer.

In any traditional film-to-tape transfer there is a certain amount of film weave. It may be hard for you to detect this weave when you are looking at your dailies, but the weave is there. Many facilities have taken steps to minimize the amount of normal film weave by using special gates for the film to pass through when it rides over the scanner—or by using a special scanner designed to minimize the appearance of film weave.

Weave can also be caused by a camera problem. Unfortunately, this will not be known until the film is actually processed and viewed. Certain types of telecine transports can help to reduce the appearance of this weave. Film stock problems can also cause visible film weave. Film shrinkage will cause film movement as the perforations no longer line up properly with the pins that pull them through the path.

For worse cases, there is equipment currently in Research and Development (R&D) that has seen some very promising results in image stabilization. This equipment won't help a film-finish project unless you run your material through this box then back out to film. But for tape finish, the process has proven quite impressive. This technology is now only available in standard definition, but high definition can't be far behind now that the technology has proved viable and put into commercial use.

Footage Calculations

There is a trick for calculating how film footage translates into running time. While labs and transfer houses are very comfortable working in footages when discussing your film, the people in the production company, including your editor, may not be. Therefore, it will be very handy (and maybe somewhat impressive) for you to be able to accurately convert how much film you have shot or transferred into actual running time. This is also useful for knowing what length of videotape stock you will need based on the amount of film you are transferring. You will be able to avoid paying for stock that is longer than you need. To determine running time estimates use the following formulas:

35 mm four-perf:
  number of feet divided by 90 = number of minutes
  number of minutes divided by 60 = number of hours
35 mm three-perf:
  number of feet divided by 90 = number of minutes of four-perf
  number of minutes divided by 60 = number of hours of four-perf
  number of hours multiplied by .25 = number of hours of three-perf
16 mm:
  number of feet divided by 36 = number of minutes
  number of minutes divided by 60 = number of hours

A convenient rule of thumb to quickly figure approximate run time:

35 mm four-perf:
  1000 feed of film = approximately 10 minutes
35 mm three-perf:
  1000 feet of film = approximately 12 minutes (25% more than four-perf)
16 mm:
  400 feet of film = approximately 10 minutes

Dirt and the Film Transfer

Dirt and hair on film are problems that are faced by anyone who shoots film. Dirt is more noticeable on 16 mm film than on 35 mm film, partly because the surface is much smaller and dirt shows up more easily. Another reason is because 16 mm film is blown-up to size for use in TV or up to 35 mm for theatrical projection. This blow up enlarges every imperfection captured on the 16 mm film frame—especially dirt and scratches and the film grain itself. If you're shooting on videotape you can skip this section, all others read on.

Dirt is everywhere. It can originate in the camera, or it can be picked up at the lab or during any part of the film-to-tape process. You can't avoid dirt, but you can minimize it.

One way to cut down on excess dirt is to practice good production values. If the telecine colorist has to rock the film back and forth over the gate trying to find a sync point or to sync tail slates, the film has a greater chance of picking up extra dirt. When synchronizing a tail slate, the colorist has to run the film to the slate at the end of the take and establish the sync point, then run film back to the beginning of the take, and then run the film again to lay the take down to tape. Even if sync is perfect the first time, your film runs through the telecine system a minimum of three times. This is an opportunity to latch on that dirt and hairs just live for! Doing away with tail slates will eliminate this problem.

In the field, make sure the magazine and gate are clean. If your camera people do frequent clean-outs on the set, make sure they mark the frame that's in the gate when they remove the magazine so they put the film back in the same place. If they don't do this, the telecine colorist has to stop the telecine at each camera clean-out, physically go out and realign the film in the telecine gate, and reset the counter before transferring the next take. This is extremely time-consuming and can add expensive time to your telecine transfer. It is also a chance for the film to pick up dirt from the extra handling.

Wetgate printing of your final film element also makes a big difference in the amount of dirt and scratches seen in that print. If you wetgate your inter-positive or locon print and then use that element for telecine, you'll greatly reduce the amount of time you will have to spend cleaning your videotape master. If you use that wetgate print to make your IN for theatrical printing, your prints will be cleaner.

The lab cleans the film after processing, and negative assembly is completed in a very clean environment by people wearing white cotton gloves. The film is put into plastic bags before going into the boxes or cans that are delivered to the transfer house. Despite this care, some dirt or hairs will make it onto your film. Film can also pick up a small amount of dirt as it travels through the transfer path. Even if the equipment is housed in an enclosed area, there will be some dirt that can end up on your film.

In Summary

In summary, remember not to let dailies make you too crazy. If you are the client, the lab should bend over backwards to help you (if they don't, seriously consider switching labs as life it too short to fight everyday to get your material when and how you need it). The facility needs you to be happy so you will come back again and so they can move on to the next job.

If your job takes you into uncharted territory, don't feel like you are all alone with your problems. There is *almost* always someone else who has been there and can help you. The trick is to find that person. If all else fails, call us.

Granted, high definition is bringing with it some new and exciting issues to post-production. But quite a few shows now have experiences to share. Ask around and ask for help. One of us bought soy milk recently and the carton read "Shake Well and Buy Often." Maybe that applies here, too.

If you work for a postproduction facility—KEEP YOUR COOL. From time to time your dailies clients will drive you crazy—it's their job. Just remember to remain organized and when all else fails buy time with kindness. Your job can be very stressful so remember to take a few moments throughout the day and breathe, turn up the music, stare at a picture of your dog or baby, reconnect, and then go on. If all of this fails, remember two things: 1) they can't really kill you and 2) the day will eventually end.

6 Editorial (Film Editorial and Video Off-Line Editing)

Editing is a multilayered creative process. Takes are assembled from dailies to create scenes, and scenes are assembled to make a show, all according to the blueprint provided by the script.

The editor, being familiar with all of the footage, chooses the better takes of each scene to assemble into the first picture cut. Many variables are considered when choosing shots and cutting them together. Performances, the look of the shots, visual coverage, and the pace of the storytelling all contribute to the decisions made by the editor.

Editing begins with the first day of dailies and ends when all of the changes have been made and the opticals and stock footage have been cut in. At this point the picture is considered locked, and you are ready to go into on-line and/or have your negative cut.

In the course of a project, editors have countless reels of film or videotape to review, an impossibly short schedule, and changes to incorporate at every turn. Working daily with the photographic images, the editor can give the director timely updates on missing shots and film scratches or damage that render a take unusable.

Feature and movies-of-the-week editors start work the first day of production and are usually employed until the last day of the dub (mix). Some television producers cut their budgets in editorial by letting the editor go upon picture lock and keeping the lesser-paid assistant through the dub. This is predicated on the budget and the producer's style and experience.

Editors employed on TV series are with the show for the run of the series. There is normally more than one editor employed. Each editor works on a different episode, and two or more episodes are often in different stages of completion at the same time. Depending on the complexity of the series and the budget, two editors sometimes share one assistant. Both multicamera and single-camera sitcoms often opt to hire a "digitizer" instead of an assistant editor. The digitizer is on a show long enough to input the dailies into the off-line system and verify that the data is accurate. The digitizer still handles some of the paperwork normally organized and tracked by the assistant editor, but much of that responsibility falls back on the editor.

Once all the dailies are shot and delivered to the cutting room, the editor has 1 to 2 days for assembly of episodics and sitcoms, and 6 days for MOWs and TV movies or projects that have a running time of more than an hour. These timetables are regulated by the Director's Guild of America (DGA). Any deviation from this schedule will be up to the editor's discretion.

The Film Editor

Film editors will usually sit in a semidarkened room all day and sometimes all night. Those experienced in the demands of editing come to recognize good editors as talented artists. Paid by the producer and answering to the director (who, in turn, answers to the producer and studio), editors often find themselves walking a tightrope in many situations, trying to keep everyone in agreement.

Respect your editor (unless the editor's just difficult, and then figure out the best way to get through the situation and still get a good product). The editor and assistant editor are your communication lines to the production battlefield.

An important note regarding editors: It has been our experience that an impossible editor is often reacting to a "less than ideal" situation. Be sure to weigh all the facts and try and ascertain the true problem before passing judgment. Inquire about how you might help. It may turn out to be something as seemingly trivial as a supply of chocolate bars . . . don't laugh; we know of what we speak!

Film Editing

During principal photography, takes that the director wants to see printed are circled on the camera and sound reports. The camera reports accompany the dailies negative to the laboratory for developing. The entire negative is processed. Once developed, the circled takes are physically cut out of the negative and spliced together, and a one-light print is made. This print is always referred to as a *work print*.

The production sound, along with the matching sound reports, is delivered to the appropriate facility. At the same time the film is being processed and printed at the laboratory, the sound is being transferred at a sound house. The circled takes are transferred to magnetic tape. This magnetic tape is usually called a single-stripe mag or referred to as one-to-ones. Any audio recorded on the production sound element is combined onto one single track on a mag.

Once the work print and mag (sound track) are ready, they are delivered to the editor's cutting room. Once together, these elements are referred to as "picture and track" or "double system." It is now the assistant editor's job to prepare the film for dailies viewing, coding, editor's use, and possibly transfer to videotape. The assistant editor's daily duties do not vary much—even if dailies are transferred to videotape or dailies screenings are only projected in a screening room for the first week or so.

Film Edit Room Equipment

Film editors need two rooms, Moviolas and flatbeds, sound heads, rewinds, film benches, bench stools, banners, film splicers, splicing tape, take-up reels and film cores, grease pencils, boxes, gloves, cleaner, tape, and on and on. The assistant editor may make the list and can help double-check that nothing has been left out.

In addition to cutting-room equipment, each editor and assistant will need the following:

- Time cards, I9s, and any other accounting necessities;
- Script plus all changes;
- Crew list/cast list;
- Shooting schedule;
- Postproduction schedule;
- Film laboratory and sound and videotape facility contact names and numbers;
- Delivery requirements (domestic and foreign);
- Credits (as soon as available); and
- Purchase orders (we suggest you set up a procedure that requires purchase orders be issued for all work done through your postproduction facilities).

Viewing Film Dailies

For print dailies viewing, the film is projected and the editor, producer, and possibly the postproduction supervisor view the new footage in a screening room. Each day, using the camera and sound reports to help locate the individual takes and determine sequencing order, the assistant editor will prepare the dailies for this screening. This preparation involves syncing picture and track and adding the leader necessary to thread the footage through the film projector. Oftentimes a framing chart will be spliced to the head of dailies. During the screening, the assistant editor may attend, making notes of film damage, scratches, and preferred takes.

It is the responsibility of the associate producer or postproduction supervisor to schedule the screening-room time. Do this through your film laboratory, they have projection rooms available for viewing dailies. There is no charge for using these rooms—unless you abuse the service. Scheduling several screenings in a day or constantly changing screening times will make it difficult for the laboratory to service both you and its other clients, and the lab may begin to charge you for extra screenings or cancellations.

Depending on the producer's style, this screening process may continue daily or, after a week or so, print dailies will be projected for the editor and then transferred to videotape for distribution on cassette to the other parties.

In another scenario, print dailies can be transferred to videotape from the first day of principal photography—even if they are also viewed on film in a screening room.

Film Coding

As soon as the day's printed takes are organized and the reels are leadered for projection, the assistant editor codes the synced picture and sound. If you have ever walked through a hallway of cutting rooms and smelled a strong burning plastic smell, you have experienced the smell of coding. The picture and corresponding sound, in sync, are passed together through a coding machine which stamps a number into the exact same spot on both the film and sound. This way, if scenes are recut or takes edited, you will always be able to resync by lining up these numbers.

Preparing for the Film Cut

Each day after the initial dailies screening or videotape transfer, the assistant editor breaks down (cuts apart) the selected prints and groups them into scenes with other takes from the same scenes.

In the course of breaking down reels, the assistant editor is also cataloguing each take so it can be found instantly when requested by the editor. Now the editor is ready to start cutting scenes together.

Editor's Log and Script Notes

The assistant editor will create an editor's log or script report that organizes scenes shot, footage shot, and number of setups and run time of each take. This is done for each production day and may look like Figure 6.1.

Figure 6.1 Editor's Log

SCENE	ACTION 9-27-97	LENS	CAM ROLL	SND	TAKE	TIME	COMENTS
6	Master: sign Will→Steve joins her 3 shot thru end	32m 4′6′	A2	1	1 ②(circled) ③(circled)	1:19 1:27 1:35	thru 1B some good
6A	Will→2 shot Will: Steve	70m 7′5′	A3	1 1	①(circled) 2	:23 1:45	incomp. good
6D	Don's POV of Steve	70m 12′4′	B1	1	1 2 ③(circled)	:07 :10 :06	
6F	OS Steve	70m 45′	A4	1 3	1 ②(circled) :21 ④(circled)	:18 :34 :35	*print forsnd inc. NGA birds!
6G	OS Will	50m 5′	A4	1	①(circled) ②(circled)	:33 :35	great
6H	Don enters w/ chef w/pastries	50m 15′	A5	1	1 ②(circled) ③(circled)	:10 :18 :17	camera *tighter

The script supervisor's notes are the primary source of information for this log. If your script supervisor's information has proved unreliable, then you may need to look elsewhere to verify the information. These other sources will include camera and sound reports, production reports, and call sheets. The script supervisor holds a very key position on a project, and many aspects of production and postproduction depend on the information contained in the script supervisor's notes.

Figure 6.2 shows some sample script supervisor pages that correspond to the editor's log sample. The circled scenes and takes from the script supervisor notes are organized in order onto the editor's log. The wavy lines indicate the length of the take and are often accompanied by timings that tell the editor if the takes are complete or were aborted.

Figure 6.2 Script Supervisor's Notes

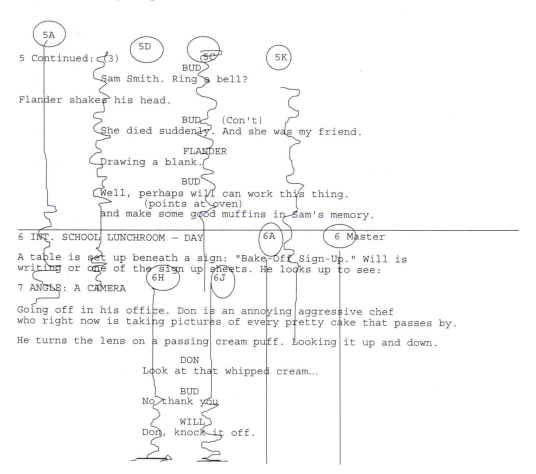

Off-Line Editing

The terms "nonlinear" and "off-line" editing are used to describe the electronic editing process prior to on-line or negative cutting. The creative process is the same as the film editor uses to create the editor's cut in film editing. The end goal is the same: picture lock.

In off-line, you can cut, paste, move scenes, change which takes are used, add sound, add sample sound effects, and incorporate simple titles. All of this is accomplished without any physical alterations to your source material. Off-line has gained much popularity over the last few years, and even features are cutting electronically. This popularity stems from two factors. One is the speed with which changes can be tried and then changed again. The other is that scenes or partial scenes can be cut in random order instead of having a continuous roll of physical film that is affected every time a change is made in the middle—hence, the term "nonlinear."

The flexibility for making changes instantly is very appealing. Scenes can be cut and recut endlessly without worry about film damage, resplicing reels, or waiting for reprints. Off-line equipment also offers the ability to insert simple effects and titles into an unfinished picture without incurring extra costs.

A variety of electronic nonlinear equipment and corresponding software is available. These computers are specifically designed to take in video (originating on film, video, or both), interpret the information, and spit out accurate lists for use in on-line, negative cutting, and sound services.

Correct Opticals and Effects

One of the great advantages of the off-line system is that you, at any point, can see how the project is coming together, complete with at least rudimentary dissolves, fades, titles, color correction, and other effects. This sounds terrific and it is. This can help the creative team test artistic decisions without getting into expensive on-line and effects bays. As cool and practical as this is, this magic must be accompanied by a word of caution.

The effects you create in your off-line are "temp" effects and can only be used as a gauge. Once created, the real film effects will look slightly different than the effects you build in your off-line system. The manufacture of film prints is a mechanical process. Light valves and camera irises open and close letting in light and color to create the effects you envisioned. Yet, these delicate machines do have limitations.

Ultimately, what comes out as dissolves, fades, and other opticals will only be as good as the information going in. Without accurate footage counts, those beautiful effects will be useless to you if they do not fit into your negative perfectly. Any deviation that changes the physical length of the cut negative will cause sync problems when your track is lined up with your picture. Your editor must provide precise footage counts for the lab to create fades, dissolves, and color changes accurately.

Years of working with video material in the video world can make editors forget the rules in the film world. In video, if a shot is too short or too long it can be sped up or slowed down to help it fit into its designated spot. Animation a few frames short? Fix it in post. You don't necessarily have to draw or shoot more frames. None of these tricks work in the film-finish world. And, editors who work primarily in the electronic world can quickly forget these limitations. They then become frustrated when their opticals transition too quickly or the color isn't the same as their monitor in the cutting room. But, as with most things in life, the harsh realities of the celluloid world come crashing back rather quickly.

To try and avoid these frustrations and wasting a bunch of time and money needlessly, we recommend a little "better safe than sorry" test. Before creating the final cut list for the negative cutter, pick up the phone. Call your rep at the laboratory that is going to print your negative and ask a few questions. You might start with how short/long can my dissolves be? Can I get a color timer involved before the final film opticals are approved? And, here's another favorite, what do I have to know about cutting A and B rolls prior to submitting my negative to the lab? Seeking technical information with opticals and color timing from the start will solve many of your problems before they even happen.

Beginning the Off-Line

The first step in off-line is the downloading of your transferred selected takes or videotape dailies into the off-line system. This is digitizing and it is done by the assistant editor, apprentice editor, or digitizer.

The editor's cassettes of your telecine material are loaded onto the hard drive of your edit system. The individual scene and take information is loaded off a floppy computer disk created by your telecine facility. This disk contains information about your dailies that includes camera roll number, sound roll number, scenes, takes, film edge numbers, audio timecode, and videotape timecode for each take transferred. If you shot your project on videotape instead of film, there will be no disk of information and any facts about each take will be entered manually by the assistant editor.

Dailies Transfer Direct to Hard Drive

Digitizing describes the loading of the dailies videotape work cassettes into the off-line (or on-line, if they are one in the same on your project) electronic editing system.

The loading process happens in real time, so digitizing shows that shoot with multiple cameras and produce a high volume of daily footage is time consuming. The assistant must load the action and track into the computer at real time. The editing equipment, daily footage, and an assistant editor/digitizer are monopolized for hours.

To help meet the demands of shortened postproduction schedules and miles of daily footage, facilities have teamed up with manufacturers of editing software to create an alternative. Their idea is to load the dailies directly from the telecine into the editor's hard drive. Bypassing, or in addition to, recording to videotape thereby eliminates the need to digitize and editing can begin immediately.

If this method appeals to you, check with your video facility to confirm they can accommodate you. If so, the facility will need to know the following:

1. The type of hard drive are you using,
2. The type of editing software you are using,
3. What resolution you are working in,
4. The set up information for the telecine file, and
5. The usual dailies telecine specification.

This straight-to-hard drive system can be great for certain projects and a big help to editors. But, it does cost a little more than the traditional method. The assistant editor is still needed, but instead of being a digitizer the job becomes about media management.

Off-Line Edit Room Equipment

Nonlinear or electronic off-line cutting rooms will need less, although more expensive, materials than film cutting rooms. They will need an off-line editing system and black and coded tape stock (you can purchase stock already coded, code it yourselves, or pay your facility to code it for you). The editors will need to lay off their various cuts to timecoded stock if those tapes will be used to generate work cassettes or as check cassette for the on-line. They will also need chairs, phones, fax machines, desks, and general supplies such as binders, hole punches, pens, and pencils. Remember when choosing office furniture that at times there will be several visitors in the room at once and they will all want a comfortable place to sit.

When ordering your nonlinear editing system, the number of gigabits (amount of hard-drive storage) you will need for the duration of your project depends on several things. It will depend on how much money you have in the budget, how much information you will need to store, and how defined an image (or how much resolution) you need to see on the monitor and output to cassette. Consult your producer, editor, and equipment supplier when making these decisions. Try to be honest and accurate about the amount of storage you'll need. Unexpected delays in production and cut approval can require that several shows stay stored on the off-line system. This may require that you order additional storage space (larger hard drives) so your editors can continue working while you are waiting for shows to be locked.

In addition to editing room equipment, each editor and assistant will need the following:

- Time cards, I9s, and any other accounting necessities;
- Script plus all changes;
- Crew list/cast list;
- Shooting schedule;
- Postproduction schedule;
- Film lab and videotape facility contact names and numbers;
- Delivery requirements (domestic and foreign);
- Credits (as soon as available); and
- Purchase orders (we suggest you set up a procedure that requires purchase orders be issued for all work done through your postproduction facilities).

Desktop Editing

The filmmaker has many choices when deciding how to shoot, post, and deliver a project. There are traditional motion picture film and standard and high definition videotape for use in shooting. There are also several means for viewing and posting what has been shot. There are film print dailies, videotape dailies, dailies direct to hard drive, dailies on CD-ROM, and the possibilities seem to grow and grow. What does not seem to enjoy the same growth are postproduction schedules and budgets.

As technologies in postproduction *editorial* evolve, the nonlinear editorial suite is also changing and improving. In fact, over the past few years, some independent low budget filmmakers have borrowed an idea from the news media and have begun working with digital video cameras.

Always on a mad dash to make deadlines and be first with "on the scene" footage, news was the perfect market for professional grade digital video (DV) cameras. These cameras are small, easy to handle, and use high quality tape stock. With the proper hardware and software, you can plug a DV camera into your desktop or laptop computer and download the images recorded. Once downloaded, editing can be done right on the same desktop computer. The speed at which you can edit a project, the cost savings, and convenience have made this method attractive to industrial, documentary, low budget, and first time filmmakers.

Shooting Film—Editing on DV

As a filmmaker you may want to retain the ability to create a negative cut list while being able to edit on your desktop. This requires a telecine transfer of your film dailies. A video facility can transfer your film negative directly to DV. However, they may suggest you add a Betacam SP or Digital Betacam to your order. The Betacam SP or Digital Betacam are backups in case your DV crashes or you need a new DV dub. Dailies telecine transfer specifications will be the same as regular videotape dailies. You'll have the facility capture the edgecode, sound timecode, and running timecode information. Many telecine facilities won't have a DV deck on hand to use as a recording device and will need to borrow your camera for the telecine sessions. Once the dailies are transferred to DV, you can download them into your desktop and begin editing. Depending upon the software you use, you may have the ability to add titles, effects, and even edit your sound and complete the project right on your computer. When finished, the project can be recorded back to DV and then upgraded to another tape format. If needed, a cut list can be generated for a negative cut.

Shooting DV—Editing DV

If you are shooting on DV, dailies telecine (film-to-tape transfer) is obviously not necessary. The tape used during production, which is your master original, is rewound, the DV camera is plugged into the computer and used to download the dailies information right into a hard drive. Once editing is complete, the project can be recorded back to DV, again via the camera. The DV can then be transferred to another video format for duplication or delivery. If a film element is required, the project can be recorded out to film. Realize, however, that due to significantly lower resolution and the high compression rate of the DV, the quality and sharpness will not equal film or even high definition video.

DV Tape Stock

You will need to keep extra tape stock on hand for dubbing directors cuts, alternate cuts, work tapes, etc. Stock cassettes come in two different sizes, DV and Mini DV. Both tape stocks are the exact same tape packaged in different sized cases for use in both the regular DV, a professional grade camera, or a smaller case for use in the Mini DV, which is a consumer grade camera. A Mini DV tape is about the size of a DAT. The regular DV case is about the size of a VHS. Both sizes come in several stock lengths.

Timecode and the Mini DV

Because the Mini DV camera is consumer grade it does not generate it's own time-code. Regular DV does generate a record timecode and therefore has a reference to edit to. When shooting a Mini DV, you will first need to dub all of your dailies to another piece of videotape (such as regular DV, 3/4″, or Betacam SP), generating timecode as you record. Then you can download to your computer for editing. Without this timecode, you won't have a reference to mark your edit points and cutting your project will be nearly impossible and much more costly.

The DV camera reception has been good and it seems this format is here to stay for a while. It has even been used to create the newsreel or documentary look in a movie-of-the-week TV project.

Preparing for the Nonlinear Cut

Several items are vitally important to the off-line cutting room. For shows shooting on film these consist primarily of paperwork on the previous day's shoot, provided by the script supervisor, and the telecine transfer information, provided by the telecine dailies colorist.

Someone needs to track the daily amount of film that was shot, the camera rolls and sound rolls that were turned in to the laboratory for process and prep, and any B negative or reprints (or retransfers) that are due. Traditionally, the associate producer or postproduction supervisor gathers this information, which they receive from production. For videotape shoots, someone needs to make sure that all of the dailies master tapes are accounted for and delivered to the facility for vaulting until the on-line. Sometimes this tracking falls to the editorial staff. The same person must also make sure that one off-line cassette for each master tape is delivered to the editing room. Sometimes on a videotape show, the producer may even handle this. If these off-line cassettes were not recorded simultaneously on the set during shooting, then they have to be created. There is additional information on the creation of these videotapes in the "Dailies" chapter under "Editing Nonlinear Off-Line Cassettes."

In this section we will refer to "film transfer dailies videotapes." Naturally, the dailies for a videotape-shot show will not come from a telecine transfer or work print. The assistant editor and off-line editor duties are, however, similar in all three scenarios.

The assistant editor must have a technical understanding of the dailies information that is provided from the telecine transfer. While dailies colorists are usually accurate in the information they record, they are keeping track of many things at once. Colorists and their assistants constantly monitor their equipment to assure it is functioning accurately. They check that they have laid down all of the circled takes. They check camera reports against sound reports to verify nothing has been missed. They decipher misslated takes and incomplete camera reports. There is a window of opportunity for human error in every dailies transfer session. There are, frankly, too many areas to keep track of during the transfer to guarantee that there will be no mistakes.

Because of the human error factor, it is incumbent on the assistant editor to verify the accuracy of the information they receive and load into the off-line system before the editor begins to work with the material. It is also critical that the assistant editor be very organized. An accurate list of shots, circled takes, B negative, and retransfers must always be available and up-to-date.

Editorial Specifications

When you are transferring film to tape dailies, have your editor or assistant editor speak with your telecine representative at the postproduction facility about the dailies transfer specifications. It is important to make sure there are no questions or misunderstandings regarding these specifications.

Be sure that your editor is aware of your delivery needs down the road. Even if negative is going to be cut sometime later, the editor must gather the necessary negative cut information and prepare the negative cut list from the start of the postproduction process.

We know an editor who was never told there would be a negative cut and film opticals. Therefore, none of the work required to produce an accurate negative cut list and opticals list was done. This caused a huge problem, as no EDL for the negative cut could be produced. Another editor had to be hired to spend two months reentering data to produce a workable EDL, at great expense to the project.

It is important to order any transfer data you might need for your project at the beginning of the dailies transfer process. All of this information is explained in the "Transfer Data" section in the "Dailies" chapter.

Nonlinear Editing for High Definition On-Line

Even if you plan to on-line edit your show in a high definition editing bay, you will probably still choose to off-line your project using traditional standard definition nonlinear editing equipment.

Once your film-to-videotape dailies are transferred to a HD format, they are then down converted to a standard definition tape format, such as 3/4″ or Betacam SP. This is done through the use of either a universal standards converter or some other down conversion equipment. You will edit exactly as you would for a standard definition show. Once the picture is locked, you'll create your output for visual reference to use once the on-line is completed.

Why Off-Line in Standard Definition?

The biggest advantage is money. This method allows you to spend more time in your off-line getting the show right. So, it is cheaper and faster to do the creative work this way than on a HD nonlinear system. It also avoids the high cost of down converting viewing cassettes for the different phases of the project (i.e., editor's cut, director's cut, and producer's cut) and down converting work cassettes for various editors (such as the music editor, composer, sound effects editor, etc.).

As you near the end of your off-line, we recommend sending a sample EDL to your HD on-line facility to make sure there aren't any problems before you get into the on-line session itself and are on the clock.

There are additional editing costs when compared to doing your entire show in standard definition. There are the initial costs to down convert the dailies materials. Whether you shoot on film or HD camera you'll have this cost. This needs to be done so the dailies can be digitized into the off-line system. There is also the added cost of a HD editing suite. However, this is the most cost-effective way to do a HD video completion and not compromise the creative end of your project.

B Negative and Reprints

In the course of editing, the editor may determine that takes not originally circled and printed are now needed. This may be because the existing printed take contains film damage, missed cues or lines by the actor, or some other continuity issue not apparent during shooting on the set. These originally unprinted takes are referred to as "B negative" or "B neg." This term applies to all uncircled takes, whether or not they are ever printed.

When scenes are recut, reprints are sometimes required. Film editing involves the physical cutting of the film to put scenes together. If a scene is recut, the original printed take may have been cut apart. A reprint then has to be made of that take. Reprints may also be necessary if a take is torn or otherwise damaged in handling. Reprints are common in film editing. Normally, reprints and B negative are ordered, usually sound for those takes must be ordered also.

The assistant editor is responsible for organizing the elements to be reprinted or locating any B neg. Depending on the structure of the project, either the assistant or, more commonly, the associate producer/postproduction supervisor will actually order the materials to be made.

Be aware that when B negative is ordered for film print dailies, this is the first time a print (or sound) is being struck from this negative. This piece of negative has been cut out of the original negative reel and now needs head and tail leader before the lab can print it. It is usually the negative cutter's job to leader the B negative. However, if your negative cutter is not available the laboratory's negative assembly department may do this (usually for a fee), or it will fall to the assistant editor. This does not apply to videotape dailies, as the negative has not been physically cut apart.

Stock Footage

Stock footage is picture that is nonspecific to a particular movie or television show. It could be a shot of a famous building or skyline, used to establish location, or it could be just generic locations, buildings, weather, catastrophic events, large gatherings, wildlife, or military shots. If a production company determines that it is not cost-effective to send out a camera crew to shoot stock footage, they turn to any of the numerous established companies that keep a stock footage library for licensing. Some stock houses specialize in particular types of shots. Some stock houses have contracts with film studios to buy their footage for relicense.

The ordering of stock footage usually falls on the assistant editor's shoulders in a film show. Again, depending on the company structure, it may also be ordered by the assistant editor. Regardless of who actually orders the stock footage, it still must be looked at in the cutting room to determine if it is appropriate and usable.

To order stock footage, determine which stock house you will be dealing with (several stock houses may be used on one show). Then call the stock house and describe what you are looking for. They, in turn, will send out film prints of several different shots for evaluation. Some stock houses will send out videotape instead of film—which may or may not cost extra.

The producer, director, and editor will view the shots and decide if any are appropriate. Once a shot is chosen, the stock house will provide an internegative of the shot to be cut into your final cut negative and a work print for use in the rough cut. The associate producer handles the paperwork for the licensing of the clip. Part of this paperwork requires an exact footage count of the amount of the clip used. The associate producer will gather this information from the assistant editor. Detailed information on licensing stock footage is located in the "Legal" chapter.

16:9—There Is No Stock Answer

If you are working in the 16:9 format and your stock footage material is only available in 4:3, then the short answer is that you have to blow it up . . . really. If you are taking your stock footage in film-form, then the original aspect ratio in which the film was shot will determine if it can be used as a 16:9 image.

Film that was shot in widescreen (such as 2:35) can be made into a 16:9 image by either letterboxing the image or extracting just the picture that fits into 16:9 (the same holds true for 1:85). If the film you are using was shot in 4:3 (such as an older TV series), then your only option will be to blow up the image to fill in the 4:3 top and bottom. You will, however, lose significant image from the sides. To control how much of the image you lose, you can manipulate and pan and scan the image to choose what part of the shot stays and what part will no longer be in frame. Existing stock footage on videotape will probably not be available in the 16:9 format. Therefore, you will have to enlarge the image optically. As with film shot at 4:3 you will lose image from the sides to fill up to the top and bottom of the screen. You can do some pan and scan, but you will have a lot less material to work with than you do when you are panning and scanning film. Part of any blow-up from 4:3 to 16:9 will include repositioning of the image, and some picture will be lost from either the top or the bottom of the shot.

Clips

Clips are entire programs, scenes, or partial scenes that are particular to a specific movie, newscast, or television production. Clips are used for playback on a set, dream sequences, flashbacks, to establish an event or mood, or to provide information vital to the telling of a story. There are companies that specialize in licensing vintage, news, or public-domain clips.

As with stock-footage, call the clip house and describe what you are looking for. They provide, on film or videotape, what they have available, and the producer, director, and editor will work to choose what they need. Once a clip is chosen, the associate producer handles the licensing paperwork. Clips traditionally are licensed without sound, due to complications with music clearances. Detailed information on how to license clips is located in the "Legal" chapter.

Clips from movies still under copyright must be licensed from the copyright holder. This is usually a film or television studio. Again, more details are available in the "Legal" chapter.

Editor's Cut

The editor cuts with all of the elements that the assistant editor has gathered, in conjunction with script notes and producer and director notes. The end result is the editor's cut. This version is the foundation for, and often closely resembles, the final cut of a show. Scenes are assembled from dailies according to the blueprint provided by the script and script notes. Being familiar with all of the varying takes, the editor chooses the better takes of each scene and orders B negative and reprints, as needed. The DGA agreement specifies the number of days the editor is legally allowed to complete the editor's cut.

Know that there will be editing changes before the show can be called "locked." Many times an editor will leave room in scenes for editing changes, pacing, and continuity. When the editor signs off on this cut, the director takes over and creates the director's cut.

Director's Cut

Once the editor's cut is complete, the director screens it. All changes made by the director become part of the director's cut. Now the director sets the pace of the show, shortening (tightening) and lengthening scenes as necessary. This cut shows the producers how the director envisioned the movie when it was shot.

Unless the director invites them, it is illegal (per the DGA) for anyone other than the editorial staff to be in the cutting room before the director has finished. Breaking this rule can result in costly fines to the production company. The DGA also sets the rules governing the number of days allowed for the creation of the director's cut. If in doubt about the rules, call the DGA. Some directors are very strict about these rules, so exercise caution.

Sometimes the director will ask for insert shots or second unit shots to enhance the story. The producer and the director will determine feasibility. If additional takes are shot, a minicrew is assembled and sent out.

Inserts can sometimes be shot on an "insert stage." Insert stages vary widely in size depending on the requirements of the shot(s). Insert shots can run the gamut in terms of difficulty, from something simple like an object falling to the floor or a hand gesturing. They can also be more complicated shots requiring that pieces of the original set be brought in. Because these shots occur after principal photography, it is often incumbent on the associate producer or postproduction supervisor to organize the insert shoot. An insert stage will be equipped with camera(s) and operators, lighting, and sometimes even makeup. Insert shots are normally MOS.

If a crew goes out to shoot additional second unit footage, a call sheet and production report will be created. Hopefully, the production manager is still on the payroll and can handle the DGA paperwork. If not, see your producer for instructions or to handle the details.

The director's cut is formatted to include film slugs (placeholders) identifying act breaks, commercial blacks, missing insert shots, and title cards. It goes to the production company and sometimes to the network executives to view.

In TV, the director's job is officially done when shooting is completed and the director's cut is delivered. Because of TV's fast pace, a new job is often waiting and the director leaves before the picture is locked. However, the director may supervise the automatic dialogue replacement (ADR) or looping session and the second unit shoot, and also be present at the final audio mix. Even if it is not specified in the contract, it is usually considered good form to invite the director to participate in each of these steps.

Producer's Cut

Following the director, the producer creates the next version of the show. For television projects, producers usually take 2 to 5 days to screen the director's cut and complete their version. Longer periods of time are allotted for features.

As with the director, the producer may feel that insert shots or additional footage is necessary. If approved, the process for arranging inserts shoots and second unit will be identical to the scenario described under "Director's Cut." Traditionally, any extra inserts and second unit shoots are coordinated by the director and producer, who together determine what is needed. This way, all of their requests are covered in a single shoot or insert session.

The producer's cut will then go to the production company executives and usually the network for viewing. Even in a half-hour sitcom several versions (called producer's cuts and labeled PC #1, 2, 3, etc.) may be created for executives and the network to view. We have seen seven and eight producer's cuts go out for a single show before everyone was satisfied. In one instance, four copies of each version were sent to the production company and seven VHS copies were sent to the network executives. The costs of duplicating multiple cassettes of each version can really add up.

Temporary music and effects may be incorporated into the producer's cut. With film, any special effects not created during production are often too expensive to make just for a screening—in case they are not used in the final version. With electronic off-line editing, simple special effects can be created quite easily by your off-line or on-line editor. Simple titles can be added to help round out the effect. These "extras" are traditionally saved for use on MOWs and pilots, as are temporary on-lines and temporary dubs.

Temporary On-Line/Temporary Dub

Depending on your project's budget and the importance attached to the network screening, the producers may decide to create a more completed version. Rather than simply making copies of the off-line cassette or sending out the work print as is, they spruce up the off-line cut a bit with a temporary on-line and temporary dub. These added steps are the exception to the rule and are often saved for use on pilots, MOWs, and cable shows with anticipated foreign theatrical releases.

Producers incorporate temporary music and effects because they want the network and studio executives to visualize the finished product as clearly as possible during the various stages of the cut. This is an added expense that may not have been included in the budget at the start of the process. The money to do this may have to come from somewhere else in your budget. One option when doing a temp audio mix may be to first do a prelay (see the prelay/predub section in chapter 8, "Sound") and then do the temp mix. This can limit or even eliminate the need for a prelay session when the final mix is done.

A temp on-line provides a far superior picture quality by on-lining this cut from your dailies masters. A temp on-line, temp dub, or temp mix may be done with your sound services vendor. Here temporary sound effects, mood music, and voice-overs can be added prior to sending the picture to the network for their viewing. As rumor has it, network executives often have little imagination and pretty much need things spelled out for them. Of course, this has not been our experience.

Network/Studio View

In the early days of recorded television, a producer's cut work print would be viewed with the network executives and legal department in a network screening room with the director, producer(s), and postproduction supervisor or associate producer present. Later, the network simply had a work print delivered and screened it by themselves, calling afterwards with their comments (referred to as network notes). Today videotapes are delivered (on VHS or 3/4″) and everyone waits (and waits and waits) for the network notes—usually 2 or more days later.

Picture Lock

As with the completion of principal photography, picture lock is a big step toward the completion of your show. Once all the studio/network notes have been addressed, your picture is considered locked meaning, in theory, that all of the changes that will be done have been done.

At this stage, the work print is locked, slugged (meaning that correctly sized pieces of leader or clear film inserted into the print to hold the place of missing opticals or shots), and balanced. In a film show you now order the negative cut to begin. The editor hands the work print (sometimes reel-by-reel if there are opticals still being made, approved, and cut in) to the negative cutter to begin their job. Sound and music editors and given black-and-white film prints and sound one-to-ones.

For electronic shows, you are ready for on-line. If you are doing a tape finish and time is short or the music, sound, or effects are complicated, you might need to make work cassettes from the off-line. Work cassettes are traditionally made from the on-line master, time permitting.

The editor and assistant editor will also wrap up any paperwork and organize, inventory, and box the film or tape elements, such as trims, outtakes, and work cassettes, for storage.

If your show is a tape-finish show, the editor must go through and check that the EDL is accurate and formatted properly according to the network-required act breaks. The EDL, disk and output cassette, and source elements are delivered to the on-line facility.

Balancing Reels

One very tedious but important job the editor must complete for shows doing a film-finish is called balancing the reels. Balancing the reels is required if a scene is split between two reels and a music cue is involved. It is mandatory that the scene be left in its entirety and not split up. It will be difficult or almost impossible for the music supervisor to cut a cue if it has to be split between two reels.

Act Timings

The editor also provides the act timings and final running time for your network delivery requirements. (See the "Delivery" chapter for more details.) The act timings will tell you if you need to varispeed to come "to time" providing the executives and your distributors find this solution acceptable.

All TV shows are delivered in drop-frame timecode (DFTC). If your show is staying in nondrop-frame timecode until air masters are struck, it would be prudent to double check that the act timings and final run time have been converted to DFTC.

A word of advice: If your show is just slightly over or under the run time designated in the delivery requirements, call the network to see if they will allow you to deliver your show at its current time before going to any expense to varispeed the show. There is more on varispeed in the "Completion" chapter.

Opticals/Simple Visual Effects

If you must create a cut negative to satisfy your delivery requirements, the editor will start ordering your film opticals as soon as possible. Film opticals are created on film at a laboratory or optical house. A copy of the original negative (called an internegative) is made and then altered to create fades, dissolves, scene transitions, titles, and other effects.

For a tape-finish, simple opticals can sometimes be incorporated into the on-line session. Be aware that the postproduction house will probably separate out the time spent in the edit bay creating opticals and visual effects and charge that time at a higher rate. Double-check the breakdown of your charges before the session begins.

When the electronic opticals are too complicated to be done during an assembly, you can build your electronic opticals or effects before or after your on-line. This optical reel is now part of your on-line source material. Just make a cassette for the editor to load into the off-line system. The shots taken from this optical reel will then be incorporated into the final list of edits. If they are not completed before the on-line, the opticals and/or effects can be created after the on-line in a separate session and dropped into your master.

Often the effects or music department will have questions and will want access to the editor. If your show is effects-heavy, it would be wise to have the editor oversee the effects and attend any optical/effects sessions at the postproduction house.

Negative Cut

Negative is never cut before the picture is locked, and the negative cut is never complete until all opticals are approved and have been cut in. All features cut negative. Not all television shows that shoot on film cut negative.

If your show has film dailies and is finishing on film, the editor will provide the negative cutter with a complete work print. If you have done an electronic off-line, the negative cutter will need a cassette (called a LokBox cassette) and a paper list called a negative cut list or negative conform list. This list is generated either on paper, computer disk, or both and provides the negative cutter with a list of each shot and its location on the negative. See the "Completion" chapter for additional information on negative cutting, negative conforming, and creating LokBox cassettes.

Summary

Whether you are finishing on film only, finishing on film and videotape, or finishing only on videotape, everyone involved plays a critical role in the postproduction process. The dailies information must be accurate, be it work print or videotape-based. Many creative and technical decisions throughout the process are based on this information. The assistant editor plays a key role in verifying the accuracy of your information, organizing the editor's materials, and tracking your shots. The editor is a vital creative link in the end result—locked picture. When your editor is thorough and talented, your cut versions will mirror these talents all the way to picture lock. Finally, the success of your negative cut (for film-finish projects) or your on-line (for videotape-finish projects) is completely dependent on the work that is done prior. So often with electronically completed programs the emphasis and the spotlight are on the on-line process; when in reality, most of the creative work is done before the show ever steps into an on-line bay. The on-line bay may contain the equipment designed to give your show that polished look with fancy moves and effects, but all of that is only possible when the editorial work that is done prior to on-line is done well.

7 On-Line Editing

Lies Producers Tell Editors

1. It's pretty simple. It should only take an hour.
2. I'm positive we've got this shot on another tape.
3. I've never had this problem at any other facility.
4. I thought you'd be able to just paint it out.

Lies Editors Tell Producers

1. I'll fill out the paperwork tomorrow.
2. Oh, don't go by *that* monitor.
3. It's on the source tape.
4. I think it looks just fine.

On-line editing is the electronic equivalent of negative cutting. This process is used if you will not be cutting negative or if you are not cutting your negative until after you deliver a finished videotape version. Sometimes an on-line is necessary to provide the promotional department with advertising material before the show is actually finished and delivered. Very often, due to production schedules, the final version of a television show (with sweetened audio, visual effects, corrected color, and titling) is not available until a day or two before the airdate.

In your videotape on-line you will use your master materials to carry out all the creative decisions made in the off-line process. All of the various pieces that make up your final version will be assembled together to create your final picture. In this assembly session, you will use the highest quality materials available to you.

These elements may include dailies master tapes, graphics reels, main title reels, stock footage, and any other source material. For example, if you are creating an episode of a one-hour drama TV show, you will have 5 or more days of dailies, a main title reel, and maybe 1 or more effects reels. For a biography or clip show, you may have hundreds of source masters coming from many different places, such as movie clips, interviews, graphics reels, etc. Regardless of what type of show you are creating, up to this point your off-line editors have been working with copies of your master materials to cut and recut, getting the show just right. Now you're going to reproduce those final edit decisions with your master materials. Selected shots and sections from your source tapes will be strung together. A whole new tape will be created. This will be called your edited master, assembly master, or video assembled master (VAM), depending on your preference. The session in which you string these together is the on-line session. (Sometimes referred to as an auto assembly.)

To summarize, the off-line is the creative process where all available shots are analyzed, and shots that will make up your program, and the order and way they're put together, is decided. Copies or "work tapes" of all those materials are used for this process. This preserves the pristine quality of your master materials. The on-line is the putting together of those shots from your master materials.

On-line editing utilizes computers and electronic effects equipment to emulate a "negative cut" on tape. It seems these days that for all but theatrical releases, there is an on-line in almost everyone's postproduction experience. Depending on the complexity of the on-line and time frame allotted for fixes, you may or may not need to supervise the on-line.

When it is time for your on-line, you essentially add a new member to your team: The on-line editor. The on-line editor sometimes referred to as an assembly editor, becomes an important component in the successful completion of your show.

In an on-line session, the editor is merging your EDL (list of cuts and effects generated from your off-line) with your dailies masters. An EDL may be a video-only list, audio-only list, or a combination of both your video and audio edits. The edit system assembles each cut specified in the EDL from the master videotapes, incorporating simple effects such as fades and dissolves along the way. What you end up with is a master tape of your locked picture.

For picture-only assemblies, a guide track is often laid down to your on-line master. This guide track can be simply the layback of audio from your off-line cassette. The guide track is there to help the sound facility ensure sync.

The advantage to editing picture and sound from your digital dailies masters is that it will most likely cut down on the amount of sound editorial time required. Any production sound that can be used from the on-line eliminates the need to go back to the original sound sources to locate that audio.

On-Line Edit Decision List (EDL)

The on-line editor needs an edit decision list (EDL) on a computer disk and a paper printout—both generated from your off-line system. The postproduction house will provide specifications for the format in which you should deliver your EDL. Don't assume that a Grass Valley or CMX list will do. There are several brands of on-line equipment and it may be difficult for the facility to convert your disk to the format they need. On the other hand, most off-line systems can spit out an EDL disk in whatever format is requested. "Clean" the list before you deliver it to the facility. Off-line systems contain software bugs that create unwanted anomalies in edit lists. It is incumbent on the off-line edit team to go through their list and text-edit any problems that have been introduced by the off-line system. Naturally, the on-line editor can clean the list, but list management usually bills out at the edit-room rate, which can cause unnecessary costs and possible delays in the edit session. A producer supervising a session won't appreciate sitting for an hour while the on-line editor cleans the list. And it makes the off-line edit team look unprofessional. You should also provide a videotape cassette of the final output so there is a source to check and reference to. This check cassette is also generated from your off-line system.

To avoid confusion between the way your source reels appear in your EDL and the way the actual source tapes are labeled, send a legend so the editor can match the source names in the EDL with the actual tape labels (for example, OPT = Optical Reel, MT = Main Title Reel).

On-line editors work almost totally at the mercy of the client and the client's editing team. If any of these folks has made an error anywhere along the road to on-line, the on-line editor is going to be very, very unhappy and possibly, deservedly, crabby. Because on-line editing is a very data-driven function, there are simple guidelines that, when followed, will pretty much guarantee a smooth and efficient on-line session every time. A smooth on-line makes the on-line editor look good (which they like) and makes you look good (which may help ensure continued employment), all the while creating a really top-notch, professional-looking product. Two items that top this list of guidelines are 1) clean and check the EDL before delivering to the on-line session and 2) make sure there is a clear correlation between the source names in the EDL and the source tape labels.

Talkin' Trash

Remember garbage in, garbage out. If you've sent your on-line editor a problem list, it may greatly increase the list management time required before the actual on-line session can start. It may even cause the session to be aborted, meaning you will have to pay for a session you cannot use.

On-Line Session Requirements

For your on-line session(s) you will need to provide all of your source elements. This will include any dailies masters, logo reels, main title reels, and any stock shots that are available—and, of course, the edit decision list (EDL), both on a computer disk and on paper. You will want to provide an output cassette (sometimes called a chase cassette or check cassette) to be screened against your on-line master at the end of the session. This is done to double-check that the on-line picture and sound edits match your off-line cut. Also bring your delivery timing sheet and title/credit information (if you're planning to format and title during your on-line session). If you did not off-line using an electronic off-line system (such as an Avid or Lightworks), the on-line editor will have to manually input the edits from a paper list.

Traditionally, a half-hour sitcom tries to on-line, create opticals, dirt fix, and title all in one session. The speed of some of the current editing systems has cut the actual assembly time so drastically that accomplishing all of the above in a normal on-line session is very doable. The exception is for shows that are doing tape-to-tape color-correction. You will need to color correct your show before you can title. Dirt fixes can be done either before or after the color-correction. Be aware that if you do your dirt fixes after you color correct, you will have to fix both the on-line master and the color-corrected master in order for both of them to contain the dirt fixes.

What the On-Line Facility Needs to Know

When you book your on-line time, the facility will have a list of questions you will need to answer regarding the following:

- What type of editing bay you will need;
- What editing room equipment you will require;
- What types of playback and record videotape machines you will need access to;
- Which of their editorial staff will best be suited to your project; and
- A realistic timetable for the completion of your project.

Be prepared when you call to schedule your on-line. If you cover all of the following points, you will have made a giant leap toward making your on-line a successful experience.

- Know what tape format your dailies are on;
- Know the audio configuration on your source reels;

- Know the timecode on your source tapes (drop-frame timecode or nondrop-frame timecode);
- Pass any necessary VITC information from your sources to your on-line master;
- Know what off-line editing system you use;
- Make sure your off-line editor receives any on-line specifications (your post-production house should have these ready to fax to you);
- Know the amount of time it will take to complete your on-line—based on the number and difficulty of edits (again, the postproduction house will be able to help you estimate the time needed);
- Send a test EDL to the on-line editor;
- Know what format the facility requires your EDL to be in (e.g., Grass Valley, CMX, Macintosh or PC disk);
- Know the EDL computer disk format;
- Be aware of any opticals or visual effects in your on-line that might require a separate optical or effects session;
- Be aware of any other elements needed for your session that are on different formats (e.g., stock shots, opticals reels);
- Know the location of your source elements and how they are getting to the on-line facility;
- Deliver all the elements for your session in a timely fashion to the on-line facility; and
- Provide the facility with an inventory or pull list of the elements for your session so they can confirm that all tapes have been received.

You must also have a clear understanding of what you must end up with at the end of your on-line session:

- Know the format are you mastering to;
- Know the audio configuration you need on your on-line master;
- Know the timecode you will need on your on-line master (DFTC or NDFTC);
- Determine if you will require pre-timecoded stock (referred to as black and coded stock) for your assembly;
- Find out whether your on-line editor feels the time booked is sufficient for the number and difficulty of edits (after starting the session and seeing your material, the editor may feel less or more time will be needed to complete your session);
- Know what effects or moves that are built into your EDL can be done as part of your assembly session; and
- Know if titling will be part of your session.

The above list can also be a helpful guide when choosing your on-line facility and when you actually schedule the session(s). An even better suggestion is to ask the facility if they have a form you can fill out and fax back to them that will outline all of your specifications and requirements.

The 16:9 On-Line

If you transferred your dailies in the squeezed 16:9 format, you will probably be required to unsqueeze the image for broadcast delivery. To do this you will first on-line your project squeezed (from your dailies masters). Any opticals you are creating, either as part of the on-line session or in a separate optical session, will also need to be created in this format (this happens naturally, as the dailies source reels are already squeezed). Once your on-line is completed, you will take this 16:9 edited master and play it back through an aspect ratio converter, thereby creating a 4:3 unsqueezed version.

The following two points are critical when creating this 4:3 version:

1. A copy of the framing chart used in the dailies transfer must exist at the head of the 16:9 master. This will be used to frame the image when converting it.
2. You must create this 4:3 master *prior* to titling the 16:9 master. You will be titling twice—once for the 16:9 version and once for the 4:3 version.

You may also want to consider color correcting the 16:9 version of your show prior to laying it down in 4:3. This way you are only going through color-correction once for each show.

24P Editing

Editing in 24p is here and appears to be the industry's answer to creating both NTSC and PAL masters from one source without all of the undesirable artifacts that come from even the most advanced standards conversion system.

24p editing is a high definition system that for film-originated videotape completion mirrors the film finish by creating one video frame for each film frame. The method is progressive (denoted by the "p") and, therefore, avoids the interpolation problems that exist in the interlace format and the 3:2 pulldown of film to video in the NTSC format. Both NTSC and PAL can be output from the 24p master. This also allows for one color correction, one titling session, and one dirt fix session.

You shoot in film or high definition, transfer your film dailies to high definition, then down convert for your off-line. Being able to still off-line on a standard definition nonlinear editing system is less expensive. This means you can use your existing equipment and spend more time getting it right. The list is converted for use in the 24p on-line suite. You can mix your on-line with interlace materials provided the 24p on-line system you're using has a 24sF interlace. *24sF* is a segmented frame interface, which allows progressive signals to pass through interlace material. It is very simply a system that processes the 24 progressive frames into a 48 Hz signal. Each frame is represented by two segments. The two segments can then be utilized in nonprogressive equipment in the postproduction process, provided they have a 24-segmented frame interface. At any point the two segments can be reconnected together again if you want a progressive frame.

On-Line Specifications

The form the on-line department provides for you to fill in might look something like Figure 7.1. There are places for you to list when and from where your materials are coming. There is also a section for you to fill in regarding any duplication you may need following your session.

Trust us. You can't be too prepared!

Figure 7.1 Videotape On-Line Specifications

PRODUCTION COMPANY:_____
TITLE:_____
CONTACT:_____PHONE:_____
Type of Session:_____   Client Supervised _____Yes_____No

SOURCE ELEMENTS
_____D1 _____D2 _____DIGI BETACAM _____1" _____3/4" _____OTHER
_____Client to Deliver Elements   _____Elements Delivery Date
_____Client to Bring Elements to Session _____Facility to Pick up Elements
                                                                 (arrange with facility prior to session)

MASTER
Record To:_____   Audio Configuration: CH 1:_____ CH 2:_____
_____DFTC   _____NDFTC   CH 3:_____ CH 4:_____
Vertical Interval Information:
Pass Source VITC   _____Yes   _____No   _____(Note lines)
        Record Timecode   _____Yes   _____No   _____(Note any line)
Record Stock Length: _____30 Min. _____60 Min.   _____Other _____Client Stock

_____Off-Line System Used
_____Client to Supply EDL Floppy Disk   _____Client to Supply EDL Printout
_____EDL Format

OPTICALS/VISUAL EFFECTS (Please discuss any special requirements with scheduling)

DUPLICATION
_____ # and Type
Visible Timecode Windows: _____Timecode   Position _____
                                            _____Keykode   Position _____
                                            _____Audio Timecode Position _____
                                            _____Foot and Frames Position _____
_____Address Track Timecode
Audio: CH 1:_____ CH 2:_____ CH 3:_____ CH 4:_____
Vertical Interval Information: _____Audio   _____Keykode _____Timecode
Record Stock Length: _____30 Min.   _____60 Min.   _____Client Stock
----
_____ # and Type
Visible Timecode Windows: _____Timecode   Position _____
                                            _____Keykode   Position _____
                                            _____Audio Timecode Position _____
                                            _____Foot and Frames Position _____
_____Address Track Timecode
Audio: CH 1:_____ CH 2:_____ CH 3:_____ CH 4:_____
Vertical Interval Information: _____Audio   _____Keykode _____Timecode
Record Stock Length: _____30 Min.   _____60 Min.   _____Client Stock

Summary

Off-line and on-line editing are both equally important steps in your quest to meet your videotape delivery requirements. The success of one (off-line) will dictate the success of the other (on-line). Even though we split dailies and editorial into different chapters, they are in no way independent of one another. We just did it so the information wouldn't seem so overwhelming and you'd continue reading.

Remember that the best way to help guarantee a successful editorial experience for your project is to be as prepared as you can be. Don't leave anything to chance and choose carefully whom you depend on to provide you with information that is accurate and complete. At each step, double-check what you are asking for and what you are receiving.

Your postproduction facility contacts are a valuable resource for guidance and information. Use them. The more they know about where your project has been and where it is going, the more help and insight they can offer to you.

Don't be shy. Sure, there are dumb questions. But we continue to stress that if you don't know something, you should swallow your pride and ask anyway. They can't kill you, but your producers can! Save yourself!

8 Sound

Okay, it's time to talk about sound. Listen up. This is a big topic and an important one. Even in the days of silent pictures, there was sound. Someone played the organ or piano offstage, in the dark, giving life, emotion, energy, and flow to quiet images. These guys could be called the first film sound composers.

Audio Sweetening

Taking your production audio and finalizing it with enhancements, looping, music, sound effects, and various clean-up procedures is called audio sweetening.

Audio sweetening includes the manipulation of the production sound track on many levels. Extra sound "material" can be added, production tracks cleaned up, existing sound enhanced, music bridged between scenes, music and effects added, and ADR or looping combined with production audio.

Your sound is "built" under the supervision of a sound supervisor. This applies to dialogue, effects, and music. The person actually responsible for building the tracks will be either the supervisor or, depending on the time constraints and complexity of the project, a specially hired editor.

Sound is as important in television as it is in film. Some may argue that it is even more important to TV because the images on the screen don't have the power and size of those on a movie screen.

When done well, TV sound tells the audience when to laugh, when to cry, and when a commercial is coming up so they can get a beer or go to the bathroom. In fact, we owe it to the American viewing public to give them the sound they need and expect. On the other hand, put an inappropriate sound in the wrong place and you could have Dad getting a beer during the climax of the show. Just something to think about.

Because sound is complex, we have broken our discussions into the following topics:

1. Production sound
2. Temporary mix/temporary dub
3. Laydown
4. Predub/prelay
5. Sound effects
6. ADR/looping
7. Foley
8. Music/scoring
9. Mix/dub
10. Layback
11. Music and effects tracks (M&E)
12. Foreign language dubbing
13. Foreign language film prints
14. Foreign language videotape masters
15. Dubbing materials
16. Anti-piracy issues
17. When do you dub?
18. Foreign laugh pass

And, for those of you who prefer a visual reference (this is TV, after all), we've drawn a nifty diagram to help you (see Figure 8.1).

Figure 8.1 The Sound Path

Nifty Diagram (The Sound Path)

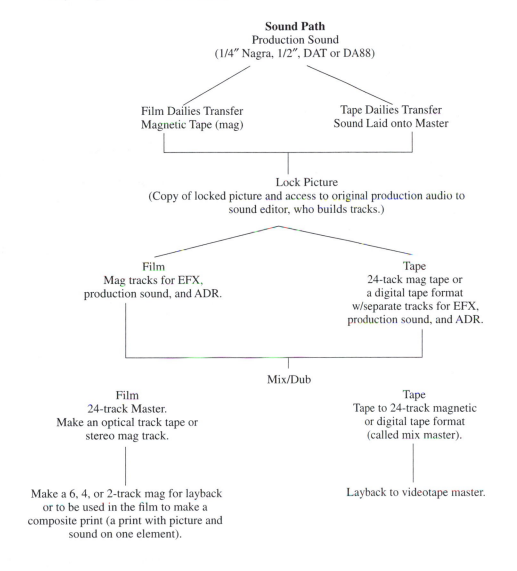

Sound Path
Production Sound
(1/4″ Nagra, 1/2″, DAT or DA88)

Film Dailies Transfer
Magnetic Tape (mag)

Tape Dailies Transfer
Sound Laid onto Master

Lock Picture
(Copy of locked picture and access to original production audio to
sound editor, who builds tracks.)

Film
Mag tracks for EFX,
production sound, and ADR.

Tape
24-tack mag tape or
a digital tape format
w/separate tracks for EFX,
production sound, and ADR.

Mix/Dub

Film
24-track Master.
Make an optical track tape or
stereo mag track.

Tape
Tape to 24-track magnetic
or digital tape format
(called mix master).

Make a 6, 4, or 2-track mag for layback
or to be used in the film to make a
composite print (a print with picture and
sound on one element).

Layback to videotape master.

Production Sound

Production sound is recorded on the set during shooting. It is the raw audio that much of the final audio for your show will spring from.

The Sound Recordist

The sound recordist uses the following equipment and materials: The record machine (1/4" Nagra T, 1/2" 4-track, DAT, DA88) in the format chosen by the production company and any backup format, if used, along with plenty of stock, sound reports, and labels for each piece of tape and its box. There will also be one or two assistants.

The job done by the sound recordist often determines the amount of additional ADR and looping required later. As an experienced professional, the recordist will notice extraneous noises from planes, cars, wind, actor movement, and fluorescent lights, that will affect the usability of each take.

The sound recordist can also make or break the film to tape dailies transfer. Sound for standard definition shows should always be recorded at 30 fps and at 60 Hz (50 Hz is for PAL). Nondrop-frame timecode is usually preferred, but DFTC can also be used successfully. DFTC drops frames at predetermined intervals, thus making it impossible to confirm that all of the frames are accounted for. Timecode must be recorded on the center channel or timecode track—not on a standard audio track. The resolution of 30-fps sound to 24-fps film is a function of the telecine process. Do not let a sound recordist convince you that the sound needs to be recorded at 24 fps or 29.97 fps. The telecine facility will have to resolve the audio, there will be drift in long takes, and the nightmare of your sound will haunt you throughout the entire process. Off-speed film transfers, of course, cannot have sync sound.

The Sound Report

The sound report is the form that the sound recordist fills in so there is always a written record of what is on an individual sound reel and how that sound was recorded.

One sound report goes in each box of audiotape. If there is a primary sound source and a backup sound source is also recorded, each format gets its own report. If at the end of your day you've shot three DA88s and three DAT backups, then you should have six separate sound reports. Figure 8.2 is a sample sound report.

Figure 8.2 Sample Sound Report

A   **SOUND COMPANY NAME**
B   **SOUND COMPANY ADDRESS**
        AND
        PHONE#

C PROJECT TITLE: In Your Face#3326   *D* DATE:8/20/96

E PROD. COMPANY: Pie Throwers   *F* ROLL# 3

G RECORDIST: Rocky   *H* REEL NO. 2 OF 3

I ☐ WILD ☒ SYNC 60 TIMECODE 30 FPS
DFTC

HEAD TONE: -10 bm
PRINT ☐ ALL ☒ CIRCLED TAKES ONLY

J SCENE NO.	*K* TAKE	*L* NOTES	*M* SMPTE START
			10db Tone
4B	①(split tracks)	split tracks	06: 00: 00: 00
4B	②(split tracks)	split tracks	06: 10:03
4C	1	Incomplete	(Inc.)
4C	②		06: 29: 34:
	N TAILS Out		

The Sound Report Breakdown

Following is a breakdown and explanation of each section of the sound report and how the information in each section is used. Sound companies may set up their reports with slightly different forms, but all of the information listed here must be listed on each sound report. If any information is missing it means your sound recordist has omitted information that will be necessary to you down the road.

A. *Sound company name.* This is usually preprinted on the sound report.
B. *Sound company address and telephone number.* These are usually preprinted on the report.
C. *Title of the project.* If a separate line is not included for the episode number, it should be included here.
D. *Date the sound was shot.*
E. *Name of production company.*
F. *Sound roll number.*
G. *Name of mixer or sound recordist.*
H. *This reel's number out of total number of reels.* If there are multiple rolls, this allows the postproduction facility to check that they have received all of the sound rolls.
I. *Technical information.* Note here such details as the sync reference (so the telecine operator knows how to set up the tape for playback), timecode type, and head tone (so the telecine operator knows how to reference tone to zero so that the playback levels match the levels at which the tape was recorded). Sometimes the instruction to transfer circled or all takes is included here.
J. *Scene number.* This references the script scene number and is included here so the sound can be matched to the proper picture.
K. *Take number.* This references the number of times a scene is recorded and is included here so the sound can be matched to the proper picture.
L. *Any special notes about that scene and take.* Details such as incomplete take, split tracks, and interference.
M. *The start timecode off the record machine for each take.* It is common for electronic slates not to work properly. This notation of the general beginning timecode of each take gives the telecine operator some clue as to where the take exists on the audio source if there is no electronic slate reference and the operator has to search for and hand-sync the takes.
N. *Threading information.* This tells the telecine operator whether the audiotape was left *tails out* or was rewound back to the head. If using a reel-to-reel format, the operator needs this information to know how to thread the tape onto the playback machine.

Any time you find a member of the production crew providing incomplete information and it is information you will need in the postproduction process, correct the problem immediately. Sound reports definitely fall into this category. Any information left off these reports affects you directly in the electronic dailies process. There is no reason for any information pertaining to your project to be left off sound reports. It may seem as if we are being repetitious in saying this, but every piece of information is necessary. Ultimately, heeding this warning will save you valuable time throughout the postproduction process and time *is* money.

Production Sound Record Formats

Here are a few rules and some information about the various production sound formats available for recording:

Quarter-inch Nagra two-track analog tape: 1/4" is recorded with a sync pulse that is either a tone or a timecode. Today, most houses require that 1/4" be recorded with center-track timecode. Some facilities have modified their machines to read pilot tone, but this is something you have to check ahead of time. If not, the facility may have to stripe the 1/4" or dub it over to another piece of timecoded stock before the transfer so the Nagra machine has reference on which to lock. This reference is the only thing that keeps the sound from drifting out of sync. There is a really boring explanation as to why this is so, which we won't describe here. Just believe us, it's true.

Quarter-inch has two audio tracks. Therefore, you can record split tracks. Split tracks are when individual and different sound is recorded on each audio channel. If split tracks are used, most sound recordists note this on the sound report. Make sure yours does. As with everything you do, give the facility as much information as possible about what you did in the field. Traditionally, when transferring dailies, facilities transfer the audio channels straight across—channel 1 of production sound element to channel 1 of dailies master and channel 2 of production sound element to channel 2 of dailies. But clear this up with the facility before the transfer begins.

Half-inch four-track analog tape: This is a pretty straightforward, tried and true method for recording production sound. There are three analog audio tracks along with a timecode track. Be sure to let your postproduction facility know how your tracks are configured and how you want them transferred to your dailies. Half-inch four-track is also a popular backup format for DA88. If you are delivering both formats to your transfer facility (and ultimately the sound facility), be sure to let them know which format you prefer they use in your transfer.

DAT: DAT stands for digital audiotape. It is reportedly a superior sound source to both 1/4" and 1/2" analog formats. But there are people who argue that for television dailies that are transferred to a digital videotape master, the difference is not significant. With only two audio tracks, it is not very practical for sitcoms, which usually record multiple tracks.

DA88 digital 8-track tape: DA88 has fast become a popular production audio recording choice. It has eight audio tracks. The critical step when using DA88s is that they must be formatted before they are used. Either 44.1 or 48k sampling rates are usually acceptable. If you need, your sound house can probably format your tapes for you before you use them to record your production audio. Use only Hi-8 mm metal particle tape.

Deva: The latest digital sound format to hit the dailies scene is Deva. This is a computer controlled disk format, which will record hours of program on as many tracks as your field mix equipment will handle. The main attraction to this new format is that it does not need to pre-roll prior to recording. All tape and mag based recording devices need a minimum of 3 to 5 seconds of pre-roll to get the machine up and running at optimum speed. Deva is ready when you hit record. This is a great advantage for fast-paced productions and first time directors who often aren't used to this requirement and cause problems for themselves with their production audio. It will even generate a sound cue sheet on demand. The disadvantage is that it does not record or slave to timecode, making editing directly from Deva basically impossible. Before the dailies telecine transfer, or before editing final sound tracks, the disk must be transferred to a timecoded element (usually DAT or DA88). As with all production audio, we suggest that you simo record a back up audio source. We have already seen several productions after the first day of shooting and the DEVA disks have been blank. A back up might save the day. Be sure to check with your video or sound facility, as not all transfer houses have Deva decks.

Use a SmartSlate, Dummy

While the electronic slate is not an audiotape format, we are going to deal with it here because it is so important to the speed and accuracy with which your dailies are transferred—as well as being a visual check/reference for each take you shoot.

A SmartSlate is a clapper with a rectangle in the middle that gives an LED readout of the timecode that is being laid down simultaneously on the production audio. DO NOT SHOOT WITHOUT AN ELECTRONIC SLATE IF YOU ARE PLANNING A FILM TO TAPE DAILIES TRANSFER. The costs per day for that SmartSlate will be money well spent when you get into telecine and off-line. You can read more about the use of the SmartSlate in the telecine section of the "Dailies" chapter. Essentially, it allows the telecine operator to type in the LED number and have the audio playback machine physically go to that timecode, giving the operator a very close sync point for the take prior to any manual manipulation.

The Dos and Don'ts of Electronic Slating

Having an electronic slate is not enough. Learn how to use it properly! Your transfer facility may give you some written guidelines, but if not, here are the basics:

- Do not point the electronic slate towards the sun. If you must shoot with the slate facing the sun, then shield it with something so the numbers are readable when photographed. Use the "bright" setting on the slate when shooting outdoors.
- When shooting in the dark, put the brightness switch on "dim." Otherwise, the numbers tend to bleed or blur, making it difficult or impossible to read them.
- Check periodically to make sure the numbers on the electronic slate matches the timecode being recorded on the sound source. This is a piece of electronic equipment and can be affected by loss of battery power, loose cables, and the damnable forces of Murphy's Law. If the readout doesn't reflect the actual timecode being laid onto the audiotape, try jamming the slate to reset it. If you can't get it to work and you can't get a replacement, the transfer house will shower you with unpleasantries under their breath and be very unhappy during your telecine transfer. Not to mention that the transfer will take much longer to complete. Slate timecode problems will occur in the field. When they do, your sound person can help save money in telecine by noting on the sound report the start timecode at the beginning of each take.
- Make sure the electronic slate is "in the picture frame" so that the operator can see the entire number during the transfer.
- Ask the transfer house if they prefer that the numbers stop when the clapper closes or if they prefer to continue through the closing of the clapper. Especially in a multicamera shoot, it is often good to have additional time to grab a timecode—especially if it takes a while for the slate to get around to all the cameras.

And, while we're on the subject of the clapper, let us regale you with a couple of anecdotes to give warning about some easily avoided "gotchas."

Electronic Slate Gotcha #1

Be sure the clapper closes in-frame. It is the only practical visual reference for sync. If the telecine operator cannot see the clapper close, then he has to search into the take to find a hard effect on which to sync. That means that it will take much longer to lay down that take, it may never be perfectly in sync on your dailies (which means the off-line editor will then have to sync the take), and your negative is being run back and forth across the telecine gate numerous times, picking up extra dirt and leaving it open to other possible problems such as scratches. This bit of advice may sound really like "duh!" but every show lets this happen, no matter how professional they are. It's sloppy and it causes unnecessary expenses down the road.

Electronic Slate Gotcha #2

When shooting a scene that starts in the dark, along with using the "dim" setting on the LED display, somehow illuminate the sticks so the telecine colorist can see when the clapper closes. This can be accomplished a couple of ways. Some productions simply use a flashlight shining on the slate; some use glow-in-the-dark tape on the bottom of the stick and the top of the slate where they meet. Use whatever method you want, just use something.

Not Too Bright—Electronic Slate Gotcha #3

During one pilot season we transferred dailies for a company that does lots of TV shows. We won't reveal their identity because we'd like to keep working in this town, but suffice it to say they should have known better. Anyway, the scene starts in a hotel room in the dark. The phone rings. The star reaches up and turns on the light next to the bed by pulling a string. He then watches the phone ring a second, clumsily picks it up and talks into it. You guessed it! The clapper closed with a very loud, firm clap, and not a bit of it was visible in the dark. All there was, was the LED display (blurred because it was on the wrong setting, I might add) and no way to see when the clapper closed. And there wasn't a hard effect to sync to.

We ended up trying to sync to the actor's mouth forming the words. Of course, there were many takes. We got pretty close on some of them—right on for others, even. But it took a very, very long time. The miracle was that the director, the cinematographer, the producer, and the associate producer were all in the room during this painstaking process. (This was truly a facility's dream. The client is so rarely around to see the headaches created when they don't shoot properly.) I'll bet none of them ever lets this happen during a shoot again.

Okay, enough with the testimonials. Back to the task at hand.

Production Sound Continued . . .

The original production sound is either laid down in sync during the dailies film to tape transfer, given directly to the off-line editor to be loaded directly into his system, or transferred to magnetic stripe, all depending on the way the rest of postproduction is to be handled.

The production sound is used as is throughout the postproduction process, until either the layback of the final sweetened audio or film sound is created. The exception is that when the producer's cut is locked, additional effects and temp music are sometimes added. This is done either in the cutting room by the editor or, budget and time permitting, with a temp mix. Temp mix is explained in detail later in this chapter.

Sometimes it is enough to add a couple of common generic sound-effects, such as a car horn, a baby crying, or animal noises, to help fill out a joke or story line until the final effects are mixed. Your sound facility can often provide these rather quickly and for a nominal fee.

Temporary Mix/Temporary Dub (Temp Mix/Temp Dub)

Here temporary sound effects, mood music, and voice-overs are added prior to sending the picture to the network for their viewing. This is an added expense that may not have been included in the budget at the start of the process. If you decide to go this route, the moneys to do this may have to come from somewhere else in the budget. You'll have to find a not-so-temporary solution.

Do You Need One?

Planning a temp mix for your project is the exception and not the rule. A temp mix can represent a large additional expense and is usually reserved for use by select cable producers who anticipate a foreign theatrical market. This would be a presales tool for marketing their program abroad. In another situation, the producers may use this tool for a pilot or MOW when the impressions made in early screenings with the network and studio executives are critical.

One of us had the experience of sitting in a screening with some network executives who, after viewing the program, wanted to know why so many of the sound effects were missing. Here goes . . . Post 101! This interim sound can be accomplished by creating a temp dub.

Producers want the network and studio executives to visualize as clearly as possible the finished product. When finishing on videotape, one option available to help these executives understand how the finished piece will sound is to schedule a temp dub. A temp dub or temp mix may be done with your sound-services vendor. Temporary sound effects, mood music, and voice-overs can be added prior to sending the picture to the network for their viewing.

If the sound effects are indeed simple—a dog barking or bell ringing—your effects company or sound company can provide these to your off-line editor on a format he can load into his off-line editing system. These can usually be had for a minimal cost . . . sometimes even free of charge. Anything more than this will require going into a dub stage or sound-effects room. The costs will rise very quickly. Regardless of the money you do or don't spend on a temp mix, it is still a temp. It all gets thrown out in the end, and you start over.

On film, any special sound effects not included in the ambient sounds are probably too expensive to make just for a screening. With electronic off-line editing, simple sound effects can be incorporated quite easily by your off-line editor.

Temporary Insanity

Beware that the extras can backfire. In another incident, one of us worked on an MOW in which some temp music was inserted to help set a mood. It was an original score from a popular feature. A network executive fell in love with the piece in the show and demanded that the composer match the music. Help, we're just a little TV movie. These "extras" are pretty much saved for use on pilots and big-budget cable movies.

Don't confuse a temp mix with a premix. Premixing is the mixing of minor sound elements prior to the dub to cut down on the need for additional mixing boards or even an extra day in the mix session.

Laydown

Sitcoms and half-hour programs where the tracks are usually added to or enhanced rather than replaced completely often go through a laydown process.

Once your on-line is complete and you have a videotape master with picture and production sound, the sound facility may want the master or another digital format (a 3/4" cassette won't work because it does not have the quality or enough audio tracks). They will lay the sound across from all audio channels of the videotape to a multitrack format. This is done at least 1 to 2 days prior to the mix. The sound facility can then begin the process of enhancing, correcting, and cleaning up the existing production audio. The goal, usually because money and time are very tight, is to minimize the time needed in the foley, prelay, and laugh sessions to create final sweetened stereo audio tracks.

Predub/Prelay

If your show includes a lot of effects, for example, explosions, music, sound effects, or loud noises over romantic dialogue, then your sound-effects supervisor will probably recommend a predub or prelay. Some of the sound effects are mixed prior to dubbing to reduce the number of individual effects the sound mixer has to control. This can be helpful, or even necessary, if there are more sound cues than the mixing board can handle, requiring the use of an auxiliary mixing board, or, if there are more cues than the mixer can handle at once. The mixer can only control a certain number of pots. Pots are the individual knobs that control the volume of each effect. Too many cues will be cumbersome and slow down the mix. Premixing them will make the dub go faster. Your sound-effects supervisor and one mixer should be able to complete the prelay in one 8-hour day on the dub stage.

Sound Effects

The addition and creation of sound effects (often seen written as EFX or SFX) is necessary for two reasons. First, they are added for creative composition. Secondly, many sound effects are just the replacement of "ambient" effects recorded with the dialogue track. These ambient sounds, such as room noise, doors and windows opening or closing, papers rustling, and heavy breathing, are lost when the production audio is looped. If the originally recorded dialogue lines are replaced, then the ambient sounds are lost and must be recreated and put back into the sound mix. In a show that is being dubbed into a foreign language (rather than being subtitled), the originally recorded dialogue track will not be used, and any sound effects recorded as part of that dialogue track will be lost. These effects will have to be recreated as part of a separate audio track called the effects track. These effects tracks are called filled effects, foreign-fill, or 100% filled effects.

Work Cassettes and Elements

At picture lock, sound and music editors on film projects will be given black-and-white film prints and sound one-to-ones. If you are doing a tape-finish and time is short or the music, sound, or effects are complicated, you might need to make work cassettes from the off-line. Work cassettes are traditionally made from the on-line master, time permitting. Make sure the music supervisor and effects people know whether you are finishing on film or videotape. Their preparation and tape specifications will be determined by the format you are working with.

Call your music and effects supervisors to get the technical requirements for delivering videotape elements. These work tapes have precise specifications. If at all possible, have these specs submitted to you in writing. If the people you've hired to do this work are seasoned professionals, this will be a common request and they will be able to fax their videotape requirements to you. Get these to the postproduction house that will be doing this duplication. Following are sample specifications that you might receive for sound work.

Work Cassette Sample Specifications

Sample #1:
- a)   VHS
- b)   Channel 1: Dialogue; Channel 2: Timecode −2 dB (minus 2 decibels)
- c)   Visible Timecode in the Lower Left
- d)   Record on both Linear and Hi-Fi Tracks

Explanation:
   a)   Some individuals, especially composers who work out of their homes, will request VHS tapes for their work tapes.
   b)   On the tape in this sample, dialogue only is required on channel 1. As long as you haven't laid back mixed audio tracks to your source tape, it is normal to have only dialogue on channel 1 of any master you have made.
   c)   On the tape in this sample, timecode is required on channel 2. This is what editor's equipment will lock to. The timecode must match the timecode on the playback source. This specification requires that it be recorded at a level 2 dB lower than channel 1.
   d)   The visible timecode window needs to go in the lower left according to the specifications above. The timecode displayed in this window must also match the timecode on the playback source.

With certain machines, you can record onto both the linear and the hi-fi tracks on a piece of VHS stock. The above specs require this to be so.

Sample #2:
   a)   3/4"
   b)   Channel 1: Dialogue
   c)   Channel 2: Timecode
   d)   Address Track Timecode
   e)   Visible Timecode Upper Left
   f)   VITC Lines 12 and 14

Explanation:
   a)   The above dub order requires a 3/4" work cassette.
   b)   Again, the editor has requested the dialogue track only on Channel 1.
   c)   Channel 2, again, must contain timecode. This timecode must match the timecode on the tape it was made from. The record level of the timecode will be the same as the record level on channel 1.
   d)   Three-quarter-inch videotape has a separate address track where timecode is generally laid. It too must match the master timecode.
   e)   This time the editor wants the visible timecode window to be displayed in the upper left of the picture.
   f)   You must also record timecode onto the vertical interval of the picture. If the master has VITC (vertical interval timecode) matching what your tape needs, you can simply pass it across with the picture. If not (as in the case of an output from your off-line system), it will need to be generated.

There are other variations that you will see in duplication specifications. That is why it is very important that you get this information directly from the people who will be using these tapes. If at all possible, have these cassettes made and available in time for the spotting session.

Sound-Effects Spotting

Once the picture is locked, it is reviewed with the sound-effects editor and the composer in a spotting session. There the producers, off-line editor, director, sound-effects editor, and associate producer (or postproduction supervisor) watch the entire show and determine the sound style of the picture. They decide the *whens*, *wheres*, and *hows* of all the music and effects cues.

The sound-effects editor will work from the locked dubs or working cassettes made from the on-line master, preserving as much of the sound as possible from that master. However, if there is background noise, recording problems, or other sound-quality issues, they will go back to the original production sound sources and try to clean them up as much as they can. Any sections where they are still unable to get acceptable audio quality, will be added to the list of ADR/looping needed.

Creating Sound Effects

At this point the sound supervisor will determine what special sound needs there are. For example, we did a film where a super-rocket car played an important role in the movie; therefore the sound made by that car was integral to the audience response. The effects company provided several sound samples until they came up with one that was blended and refined and met with the producers' expectations.

After spotting, the sound editor/designer will need as much as 3 weeks (15 working days) for an MOW to prepare, create, and cut the effects, dialogue, and loop tracks. An episodic averages 5 to 7 days and a sitcom can average 2 to 3 days. Features can easily be more than 3 weeks depending on the complexity of the project.

Sound effects editors are responsible for cutting production audio and ambient sounds not recorded in production. The sound designer and the audio dubbing facility may be two separate facilities. Therefore, if you have to go back to replace any words or effects in these tracks, or if you need to access the tracks for augmenting foreign music and effects tracks, you will go to the sound editorial company for this material. You'll then return to the audio dubbing facility to remix the changes and lay the new sounds back to your original elements.

The sound-effects editor(s) strip the audio. This is called building the tracks and is done so that on the dub stage there is complete control of each element and each element can be moved or altered individually, as needed. The following elements are separated out:

1. Production dialogue;
2. ADR dialogue;

   3.   Sound effects; and
   4.   Foley.

If you plan to make film prints, now is the time to remind your sound supervisor to create pull-ups for your sound rolls. This is an industry-wide practice for over-lapping the sound from each reel by 2 seconds or 20 frames. This will assure that you have continuous sound from one film reel to the next.

   It is important at this point to contact the mixing/dubbing facility to find out: 1) how many pots the mix board handles and whether an auxiliary board is available, if necessary; 2) from what formats they can mix (e.g., mag, 24-track, DAT, DA88, or optical disk). Find out what format the sound-effects company prefers, make sure the dubbing facility can handle it, and let everyone know what everyone else is using. All facilities are not created equal, and it's too expensive to wait until you get to the mix to find that the sound-effects company is delivering on DAT to a facility that can only handle mag.

ADR/Looping

After reviewing the picture, the sound-effects company will provide a chart (see Figure 8.3) of the looping they feel is necessary. You then take this chart and create a budget based on the cost of looping each person, including any group looping. The equation for budgeting how long it will take an actor to loop is not dif-ficult to use.

Figure 8.3 ••

CHARACTER	R-1	R-2	R-3	R-4	R-5	R-6	R-7	R-8	R-9	R-10	R-11	TOTALS
Beau	1	5	2	6	8	12	9	0	14	13	0	70
Blair	0	2	0	0	16	6	0	7	0	10	6	47
Charles	0	0	0	8	2	0	6	12	8	2	0	38
Dan	6	0	6	0	0	18	12	0	28	0	0	70
Dillon	0	5	0	0	6	0	0	11	0	21	0	43
Erica	0	3	7	8	0	21	18	19	6	0	4	86
Grace	7	0	0	5	8	0	5	0	15	19	0	59
Group	0	6	3	0	0	6	0	6	8	6	0	35
Group/Cops	0	0	3	1	4	4	9	0	0	12	0	33
Nick	4	0	5	5	0	0	0	7	6	0	2	29
Nora	3	4	6	2	6	4	2	0	0	11	0	36
Rick	0	0	0	2	0	0	0	18	6	7	0	33
Steve	6	0	7	9	5	5	0	0	4	0	0	36
Todd	0	6	6	4	2	0	6	15	5	5	0	49
Phone Man	0	0	3	0	4	5	0	2	0	0	0	14
TOTALS	27	31	48	50	61	81	67	97	100	106	12	680

Figure 8.4 is a partial guide of the exact location of each of the loop lines charted above.

Figure 8.4 Looping Log Breakdown Chart

| Production: | _____ | | | |
| Editor: | _____ | | | |

Reel#:	2 _____	FFOP:	0011'10	Line Count: 31
Dupe Date:	_____	LFOP:	0980'03	

Character Line #	In Out	Dialogue	Comments Notes	Tracks 1 2 3 4
Todd		0011'10 "I'm serious"	Low Level	
2001		0015'00		
Blair		0082'03 (Inhale) "Can't we wait until later?"	Bad BG	
2002		0085'00		
Beau		0116'00 "I can whip you at basketball."	Clipped	
2003		0121'01		
Todd		0121'05 "Oh yeah."		
2004		0123'05		
Group		0300'00 (Restaurant specifics)		
2005		0323'00		
Group		0300'00 (Restaurant walla)		
2006		0323'00		
Todd		0322'01 (Possible light laugh and efforts climb into car)		
2007		0324'00		
Nick		0588'00 "I don't think you you understand what the heck is going on, do you?"		
2008		0602'00		

| Production: _____ | Reel:2 | Page 1 of 3 |

The master loop log (Figure 8.3) lists the number of lines each character has in each reel that will require looping or dialogue replacement. This happens to be expressed in film reels, but it can also be adapted to apply to videotape masters and acts. The total number of lines for each character throughout the show is totaled in the far right vertical column. The number of lines per reel is totaled at the bottom.

In the breakdown chart (Figure 8.4), the exact location of each line is noted along with the line itself that needs to be replaced. Again, this chart is referring to film reels, so the locations are in footages per reel. For videotape masters, timecode numbers represents these locations.

Scheduling ADR/Looping

Professional actors can normally loop 10 lines an hour (add 10 minutes for each reel change if you are looping to film). Remember your recording crew is probably union and will need appropriate breaks. So, make the ADR list and meet with your producer to decide if there are any changes to the list.

Be One Step Ahead

Because TV has such a short turnaround, it is a wise postproduction supervisor who calls the main actors' managers/agents for their availability before spotting with the effects company. This way, when you and the producer sit down to make looping decisions, you'll know your main actors' schedules so you can factor time frames into the equation. If you are aware of an actor's scheduling conflict ahead of time, you can avoid last-minute disasters and missed deadlines. Even the most arrogant and hard-to-please producer will be somewhat impressed.

Schedule your actors according to time and availability. Try to work around their schedules as much as your schedule will allow. When they arrive at the session, make sure that they are comfortable and that they immediately receive a list of their loop lines. Traditionally, looping starts with reel 1 and works through to the end of the show. Actors are normally looped individually, unless it makes more artistic sense to pair two actors for the sake of the scene. Your sound-effects supervisor and associate producer need to be on hand to supply footage counts or timecodes and a playback reference.

A loop group will usually want to view the show prior to the session to get a feel for what is needed. Groups are used to working together as a unit and if they are well organized, these sessions usually go fairly quickly.

What's It Gonna Cost?

Some cast members (usually the main cast members) will have looping built into their contracts and therefore will be prepaid and available for 1 to 2 days to loop.

You can always check with casting; they made the deals and know who has looping built into their contracts, and for how many days. Actors are governed by Screen Actors Guild rules.

Here's a sample of the wording for a looping contract for a 2-hour pilot: "Work Period for Pilot: 4 (four) weeks plus two (2) free travel days and two (2) free looping days, which may be noncontiguous and which shall be subject to Player's professional availability." If you are in doubt about the rules, call the Screen Actors Guild.

Weekly players will cost either their day rate for a whole day of looping or one half of their day rate for a half-day of looping. Divide the weekly rate on the contract by 5 days. This gives you the rate for a full day of looping. For half a day, divide the day rate in half.

Day players must be paid a full day rate for a whole day or fraction thereof. Therefore, if you need a day player for only two words of looping, it may or may not be worth it financially to the producer. If you are already hiring a loop group, they may be able to handle the odd couple of lines here and there. Discuss your options with your producer using the ADR chart and your budget as your guide.

You can't just go off willy-nilly replacing an actor's dialogue with someone else's voice. SAG governs their members well in this area, and a producer is not allowed to indiscriminately revoice (or let a loop group actor add the needed two words) without the actor's consent. Ninety-nine percent of the time an actor will want to do his own looping. So, to make this all make sense financially, the sound-effects company may have to work a little harder to "clean" the original dialogue track so it can be used.

Sometimes you may have to arrange looping at a distant location. These things take time and coordination, so don't cut yourself short. Any early preplanning you can do will make everyone's job easier—especially yours! Plus, once again you've a chance to look good!

Foley

Foley is the addition or replacement of sound effects. This includes such things as footsteps, keys jangling in pockets, doors closing, windows opening, punches, and slaps. This must be one of the most creative jobs in the entire postproduction process.

Under normal circumstances, the only people in attendance at these sessions are the foley artists and their recording technicians—and maybe the effects supervisor. Traditionally, the sound-effects company is responsible for arranging, scheduling, and supervising any necessary foley.

For budgeting purposes, check how many days have been scheduled for the foley and keep track of any overages, you have usually 1 to 2 days for an average MOW, less for an episodic, and in some cases, none for a sitcom.

Music/Scoring

Spotting with your composer and music supervisor is done either the same day or the day after your effects spotting and is attended by the same group of decision makers.

Again, make sure those doing the scoring will deliver a format the dubbing facility can use. If you drop the ball on this, shame on you. We've told you twice now.

Scoring Methods

Composers use various methods to score and record.

Electronic method: Often this is done in the composer's home or studio. At various intervals prior to the mix date, the producer and director are invited to listen to a semicompleted score while the picture plays on a monitor. There is no scoring stage to book and there are no musicians to negotiate with. The composer does the entire process as a package.

Orchestral method: You will need to book a scoring stage, and the scheduler at this facility will need the following information: 1) how many sessions you need, 2) what is the picture playback format, 3) how many musicians will be attending the sessions, and 4) the record format.

You can usually count on completing 15 minutes of the score on tape in a 3-hour session. Remember that your musicians and technicians are probably union. Be sure they get their doughnuts and coffee at the prescribed intervals, or you're looking at penalties. You may have to factor into your budget such things as musician cartage fees (for larger instruments), and the facility will charge you to mix-down after the session. A mix-down is when all the instrument tracks are mixed down to 6 or 8 tracks. The music editor will supervise this session and can advise you regarding cost of session and stock.

Some producers will choose to fly the composer to a scoring facility in another state (such as Utah) where costs are lower. Remember that composers also have a guild (does anyone not have a guild?) that governs details such as conducting—so watch out for them union rules.

Once scoring is complete, the music supervisor has two options. The score can be mixed down and tracks built for the dub. Or, scores that are recorded in order of use are laid down in stereo pairs and a mix-down is not required. Stereo pairs refer to like instruments grouped together in stereo. Due to its multiple channel capability, DA88 is the audio format music supervisors most often prefer to record to for use in the dub.

Music in a Can

Canned background music for use in restaurant, elevator, and grocery store scenes, are called needle drops. Needle drops are short bits of premade music that are not created by your composer, but purchased. There are companies that sell the licenses for this music, just like stock houses sells stock shots. Your music editor will be responsible for finding this music. And, if your producers don't like the music the music editor has chosen, there's plenty more to choose from.

These music snippet licenses are relatively inexpensive, and unless you go way overboard in using them, they won't break your budget. It is almost always less expensive to license needle drops than it costs to score bits of original music.

Obtaining Music Clearances

If you are working on a show for a large production company or studio, they will employ a music coordinator to secure bids and finalize licenses. However, if this responsibility falls on you, refer to the "Music" section in the "Legal" chapter.

A Word of Advice

Keep in mind that obtaining stock-footage and music—especially music—clearances can be very time-consuming and expensive. Make sure before you go through the steps that your producer really wants the quote and that you're not just jumping to the whim of the editor. If you cannot cut around or substitute and your producer gives the go-ahead, then proceed.

Audio Mix/Dub

This is one of the most time-consuming and important events in the entire post-production process. The producers, director, composer, music supervisor, editor, sound-effects supervisor, and sound mixer review the show scene-by-scene. Audio levels are adjusted for all of the sound elements.

The separate edited tracks are played and mixed, balanced, enhanced, and altered to create a composite sound, which is recorded onto a multitrack. These tracks become the master sound track or final mix, which is then laid back or dubbed onto the sound track of the videotape master and becomes the final film sound. Because the original timecode from the picture master has been carried through the process, the sound lays down perfectly in sync if you lay back to a videotape master. This entire process is called the mix or the dub.

If you are making an MOW, the producer(s), director, composer, music editor, editor, postproduction supervisor, sound-effects supervisor, and sound and change room technicians (if you're working on film) will be present. A change room technician is in the machine room and is responsible for changing the mag tracks or videotape master at every reel change or moving the tracks forwards and backwards at the sound-effects editor's request.

The producer(s), director, and composer have the creative control and will call upon all the others for advice and technical expertise. This is tantamount to a miniproduction in itself!

Be Prepared

As noted earlier, arrange in advance to have all the sound properly prepared and delivered to the dub stage prior to the start of the dub. If your sound designer is contracted separately from the facility that will do the final mix, be sure to arrange to have all the necessary materials and equipment arrive on time. In addition, there will need to be a visual reference—either film or videotape. The music supervisor and the sound editor will have made road maps of the individual pieces of the sound. These are called dubbing cue sheets. These sheets tell the mixers on which reel or track any particular effect or sound bite is located. Figure 8.5 shows three sample dubbing cue sheets.

Figure 8.5a Dubbing Cue Sheet for ADR

PROD: **Pie Throwers**   TITLE: Facial Care

REEL# 1	REEL# 1	REEL# 1	REEL# 1	REEL# 1	
TRACK 1	TRACK 2	TRACK 3	TRACK 4	TRACK 5	
10:39:06	10:26:06	10:26:07	10:26:07	10:26:07	
Perry F/S	Gregory F/S	BUZZ	Arthur F/S	Raymond F/S	
10:45	Plus Bobby				
10:57:24					
James					
F/S					
Fall @ 11:25					
12:59					
		12:34:00			
	GROUP	GROUP			
	L	R			
	13:32				

Figure 8.5b Dubbing Cue Sheet for Dialogue

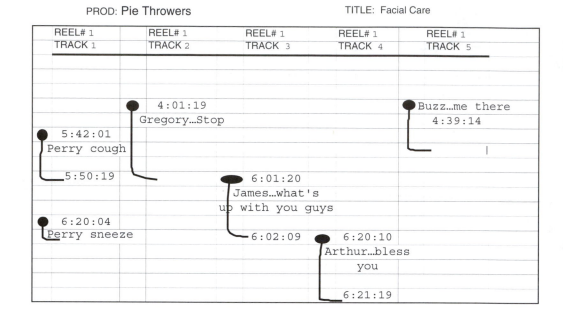

PROD: Pie Throwers   TITLE: Facial Care

Figure 8.5c Dubbing Cue Sheet for Effects (EFX)

PROD: Pie Throwers   TITLE: Facial Care

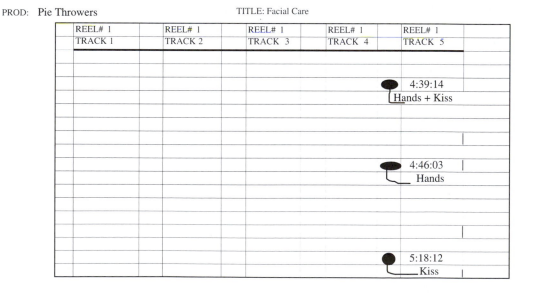

At the beginning of the first day of your dub, take inventory and make sure that all of your elements have arrived and that the crew has everything it needs.

How Long Should It Take?

The dub for an MOW will take up to 3 days and 3 mixers (1 each for music, dialogue, and effects/looping). Schedule an entire day for an episodic. The crew will probably be union and will require the specified breaks/meals.

The producer will give the mixers an overview of the movie and, if it is not painfully obvious, the overall feeling the production company is trying to achieve. Actually, they'll probably get this even if it is painfully obvious.

The show opening usually takes the longest to dub. This is where the feeling and balance of the show are set. Try to complete 20 to 30 minutes of program each day. This will help keep you on schedule.

You will be there, of course, because someone has to watch the "time is money" clock. Of course, it could be a very futile effort on your part. All the guests at this party will want the piece of cake with the flower on it.

If you see your session is going to go over the time allotted, go over and quietly notify the producer. At the appropriate time, someone will need to determine if it is more cost-effective to rack up some overtime (provided that is an option with the facility's schedule) or add another day to the dub. At this juncture, the facility may want a separate purchase order to cover the additional time. This cost is probably outside any package deal, and while many heads are nodding "yes" in the heat of passion, later they may have a hard time remembering what a good idea they thought this additional time was.

Sometimes when dubbing in Canada, and on some stages in the United States, one mixer mixes each sound source one at a time. This process takes longer—up to 5 days total (for an MOW).

Getting the Right Mix

After the picture and sound are up on the projector, or in their playback machines, the mixers will have their run-through of the opening of the show. This is where they determine the starting audio levels. The picture is run again, and it is the creative team's turn to interject their suggestions and comments. They decide the sound level and duration of each sound effect. Once this is completed, the mixers will "make it." This means they run through the scene again with the chosen levels set and record to the master audio format. Once an entire reel (or act break) has been done, the room is darkened and everyone watches that section of the picture from beginning to end with the final effects. There will be some small notes and changes. These are made, and then the process starts again until everyone is satisfied with the entire final mix.

Sibilance

Mixing your final sound track will be one of the most expensive line items in your entire postproduction budget. And, of course, the final mix comes at the end of the process—at a time when the money has usually run very low. Cutting corners and scrimping will be very tempting at this juncture. You might, for example, choose a sound facility solely based on a low bid and not on whether it is the proper sound house for your particular project. Should you yield to this temptation, it will almost certainly lead to bigger headaches down the road when your film prints are made. A poor mix and sloppy audio work don't allow enough leeway in optical printing tolerances. These are the gauges used to measure the density of your optical sound track. Laboratory tolerances vary depending upon the temperature and age of their chemical baths. All prints and tracks are expected to pass quality control (QC) inspection within several points of density. If your track is already on the edge of tolerance, and is not printed *exactly* to the proper density, you will hear a distortion called sibilance. This is a "shhh" sound that can be very problematic and maybe even unacceptable to distributors. If you suspect that your print has this problem, ask the film lab to inspect and QC a print. If they determine that it is sibilance caused by a poorly exposed track, the only recourse you have is to return to the sound facility and have them inspect their records for density and exposure. Remember that the film lab does not shoot optical tracks, they just process and print them. The sound facility will not want to reshoot a track at their expense because of a bad mix. If you find yourself here, you are in a bad way. So, don't be a knucklehead, take our advise (it's what you bought the book for, remember?), save yourself from trouble so close to the end of your project. Do it right the first time.

Final Sound Masters

Often in the film-finish process, the titles (credits) are being completed at the same time the final audio dub is taking place, and a sample print of the credits is available to view at some point during the dub. If possible, the executives will want to view their new sound against a print that has titles so they can verify that the end credit sound is mixed to time. In the video world, the dub is often scheduled after the show has been titled for the same reason.

So, the party—which you call your sound mix—is over. The executives have gone home. All that is left for you to do here is finalize the technical details of your sound masters. This will include what final audio formats you have made and how you arrange storage of your materials.

Some sound facilities store their clients' audio tracks onto hard drives. This might seem like a really good sort of futuristic idea. It's digital and has great storage potential. However, there are some possible drawbacks that you should be aware of (you knew this was coming, didn't you?). The good news is that you are relinquished of all archival responsibility. Hey, let someone else store this stuff. You're moving onto your next great gig.

What you need to consider (this could also be called the "bad news") is that each time you need to create a new audio element this sound facility is going to charge you access fees to use your own sound track. You will have to determine if this fee is still more cost effective than renting storage space at a vault. This fee is in addition to stock and recording costs for whatever new element you order. You are also married to the sound house for any future elements you may need to create on this project. Hey, you think to yourself, I'm done with this project . . . *Right*. Too often you're never done when you think you're done. They keep pulling you back. . . . Plus, you've married any future distributor to this sound facility, and its access fees, for any audio needs they may have. Not only will a distributor have to pay those additional fees to access your audio elements, but also they won't be able to use a sound facility of their choosing without it costing them just to get the materials. This could be especially problematic for an international distributor.

The Printmaster

Now your final master sound track has been made. From this a four-track master is struck with separate channels for dialogue, music, effects, and a mixed track. In the film world, this is called your print master element. This format can be a two, or more, track mag or magnetic tape; DA88; or 1/2" four-track. It is the source element that will be used to lay back to your videotape master.

Be sure to save the dubbing cue sheets. Some foreign delivery requirements ask for them.

Release Printing

When making film release prints, the sound format that will be printed onto the film needs to be determined in advance. There are several reasons for this. First, the sound facility needs to know what format to record the final mix to. They'll need to know what types of tracks will be printed onto your film (i.e., Dolby, Stereo, etc.). This will tell them what license fees you will need to pay for the right to use specific recording formats.

There are several popular digital sound formats to choose from. Each one consists of several channels of sound, which are matrix encoded. Matrix is a term used to describe an encoding device that can mix four sound channels into two stereo channels, which will then be restored to four channels upon playback. The four channels are LCRS or left, center, right, and mono surround.

The following sound formats are the most widely used. See Figure 4.4 for a visual reference of where on the film frame these formats are printed.

Dolby Surround: Many mix stages are set up to record and sell this format. It is licensed from Dolby Labs for a fee and Dolby will physically inspect your sound setup before granting the license. The sound is a four channel digital encoded format. The Dolby logo must appear in your end credits as part of the license agreement.

Dolby 5.1: This format consists of five discrete channels (left, center, right, left and right surround), and a low frequency effects channel (plays back on a subwoofer).

Dolby E or AES3: You may not be familiar with this new format, which is currently a limited distribution requirement. This new matrix trick from Dolby will take up to eight channels of high-quality audio and compress them into two tracks. This system was developed to convert TV and broadcast facilities to a multichannel audio system for broadcast in HD. The Dolby E is converted to Dolby Digital during the transmission process. One of its advantages is that unlike some other encoded audio tracks, it can be edited once it has been encoded without disrupting the encoding.

Ultra-Stereo: This is a four-channel surround format that must be licensed. A fee is charged for this license and the logo must appear in your end credits.

DTS: This surround format has six channels of audio. The encoded sound is on a CD-ROM. The final film print will have timecode information in the DTS track area that drives the CD-ROM player connected to a projector.

SDDS: This surround format is six channels of matrix sound. A license and license fee is also required along with the logo appearing in the end credits of your project.

Once you have reviewed your delivery requirements and decided what sound format to use it's almost time to have the sound facility shoot the optical sound track negative. We have cautioned you before, but it's worth mentioning again, do not shoot your optical sound track negative unless you have made a print before first trial or have mixed to a work print. These are the only elements that when played with your new sound master will insure that you will be in sync. When your comp print is made that said, "please note that the laboratory will process an optical track," note that they do not shoot tracks. See "Adding Sound" in "The Film Laboratory" chapter for more information on optical sound track negatives.

MO Disks

Not all foreign laboratories have the capability of making color corrected IPs or INs, and for this reason many foreign filmmakers find it necessary to make their final film elements here in the United States. They bring with them their original cut negative and a magneto-optical (MO) disk, containing the final audio mix in four or six digital channels.

The MO is a disk that holds 4.6 gigabytes of information, which is the equivalent of 400 floppy disks. The disk can be erased and re-used or archived for 30 years (that we know so far). From this disk a sound facility can shoot a digital optical sound track negative eliminating the need to lug heavy sound elements from country to country.

Laugh Tracks

Laugh tracks are either enhanced or created entirely in the mix.

There are a handful of "laugh people" in the world today. They operate a piece of equipment designed to create or enhance a laugh track for your show. If your show is going to have a laugh track, as it always will if you're doing a sitcom, be sure to schedule your laugh session as early as possible. These guys are busy, and they don't come cheap. They usually work on a 2- or 4-hour minimum. You can approach your laugh tracks in two ways. The way you chose depends on how your show is shot and how much time and money your producers want to budget for this step.

If you are creating a sitcom and it shoots in front of a live audience, you will already have a laugh track as part of your original production audio. That laugh track, usually labeled "audience," is recorded on your dailies masters during telecine or is recorded on your videotape dailies in a tape shoot.

From here you can elect to hire a laugh person to come in and bridge and enhance the existing laugh track. "Bridging" means that any laughs that are cut off in on-line are extended. Laughs can be filled in if you need more than the audience provided, or inserted if no laughter exists and you think it is needed.

Bridging and enhancing an existing laugh track for a half-hour sitcom should take about 2 hours, and it can be done either during the mix or after you've made a dialogue/effects pass in the mix and you've spotted the areas that need "laugh help."

Some sitcoms do not shoot in front of a live audience or choose for some reason not to use the live laughter instead having a laugh person completely replace the laugh track. Again, this can be done during the mix from the beginning, or you can make a dialogue/effects pass in your mix, spotting the laughs and then bring in a laugh person to create the laugh tracks. This method should take about 4 hours for a half-hour sitcom.

Layback

You will have a layback session if you are finishing on videotape and have a videotape element as your final delivery master.

Once you have a final sound element, you are ready to lay it back to your videotape master. This is called the "layback." It is simply the process of recording that final sound onto the audio tracks of your videotape master. If this is a domestic source tape, you will mix the tracks into combined stereo tracks (dialogue, music, and effects mixed into stereo left and stereo right) and lay them to two channels of your domestic master. Stereo left to channel 1 and stereo right to channel 2, traditionally. At this point, you can also lay down some split tracks if your master is on a videotape format with more than two audio channels. These split tracks can come in handy for meeting promotional delivery requirements. Be sure to check your delivery specifications.

If you are creating a composite print, at this point the sound facility will use the final sound master to create an optical track.

For programs that are finishing on videotape in both 16:9 and 4:3, it will be more cost-effective for you to schedule your final sweetened audio layback prior to creating the 4:3 master. This way you can avoid having to pay for two separate audio laybacks. Unfortunately, television postproduction schedules don't always allow enough time to choose the most cost-effective path, but it's still a nice thought.

Music and Effects Tracks (M&E)

Although there are separate music and effects tracks on your multitrack, you will still need to create what are called foreign-fill, or fully filled music, and effects tracks. This is normally done right after the domestic mix is completed. One exception to the rule is animation. With animated shows, the fully filled music and effects are sometimes created simultaneously with the domestic mix. Dialogue is all looped and there are no ambient affects—no on-camera action to get mixed into the dialogue track.

Fully filled tracks are used when the original dialogue track is replaced with a foreign-language dialogue track. The original dialogue track includes ambient sound, recorded with the dialogue and kept as part of the final mix. When the dialogue is removed these sound effects are lost and must be recreated. If this is not done, it will be obvious to the viewer that effects are missing. Foreign distributors always require masters with fully filled music and effects tracks.

Foreign Language Dubbing

Foreign language dubbing is the replacement of the language that the actors are speaking in a show with a language different than the one spoken in the original dialogue track.

The trick is to match the translations and timing of the way the actors recording the replacement dialogue are speaking with the mouths of the original actors as closely as possible. In addition to matching the mouth movements, it is also important to recreate the mood of the speech to carry the proper message about what is going on with the characters and the movie itself. If the actors' emotions are not also captured in the dubbing process, then the movie will not carry the same impact, and maybe not the same message, as the original dialogue track that was recorded on the set.

Foreign language dubbing may bring to mind visions of the old English- dubbed Japanese Godzilla movies. The English words were so poorly matched to the mouth movements of the Japanese actors that, sometimes, whole sentences were spoken and no one's lips moved.

The translation itself is also an important part of the process. Going back to the Godzilla movies, sometimes the phrasing was so outrageous that a serious exchange between actors became down right comedic.

Fortunately, foreign language dubbing has come a long way. Even the worst dubbing (with maybe the exception of the groans and heavy breathing in an adult film) is generally not too bad.

When you sell your movie, TV show, commercial, etc., to a foreign market, you may need to be involved in the foreign language dubbing process as part of the terms of the sale. In this case, you'll either be providing the elements necessary for a dubber in the foreign country to do the dubbing and possibly mix the new dialogue track with the M&E track. Or, you'll actually be responsible for getting the dubbing done.

In either scenario, you'll need to provide the dubber with a picture reference of the program. This is usually delivered on a work stock videotape format such as 3/4" or VHS. You'll have to provide a script and a maybe a sound element that contains the fully filled music and effects track.

The foreign dubber will use the script to do the foreign translation. Then the picture source will be used as a playback reference when the dialogue is rerecorded—matching the mouths of the actors as closely as possible.

The new foreign language dialogue track is then mixed with the foreign music and effects track making a new composite track to marry to picture.

Foreign Language Film Prints

For theatrical use, the foreign language dialogue/music/effects (DME) track will be used to shoot an optical sound track so composite theatrical release prints (picture with sound) can be struck. These will be shipped to foreign markets for viewing in a theatre. See "Adding Sound to Picture" in "The Film Laboratory" chapter for information on creating composite film prints.

Foreign Language Videotape Masters

Depending on your requirements and resources, you may: 1) have the foreign dubber actually mix the foreign language track with the M&E track and layback to videotape, creating a foreign language videotape master; or 2) you may have the dubber send the separate tracks to you and you have them mixed locally and do a layback; or 3) the dubber returns the mixed DME tracks and you do the layback only.

Dubbing in the United States

If you are considering dubbing your foreign track in the United States for a movie or TV show originally shot with union actors, check with the guild before you actually do the dubbing. You may have union residual issues to deal with. These could be costly, and create a sizeable impact to your postproduction budget.

Once you have decided to do your dubbing in the United States with a company that specializes in the language(s) you require, try to work with a company that is recommended by someone you know or trust. If that is not possible, then you may want to consider doing a test with one or more companies and having the tests viewed by either the potential client or some other representative the distributor chooses to ensure that the dubbed track will be acceptable to your client(s).

And, whether you are using a dubber that was recommended or just picking one at random, always get a credit list. You'll want to know 1) what specific programs this dubber has done, 2) get a feel for how often the dubber dubs in the language(s) you need and, 3) be sure the dubber you are hiring has experience dubbing movies in the genre of your movie. Dubbing a drama is much different than dubbing a comedy—whether you are referring to theatrical releases or network television series.

Also, dubbing is costly and you certainly don't want to get it all done only to discover that the work you've paid for is not useable. And, worse yet, that you have to pay to have the dubbing created again.

Dubbing is not new or "foreign" to our industry (no pun intended . . . okay, maybe a little pun). Don't make yourself crazy reinventing the wheel here. There are plenty of other things that will come along to legitimately make you crazy—you don't need to invent things. So, ask for help; seek out those who have done this before. Make the dubbing facility sell you on their abilities by showing you what they have done. Don't just listen to them telling you what they can do. If they're good, they should have plenty of material in the appropriate genre to show you.

Many movie studios require that foreign languages be dubbed in the country of that language (i.e., Latin Spanish dubbed in Mexico, French dubbed in France, etc.). This is certainly something to consider, especially if you find yourself in the position of having to create foreign language tracks and you haven't yet made a foreign sale so you can't know for sure who the licensee will be and what their requirements will entail.

Dubbing Materials

Dubbing for Theatrical and Video Use

To create foreign language tracks for a theatrical, TV, or home video release, videotape work materials are usually provided to the dubbers instead of film. This does not pose a problem for the dubbers, as all are equipped to play back videotape. You may be hard put to find too many dubbers that can still play back film. Additionally, film elements are very expensive to manufacturer and ship, so videotape is it.

What materials the dubber requires, will depend on how much of the work the dubber is going to be doing for you. Let's work from our three possible scenarios listed earlier in the chapter.

Scenario 1: The foreign dubber mixes the foreign language track with the M&E track. You will use this mix or "comp track" to create an optical sound track negative (OSTN), if you are making a foreign film print. (The dubber possibly lays this mixed track to videotape, thus, creating a foreign language videotape master also.)

In this instance, the dubber is going to be responsible for all of the work involved in creating the foreign language track and subsequent videotape master (assuming there is one). The dubber will not, in most cases, be creating the OSTN.

To accomplish this task, the dubber will need several items from you. You will provide:

- a dialogue script of the program;
- a picture reference of the entire show;
- an English track to use as a guide;
- a high quality sound element of the fully-filled music and effects track; and
- a copy of the show on a master tape format with at least two open channels to allow the stereo mix of the foreign language track to be laid down (if a final videotape master is to be created).

Scenario 2: You may have the dubber send the separate foreign language dialogue track to you so you can have it mixed locally with the M&E track (and do a layback, if you're also creating a videotape master).

In this instance, the dubber will require the same set of delivery materials, minus the M&E sound source and the videotape master.

The dubber will take the script and create the word translations to the appropriate language. Once that is completed, using the picture reference as playback the foreign language track will be recorded as a "dialogue-only" track. This can be recorded onto 35 mm magnetic tape, DA88, DAT, or even hard drive. At this point, the track is truly "dialogue only," no effects or music have been added. This dialogue track is then sent back to you. You take this track along with the fully filled M&E element and mix the two to create a fully mixed or "composite" track. Your foreign language track is now complete, and with the exception of a different language being spoken should match your original movie track almost perfectly.

Once mixed, this track can be used to generate an optical sound track to be married with a film print or laid back directly to an existing videotape element.

Tip: Here's a suggestion born from experience. Even if you do have the dubber mix the tracks as part of the service they provide for you, insist that you receive a clean dialogue-only track anyway. There are three very good reasons for this.

First, should you ever need to remix the composite track, you will already have all of the pieces together. It is often impossible years down the road to try and locate a foreign language track with a dubber in a foreign country.

Secondly, should there be problems with the mix done by the dubber, you have the option of simply redoing the mix yourself locally. This can be especially critical if you are on a very short turnaround . . . and, let's face it, when aren't you on a really short turnaround? I'm not sure I've ever received or made the call that starts with, "there is no rush on this so take your time."

And, third, having the separate dialogue track adds longevity to your track, future-proofing it against legal issues such as music clearances. Should you someday lose a music license in your project (and it happens more than you may think, especially with popular hit music recorded by the original artist), you can now very simply and inexpensively go into your M&E track, replace the offending music tracks, and remix your composite track. And, voila! You can continue to license your product. If you do not hold the separate dialogue tracks, you will have to cease selling this product until you can either find the separate dialogue track (which will take time, if nothing else) or redub the entire track again (an expensive solution to a problem you created yourself).

Scenario 3: The dubber returns the mixed DME tracks and you do the layback to the videotape master. The dubber will require all of the dubbing elements listed above, minus the videotape master.

Anti-Piracy Issues

Videotape provides a much more dependable way for studios and distributors to safeguard their movie against theft than some other formats. Videotape can be encoded with watermarks, which are barely perceptible visual blemishes encoded into the picture. Or, the picture can be marked up with several large text words, such as "Property of . . ." or large windows of timecode within the picture. When ordered, this is usually called "with burn in" or "spoiled." At least one movie studio places a text code visible window in the picture of all videotape copies of movies they send to dubbers. Each set carries its own unique code. Therefore, if a copy is pirated, the visible window of text will identify from which tapes the pirated copies were made.

It is nearly impossible to prevent piracy. However, it can be discouraged by marring the picture with large areas of numbers or text within the picture area.

Another option is to encode the tapes with an anti-piracy encoding that will prevent copies being made from those tapes. The anti-piracy encoding will prevent the signal of the master tape from being successfully duplicated onto another source. This is a costly procedure and not very practical for the odd tape that is sent out (such as dubbing materials). Therefore, most people just rely on the obstruction of large portions of the picture with visible information windows containing alpha or numeric characters.

Some tapes are sent out without any chroma in the picture when the dub is made, so the dubbers receive a black-and-white tape. It will certainly make piracy "less desirable."

As a reality check keep in mind that too much obstruction is going to make it difficult, if not impossible, in some scenes to see the actor's lips moving in order to sync the foreign dialogue properly. So, as you can see, you just have to use some common sense and strike a balance.

When Do You Dub?

The dubbing materials for a foreign language theatrical release often need to be provided to the dubber before the actual film-to-tape transfer is completed; or even started in many cases. This allows for the foreign language version(s) to be released about, or at the same time, as the domestic release.

Piracy in this instance is at its highest potential. Some precautions must be taken in this situation over all others to protect materials.

Foreign Laugh Pass

Not to disillusion anyone, but all the chuckles and belly laughs you hear nightly while watching your favorite situation comedy (sitcom) were probably not all generated by the live audience at the taping of the show. After the fact, someone went in and beefed up the audience laughs. This beefed-up audience reaction track, *laugh track*, was then mixed into the final sound track for domestic airing. We prefer the word "augment" to "embellish," but essentially, we're speaking of the same thing.

Just as with the domestic laugh tracks built or augmented for domestic release, for foreign release you will need to use a laugh company that will come in and generate appropriate laughs to fill your foreign track. As with other ambient effects (effects recorded while dialogue is being spoken so they are married), you have to replace the laughs and audience reactions that are lost when the original dialogue track is removed to create your foreign track. There are a limited number of laugh people and they are in great demand. So, plan ahead so you can schedule your laugh session when you need it.

Foreign effects are created to replace the ambient sounds that are married to the dialogue track and are lost when the dialogue is replaced by a foreign language track.

For sitcoms recorded in front of a live audience, the audience reactions will be recorded on the set as the show itself is being filmed. The audience is miked separately (left and right to be used later to create a stereo audience track). Because the audience is right there in front of the actors, there is no way to prevent their applause and laughter (hopefully, there is applause and laughter) from spilling over into the actors' microphones.

Now it is easy to understand that just as with any ambient effect recorded on the set as dialogue is being spoken, when the original dialogue track is removed, some of your laugh track will be removed along with it. The laughs will also be lost when the dialogue is replaced. Therefore, if your show has audience laughs, then you will need to include a "foreign laugh pass" as part of rebuilding your effects for foreign dubbing.

Okay, so you've come to grips with the fact that you are working on a sitcom being recorded in front of a live audience—and all of the special problems that situation brings to the table. And, you've accepted the fact that you will now need to add this little additional step, fondly referred to as the laugh track, into your post-production process. It seems like such a small thing, you think to yourself, but aha, there's more. There's always more.

You have to think ahead about how you are going to build your audio tracks with respect to this laugh track. Don't worry, we're now going to give you some options, reasons, and arguments, hopefully to make this all easy as pie for you. As with many steps discussed in this book, you do have choices when it comes to your laugh track and preparing for your foreign delivery (because that's really the meat of what we're talking about here).

First, there is your foreign fully filled music and effects track. Do you mix the laughs as part of this M&E track, or do you keep it separate?

As always, if you have delivery requirements, check them. If this is not speci-fied in your delivery requirements, call and ask the question. Ask your distributor specifically if they want the laugh tracks mixed in with the foreign M&Es, or kept separate. Should you have no distributor and, therefore, no delivery requirements or someone to ask here's our suggestion. Keep them separate.

The client which will use the foreign M&E track will be the client that is rerecording the dialogue into another language and completely remixing that new dialogue track with the M&E. It is no harder at that point to also mix in the laughs, should they want them. Because not all foreign clients want laughs in their broad-cast, this gives them the option without you having to redeliver, or worse, remix your M&E.

The next question is how do you deliver? What will your physical delivery element(s) be? If your delivery is for videotape that has four audio channels or less, and you *don't* mix the laughs into the M&E track, then you will have to deliver the laugh track on a separate element. The exception is a digital Betacam, which has a separate "cue" or fifth audio channel, it is, however, a mono track. But it may be preferable to your client to take delivery this way, rather than paying for a separate element. Should you need to deliver stereo comp tracks (mixed dialogue, music, effects) this takes two audio channels. Then if you need to deliver stereo M&E tracks this takes two audio channels. And you have to provide separate stereo laugh tracks, also requiring two audio channels, then you will need a secondary audio delivery element (such as a DAT or DA88) on which to deliver your six separate audio channels.

So, working on the assumption that you don't yet know how you will be required to deliver for foreign markets, we recommend you definitely maintain a separate mix. In other words, you may decide to create an audio element where the foreign effects and laughs are mixed together. We suggest that you also maintain an audio element that keeps the foreign effects track separate from the foreign laugh track.

A simple solution could be a DA88, which holds eight separate (also called discreet) audio channels, with the following configuration:

CH 1: Dialogue stereo left
CH 2: Dialogue stereo right
CH 3: Music stereo left
CH 4: Music stereo right
CH 5: Fully filled effects stereo left (w/o laughs)
CH 6: Fully filled effects stereo right (w/o laughs)
CH 7: Fully filled laughs stereo left
CH 8: Fully filled laughs stereo right

The above scenario preserves all of your tracks separately, allowing you to deliver any configuration any client may request.

For your own convenience, you may want to create a back-up element that will serve as your primary delivery playback source and not require mixing every time you use it to make a copy for someone. This would be a DA88 that is laid out as shown here:

CH 1: Comp stereo left
CH 2: Comp stereo right
CH 3: Fully filled M&E stereo left (w/o laughs)
CH 4: Fully filled M&E stereo right (w/o laughs)
CH 5: Fully filled laughs stereo left
CH 6: Fully filled laughs stereo right

And finally, on your digital Betacam videotape master, because you do have this extra audio channel (the cue track), go ahead and put down your laugh track here as a mono track. That way, whenever you make a copy from this master, the laughs will be included and delivered to the client. In many cases, this is perfectly acceptable to even the most demanding distributors overseas.

In summary, and at the risk of beating this dead horse, consider whenever you pay extra to create something, to always keep a clean, pristine copy of that thing you created . . . just in case.

Sound Advice

These eighteen areas of postproduction sound will make the difference between a really impressive show and one that's just there. Pay close attention to the details of your mix. Putting music and effects out of context and where people are not expecting to hear them will give your show a jarring, uneasy feeling. If that is your intent and it is appropriate to your piece, then great. If this is not the effect you want to have on your audience, then make sure you're giving them what they expect and what makes sense.

Sound postproduction sometimes gets the short end of the stick because the most expensive areas (such as the mix) happened very close to the completion of your project and money is usually very tight at this stage in the postproduction process. Resist the temptation to cut corners. Sound is very important to the telling of your story and ensuring your audiences have the right reactions at the appropriate times.

As we've said in every chapter in this book so far, use your postproduction house contacts. They are experts. They do this every day. And, check and double-check what you are asking for and what you are getting.

9 Completion

Once you have all of the individual components of your project completed, the elements required by the delivery instructions will determine how you will finish your project. You can deliver your show as either a film finish only (not used in television), a tape finish only, or both film and videotape. Delivering your show finished on both film and videotape does not mean that each version will necessarily be completed at the same time.

The following completion components will be discussed in this chapter:

- Film finish
- Videotape finish
- Color correction
- Color correction for digital cinema delivery
- Dirt fixes
- Video in, film out
- Formatting
- Credits and titling
- Varispeed
- Closed-captioning
- V-chip
- Video descriptions
- As-broadcast scripts
- Quality control
- Standards conversion
- Negative cut/negative conform
- Wrap-up

Film Finish

A film-finish means that all of your work towards delivery will be done on film. This does not preclude making a videotape master from your film elements, but that video-tape master will only be struck once the film and sound elements are completed. A completely finished film element must be created to satisfy your delivery requirements.

The negative is cut once the show has been locked and opticals are complete, regardless of whether or not dailies are transferred to videotape for an electronic off-line edit. What happens next is up to the client's preference and the delivery requirements.

Film Opticals vs. A/B Cutting

Prior to cutting your negative and preparing for your film finish you will have to make yet another important decision. This one covers how to complete your film opticals. Fades and dissolves, which are two types of film opticals, can be created in a couple of different ways, either as a *single strand* or *A/B rolls*.

Single Strand Opticals

Single strand opticals are created in one of two ways. The traditional method is to create an interpositive of the section where the optical is to occur and shoot the dissolve or fade with an optical camera. The result is a new negative section that includes the fade or dissolve. In the second method, the original negative background is scanned into a computer. The optical is then built, manipulated, layered, and output to a new piece of negative. Whether the new optical negative is shot optically or output from a computer, a check print is made to insure the quality of the new negative section. Once approved these new opticals are cut into your original negative in a "single strand." This method represents an industry standard and results in excellent quality opticals. Time can be a factor though as each stage takes at least a day or more depending upon the complexity of the optical.

A/B Opticals

The A/B method for making fades and dissolves requires the creation of a checkerboard of negative and leader on alternate rolls. The A roll begins with action followed by black opaque leader where the optical will be. The B roll begins with black opaque leader. At the footage where the first optical occurs, the action negative of the next scene that fades or dissolves in is cut into the B roll. This continues throughout each roll, thus creating a checkerboard of action and leader between the two rolls. No separate opticals are shot then cut into your negative; your original negative is simply cut this way. The dissolves are created when the rolls are run together for printing.

Choosing the Right Method

On the surface, the A/B method can seem to be less costly. However, you have to do your homework to do a complete assessment of the pros and cons of each method. The single strand method is a slower process whether you choose to shoot the optical or render the effect on a computer. Depending on the complexity of the optical, rendering could take several hours to several days. There are also very slight visual differences between the two methods. Your director of photography will probably have an opinion on which one is best suited to your particular project.

With the A/B method, both the negative cutter and the laboratory will charge an additional fee for a "B" roll.

Theatrical Film-Finish

To make a theatrical print, the original negative is cut and an original optical track is struck. Once your original negative has been cut, the negative is copied. This copy is called an interpositive (IP). An interpositive is an intermediate positive picture element made on special film stock. From the IP another negative, called an internegative (IN) can be struck. (Once the initial IN has been struck, a check print is made to check the overall color.) Usually several internegatives are made and the release prints are struck from these, thus eliminating the need to go back and reuse the original negative again and again for printing. This preserves the original negative's condition. An easy way to remember this process is that film goes negative to positive to negative to positive.

Should your original cut negative become damaged, new sections of IN can be created from the IP and spliced into the original cut negative. The replacement section will be two generations away from your original element.

Color Correcting Film

Creation of a color-corrected print is done at the film lab. The movie is color-corrected prior to striking release prints and can also be color-corrected for use as a telecine picture source.

When approving the color-correction, you will view a first trial or proof print. This is a slide show of one to three frames of each scene from the show. Often, the director or cinematographer attends. You may have adjustments, and two or more trial prints may need to be made before you are happy with the color correction and strike your final answer print or interpositive (IP). Be sure to order either final element with the wetgate process.

In the wetgate process, the print passes through a solution that works to mask minus-density marks and spots—normally referred to as dirt or minor scratches on the negative. These density spots show up white on the screen when light shines through them. Due to the softer emulsions of the negative stocks, embedded dirt and handling marks are not uncommon in cut negative. If successful, this wetgate process will make it appear that these imperfections have disappeared.

After you have approved the color-correction of your negative, a final first trial/answer print or an interpositive (IP) is struck. All of these can be used as the playback source for the film transfer to videotape. If the first trial is made on low-contrast stock, it is usually referred to as a locon print. Again, be sure to order these elements with the wetgate process.

Sometimes a print is created MOS (without sound), depending on its intended use. The process for creating a composite print (picture and sound on the same piece of film) is described below.

Creating Formatted Dupes

If you look at a piece of unexposed film, you will see a plain blank strip of film stock with sprocket holes (perfs) running along either side. There aren't any frame lines or blackened areas for the sound track. The entire piece of film is available for exposure from edge to edge and top to bottom. When you shoot, each film frame gets exposed according to how you are framing your shots. This is a creative choice made by the director, producer, and cinematographer. They might choose to expose only the 4:3 (a square) within the frame if you are shooting a television program; a 1:85 aspect ratio (called Academy framing); or choose to expose the entire film frame (super 35 mm) for a widescreen release. Within your choices there are standards preset by the industry for camera lenses, aperture gates, and projectors. This provides a consistency amongst shoots that ensures the aspect ratio you choose can be processed by any lab, transferred by any telecine, and/or projected on any movie projector in any screening room or movie theatre. See the Aspect Ratio chart in "The Film Laboratory" chapter.

If your project is shot utilizing any of the full frame or anamorphic exposures, you will need to create a new negative of your entire feature. Here your image is squeezed and moved slightly to the right, allowing for a sound track to be added for theatrical distribution. This new negative is called a *formatted dupe* or fully formatted internegative.

The Process

The process begins as normal. You will turn your cut negative into the laboratory and proceed through color correction just as you would with a film shot with an Academy aperture. Once the color corrections have been finalized, a full frame answer print is struck and screened for color correction approval. (This is important because the color corrections used to make this print are the same values used to create the interpositive.) This full frame answer print is run against the final sound mix, checking for sync and proper line up of the track prior to shooting the optical sound track negative. On rare occasions a composite (picture and sound) print will be struck from the full frame original negative and sound track.

At this point, you haven't created your formatted dupe yet, so in this print the track will cover the left side of the picture. That portion of the picture will be blocked. For viewing purposes, an academy gate can be placed on the projector blocking out the track area and giving the illusion of a finished print. With the academy gate, this print is useable as a pre-sales tool, for audience screenings, or for use in subtitling.

Once the full frame answer print is approved, an interpositive print is struck. After being inspected it goes in for timing. New timing lights are created in the lab to be used for making the final formatted dupe. The IP is then sent back to the printing department where a printer is fitted with a special lens that squeezes the image and moves it over a precise amount leaving room for a sound track. Then using the new timing lights the formatted dupe is created, with a small amount of picture area lost in the formatting.

Very Important: The lab will not know how much to squeeze and move the picture area unless you have provided them with a framing chart. The framing chart will consists of a few frames of film, which the DP will shoot during production. The image will be a hand drawn square, often made in production by the camera department, marking where the DP lined up the center or top of the frame. This measurement is called common top or common center, depending upon which area was used for framing. Many labs will not make a formatted dupe without a framing chart.

Once the formatted dupe has been shot and inspected, a composite print is struck. This print is called a *composite check print from the dupe* or merely a *check print*. This is usually the first time your movie will be projected as a composite print (both picture and track on the same film). The color timer, the DP, producer or director, and possibly the post supervisor screen this print. The objective is to make a dupe that will not need additional color timing. The subsequent release prints will always be within a few points (color) of printing tolerances. With the new dupe(s) you will be able to flood the theatres with your epic motion picture.

Adding Sound

Once you have finished mixing your master audio tracks, you will need to create an optical sound track negative (OSTN). This will be the element used to marry your sound to your picture.

An OSTN sounds like it would be made in a film laboratory—and it's probably the word negative that throws you. But film laboratories do not shoot optical tracks, they develop them. (See "Adding Sound" in "The Film Laboratory" chapter.) Sound facilities shoot optical tracks. They start with your master audio track (sometimes called a Printmaster, which is probably making a little more sense now), DA88, DAT, or other final sound source. And, using a special optical printer they "shoot" your OSTN. The sound track is shot onto black-and-white film stock then sent to the lab for processing.

Once processed it is returned to the sound house for quality control (QC) prior to delivery to the client. Upon passing QC, the track will go to either the negative cutter or film laboratory for syncing and then to the film lab to be printed with the original cut negative.

From your optical sound track negative an exposure of the sound track is made onto your print. This is done by printing the film negative (IN) on a continuous contact printer (CCP). This printer has two heads, allowing separate picture and sound areas of the film to be exposed. As the IN and OSTN travel over these heads, the first head exposes the picture element. The second head exposes the sound area. The exposed print stock is then put through a print processor to develop the picture. The next step is to apply a second developing solution (application) to the sound track area of the print stock. This redevelops the sound track area only, creating a higher-contrast image. When your print is projected, the light beam of an optical sound reader scans this higher-contrast image and your sound is reproduced. The light source is called the exciter lamp. The light passing through the optical track is translated into an electrical current. This electrical current is an analog reproduction of the sound track and can be amplified by the playback equipment. Because it is read by light, this type of sound track is called an optical track.

Application Splash

The part of the processing machine used to reapply the developer for the above sound track is called an "applicator." This is essentially a little wheel or sprayer that applies the developer onto the sound track area of the film. When this sprayer becomes clogged or dirty, it can spray droplets of developer onto the picture area. When this happens it has an adverse affect on the silver in the picture and the film is irreparably damaged. A new print will have to be made. This damage is detectable both visually and audibly.

Alternative Sound Application Methods

There remains an ongoing effort within the motion picture industry to improve quality and lower costs in every phase of filmmaking. In tandem there is an equal effort to become a "greener" or more environmentally friendly industry by reducing the toxicity of the chemicals used and reducing the level of water use. Film itself is not a biodegradable substance. And the developing and printing processes require the use of strong chemicals, which produce hazardous waste.

One area of interest for reducing environmental waste, excessive use of water, and increasing safety is the method used to apply sound tracks to film prints. New methods being tried should also provide additional advantages, which include a simplification of the developing process, increased stereo separation, and longer life for the illuminating track readers at the projection level.

Sighting these and other possible advantages the industry has begun to create both High Magenta and Cyan tracks. Sound tracks will continue to remain in the same physical location on the film, but will be applied and read differently. The new sound tracks will not need the addition of application to the film.

Cyan and High Magenta Sound Tracks

Cyan tracks will be exposed directly on to the cyan layer of the color print. High Magenta tracks use both a silver redevelopment of the application track plus filters which print the track on the magenta layer of the film. This allows the High Magenta track to be read with both white light and red LED readers.

The down side to these new technologies is in theatre projection. Sound is reproduced from the current silver-based sound tracks by reading the modulation of the track's application. This is achieved by shinning tungsten light (white light reader) through the track area. The new tracks require the use of a high intensity LED, "red light" reader. Theatres built within the last 6 years will have installed projectors with both tungsten and LED readers. Older theatres have been encouraged to convert to the new red light readers, however, less than 85% of these theatres have made this modification. Until this number hits 100% laboratories will continue to print silver tracks. If a High Magenta track is required in your delivery requirements you must advise your sound facility and laboratory of your intentions. The High Magenta tracks require a higher density on the optical sound track negative and must be made specifically to manufacture this type of print, it is not interchangeable with silver redeveloped tracks.

Film-Finish for Telecine Transfer

Some delivery scenarios require that you create a completed film element for your telecine transfer to videotape. For this film-finish, the negative is cut once the show has been locked and opticals are complete. This applies whether or not dailies were transferred to videotape for an electronic off-line edit.

You will provide to the transfer house a completed cut negative, an IP, or a locon print. International, home video, and PAY-TV often prefer to transfer from the cut negative or an IP. Television shows, such as MOWs or episodics, often prefer a locon as their film source. This is not a rule, just a tendency. Low-contrast stock already compensates for some of the picture's contrast (ranges between lights and darks) and is designed specifically for use in telecine transfers.

To create a print for your transfer, a first trial/answer print or an interpositive (IP), is struck after you have approved the color-correction of your negative. Be sure to order these elements with the wetgate process.

Some clients prefer to do their film to tape mastering directly from the cut negative. The transfer will have a different look than a transfer made from a print and the transfer will take longer than if a locon print is used.

Reasons to Create a Print

Consider the risk each time you use your original cut negative. While the equipment you run your film on in telecine is extremely gentle to your negative, human error or mechanical troubles could result in a tear or scratch to your negative, Once your negative has been damaged, that section of original negative is rendered useless. Often a wetgate print or other restoration method can be used to create a usable piece of film to replace the damaged area, but there is no way to repair your negative. Should damage occur and require you to replace the segment with another piece of negative, make sure your negative cutter has compensated for any frames that may have been lost.

Negatives may appear to attract more hairs and dirt, but in reality the reversed-image polarity of negatives makes these imperfections appear white instead of black, causing them to be more noticeable. Negatives needs to be sonic cleaned before it is laid down to videotape.

Another argument for transferring from a print involves problem splices. The telecine is an "edge-guided" device. Therefore, when transferring from cut negative, there could be a problem with splices if they have any roughness at the edges, the splices in the negative are too thick, or the edges of the film at the splice are misaligned. Any of these anomalies can cause the film to "bump" at each splice. This bump manifests as a shift in the picture image. A print should minimize this problem because it will not usually contain physical splices. Finally, based on your delivery requirements, you may have to deliver a locon print or a composite screening print (a print with a sound track attached). Different film stocks are used to make each of these types of prints.

Adding Sound to Film

From the optical sound track negative an exposure of the sound track is made onto your print. This sound track is called an optical track. For a complete description of the optical sound printing process, see "Adding Sound" under "Theatrical Film Finish," in this chapter. The optical track is subject to imperfections that cause distortion. Scratches, digs, and dirt can cause hiss and sound scratches, just as scratches and dirt on film cause imperfections to show up in the picture.

On nontheatrical prints, an optical track will hold only one or two tracks of audio. Therefore, the sound will be either one or two separate mono tracks or stereo-left and stereo-right tracks and will not have the flexibility for split tracks that is available with the multitrack formats, such as magnetic tape. A release print can hold more tracks of audio, as they are placed differently on the film.

An optical track can also be delivered as a separate element. This is rarely seen, except occasionally in the case of a 16 mm print. You may also see a separate optical track if the film is in the super 35 mm or super 16 mm format.

Super 8 mm film can also come with an optical track. If you find a postproduction house that can transfer super 8 mm film and your film also has an optical track, make sure the house has a super 8 mm optical head. While it is difficult to find a postproduction facility that can transfer super 8 mm film, finding one with a super 8 mm optical reader is rarer still.

Film Mags

Film sound delivered on a separate 35 mm magnetic (or mag) track will contain up to six separate audio tracks. This element could also be some other audio element such as a DAT or DA88. This allows you to deliver your sound mag with separate dialogue, music, and effects tracks, either mono or stereo. Depending on your track design, you may also have room for supplemental tracks, such as voice-overs.

For delivery requirements that call for film elements, a locon or IP and matching four-track print master (mag) are usually what you will need to provide. The four-track print master will be channel 1, stereo left; channel 2: stereo right; channel 3: stereo music and effects (M&E) left; and channel 4: stereo music and effects (M&E) right. These elements will also make very good sources for your videotape transfer should you be going from film to tape to create your final delivery master.

You will not have a composite super 35 mm or super 16 mm print if you shot super 35 mm or super 16 mm. These formats utilize the entire surface of the negative frame, placing picture in the space on the film where the sound track would be placed.

Again, these are all good guidelines and useful information. But, be sure to check your individual delivery requirements to determine which method of delivery you will need to follow.

Videotape Finish

If videotape is to be your only delivery format, and you will *not* be cutting negative prior to delivery, you have chosen what is normally referred to as a tape finish.

The Tape-Finish Process

To begin, your dailies are transferred to a master videotape format. This videotape in essence becomes your "negative." The actual film negative is put in storage to be cut sometime down the road or never to be utilized again. Any predelivery work on the show after dailies are completed will use the dailies master videotapes as the source.

In the not-so-distant past, 1″ and Betacam SP were the master videotape formats of choice. Then, as digital formats became more commonplace in postproduction houses and the networks started updating their delivery requirements to include digital videotape, D2 and D3, these formats became much more standard.

In the analog days, each time the picture was copied to another videotape there was a loss in signal quality that ultimately resulted in a delivery master with obviously diminished picture resolution. Some argue that there is still some loss of resolution when doing all your work on D2, but it is still a higher-quality tape format to Betacam SP or 1″.

One drawback to 1″ videotape is that it has only two audio channels. Betacam SP has four channels. Channels 1 and 2 are regular audio channels and can be recorded on simultaneously, with the picture recording or as a separate layback. Channels 3 and 4, also known as AFM channels, are located in the picture area and must be recorded to at the same time as the picture is recorded. Lay back to these channels will erase your picture. Conversely, recording picture will erase any existing audio on channels 3 and 4.

Recently, digital Betacam has emerged as the videotape of choice for most standard definition network shows and high-end MOWs, although D2 and D3, and sometimes Betacam SP, are still accepted. The reason for the increasing popularity in digital Betacam is that it is a component format (like D1), but the stock is less expensive. Digital Betacam is also a more resilient tape stock; it is less prone to artifacts, digital hits, and stock damage from stretching and stopping and starting than the 1″, Betacam SP, and D2 formats. Most postproduction houses can work from dailies through on-line and color correction with digital Betacam, keeping a fully digital path. This allows clients to put the videotape through limitless changes without picture or audio generation losses. The delivery master, be it D1, D2, D3, or digital Betacam, will have essentially the same signal-to-noise ratio as the original dailies transfer masters. For high definition delivery, the networks are taking HDCam.

Color Correction

Color correction is the process by which the current colors in a show (film or videotape) are adjusted, enhanced, or changed completely to bring the piece to the look you, the client, are striving to achieve. The colorist (known as a "timer" in the film world) makes the adjustments according to the specifications you have given regarding how you want your show to look on a scene-by-scene basis.

To create a color-corrected print you will view a first trial or proof print. This is a slide show of one to three frames of each scene from the show. Often, the director or cinematographer attends. You may have adjustments, and two or more trial prints may need to be made before you strike your final answer print or interpositive (IP). (For more details see "Film Finish" in this chapter.)

A color-corrected videotape is created either by running film on a telecine, using an electronic color-correction system to assign corrections on an edit-by-edit basis, or by using a noncolor-corrected videotape as your source and programming corrections where needed.

Why Color Correction Is Necessary

There is often confusion regarding the need for color correction. It is a necessary step in any project that originates on film—whether you are completing on film or videotape. A film-based project not subjected to color correction will be unacceptable to any distributor.

While film can give remarkable reproduction of the image it has photographed, it is not always a consistent medium. Color balance variations can occur between different types of film stock and even within different batches of the same film stock. Other variables such as exposure, temperature, age, and lighting all work to affect color balance. Television viewing, much more than theatre viewing, makes these inconsistencies readily apparent. Therefore, to maintain a smooth visual finish exposure and color-correction adjustments are necessary for a project shot on film and destined to be viewed on television.

Videotape more consistently reproduces from shot-to-shot and camera-to-camera. Therefore, shows shot on videotape do not usually require any scene-to-scene color correction. The exception would be if color or white balance of the cameras in a tape shoot was not set properly, and the picture was off drastically from the other cameras when the shots were cut together. Color correction can also be used to achieve color effects scheduled to be done in postproduction, rather than on the set.

The merits of one brand of color-correction system over the other should not be discussed without beer. Da Vinci seems to have become the color-correction system of choice.

Color Correcting Dailies

Color correcting during the actual dailies telecine transfer is realistic only in productions with very few setups. The best candidate for color correcting during dailies transfer is a sitcom with a limited number of changes in sets, lighting, and exposures. In any other situation, color correction needs to be done when the film has been cut or picture has been on-lined and the element can then be color-corrected scene-to-scene.

At the beginning of the transfer session, the telecine colorist sets the color of each location setup (often with the supervision of the director of photography), saves these color-corrected shots in a still store, and matches back to these stored images each time that setup is photographed. This ensures an even look across all takes of a particular scene. This type of dailies color correction will add considerably to the time it takes to transfer your dailies. How much additional time will depend on the amount of film and the number of set changes, takes, and lighting changes made while shooting.

The Color-Blind Producer

Once during a very busy period, one of us was unable to supervise the color-correction session for an MOW she was working on. One of the show's executive producers offered to go in her stead. It must have seemed unimportant to him at the time that he didn't know exactly what a color-correction session was, because he neglected to inquire. Off he went to his session.

After the session, someone at the office asked this executive producer how the session had gone. He said he was surprised at how difficult it had been to match all the gray values. Turns out the guy is color-blind. Yikes! Makes you wonder what the colorist must have thought. Anyway, the facility's colorist was very good, the show aired, and it looked all right.

Color Correcting Film to Tape

For shows that cut negative and finish on tape, color correction is done in the final film to tape process. The film is played and the telecine colorist sets color for each cut. This color-correction information is then saved in a computer as data. This applies whether or not the telecine transfer is done from the cut negative or a print made from that cut negative.

Laying Down Your Color-Corrected Image from Film

When the colorist has gone through each film roll and timed the entire show, the film reels are put back up on the telecine and transferred to videotape. This is done in reel order, starting with reel 1. The color corrections are recalled as the film runs through the system and the film is laid to videotape. The image recorded on the video-tape is color-corrected. The film itself is not physically altered.

Some colorists and clients choose to lay down each reel after is it color-corrected instead of waiting until all of the reels have been corrected. There is little advantage to one method over the other, so the decision is usually based on either client or colorist preference. Laying down each reel, as it is color-corrected could cause delays, as each roll may need to be cleaned after it has run through the telecine. This is especially true if you are transferring from cut negative. Negative dirt appears white on the screen, and positive dirt shows up as black. The negative dirt is often more noticeable, giving the appearance that the film is "dirtier." Negative dirt cannot be cleaned from a film print. If the dirt is excessive, it can be justifiable cause for ordering a reprint of the affected reel(s).

Transfer Standards

There are several decisions you'll need to make regarding the transfer of your film and the standard in which you lay your images to videotape. These are decisions you'll need to make even before you pick a facility or book a transfer session. Up until a few years ago, most films were transferred standard definition, NTSC, and/or PAL. Usually, if you needed a master in both standards, you did one laydown to NTSC and then converted the telecine bay to PAL to transfer the other version. You then quality controlled and dirt fixed each master individually.

Then people started transferring to PAL only. The PAL master was dirt fixed and once approved the NTSC was created as a standards conversion (tape-to-tape). This was possible because of the great technological advances made in conversion systems. Because the NTSC is a "down conversion" (625 lines to 525 lines) and the frame-based transfer methods were so good, the resulting NTSC was nearly as good as it would have been if transferred directly from film. Costs were lowered because only one master had to be dirt fixed.

And if that wasn't the end all, along came 16:9. Now we were looking at a second laydown from film to make a 16:9 full frame and a third laydown to make the 16:9 letterbox (fourth if you were already laying down the 4:3 twice for full frame and letterbox). This also meant another set of masters to QC and dirt fix. But we then got pretty good aspect ratio converters, so we changed how we did things one more time.

Now, for a 1:85 movie, we were making two transfers; one laydown for the 4:3 and one for the 16:9, both full frame and in PAL. These were quality controlled and dirt fixed. Once approved, we introduced a hard matte into the 16:9 full frame, put that out to a new piece of stock and generated a 16:9 letterbox. Then, we took that 16:9 letterbox and ran it through an aspect ratio converter and made our 4:3 letterbox. Voila! As a final step, all the versions were then converted to NTSC— already dirt fixed and ready to go.

Of course, there is an exception, there's always an exception. All this matting and converting doesn't work for a scope picture. In the widescreen scenario, you have to transfer from film the 16:9 letterbox version also. But then you're free to make the 4:3 letterbox from that. So it actually adds only one more laydown. But, it is also one more QC and dirt fix . . . ah well.

So we went along this way for a few years but then high definition started to become viable (it had been around for quite a few years in Japan before it really took hold here and in Europe). So, here we go again, changing the rules on everyone. The most popular HD transfer method until just recently had been 1080i. Of course, there are a variety of frame rates to choose from, but we won't bore (scare) you with all those details. There are a lot of 1080i feature product out there and we can't imagine any studio running right out to remaster all of the movies and TV series that they've spent the last few years redoing at some very significant costs.

But here we are, we've changed the rules again and, surprise, we're not done! Now we are mastering everything HD in 1080/24p. This is the standard, or so everyone says. It gives us the highest resolution available today on videotape—1080 lines of active video (1125 lines total picture information)—in the 24 fps (just like film) progressive mode.

The next new thing in high definition telecine transfers will incorporate this 1080/24p but allow us to master just one time and to just one version. It won't matter if our aspect ratio is scope or 1:85 academy. The version will go to tape or as data to a hard drive and can be quality controlled, dirt fixed, and manipulated in any way it needs to be. When it is exactly as we want it, all other versions will be struck from it without ever having to hang the film again. These systems are in limited availability and R&D is still being done. But there are a few out there and they are being used.

Color Correction for Digital Cinema Delivery

Digital cinema (D-Cinema), electronic cinema (E-Cinema), and digital projection all describe the projection of digital images via a digital projector onto a reflective (theatrical) screen. At this moment as we sit here and write this book, technical specifications for doing film to tape transfer for D-Cinema do not exist—officially. However, they will be forthcoming very shortly. As the postproduction supervisor, the most important thing for you to know is that currently you have to do a separate color correction in order to create an appropriate master for digital cinema projection.

The D-Cinema Color Correction Bay

Transfers are done in a digital projection screening room that is outfitted with a color corrector, a playback system, and a record system. There may also be a monitor with which to view the supervised original film transfer for the purpose of color matching. If you are mastering from film, there will be a controller to operate a telecine machine. The sound will come from either mag or tape (such as DA88) and can usually be dragged with the film in laydown. The sound of a new feature will be laid down as 5.1. If you are mastering from data, there will be a disk array which will hold the data files for playback.

You will have the option (depending on your needs and the facility doing the work) to laydown your color-corrected image to a disk array storage system, if you are recording to data, or laydown will be recorded to a D5 or D6 videotape machine. D6 machines are not seen much anymore due to some technical problems they have been exhibiting. HDCam is not used for this purpose due to the higher compression rate at a 7.5 : 1 ratio; D5 compression ratio is 4 : 1. Your movie will be transferred at 24p or in NDFTC. DFTC causes some problems for the projectors available today. With projector improvement, this may not be an issue for long.

From film, the telecine scans your images at 6 fps in 2K. The next generation of HD telecine should scan in real time. The D5 has 8 audio channels so is perfect for recording 5.1 audio (which requires 6 discreet channels).

Preparing for the D-Cinema Transfer

Start by meeting with the facility that will be doing the transfer. Once you have cut your negative and created an answer print or created a digital master you will need to transfer to data or a digital master for projection.

If you finished your project on film, you will make an interpositive for the transfer. If you did a videotape finish, your highest quality videotape master will be used to scan at 2K resolution. The scanning will take 4 to 12 hours depending upon the process used. Some scanners only read four to five frames a second while others might scan nearer to the real running time of the project. The picture information is then saved and held on a server during the color-correction process. A digital projector is used to project the scanned image onto a special reflective screen (it appears grayer for greater color enhancement and brightness) and scene by scene color correction begins. If the project has built in image problems like lens flares or reflections they can be corrected during this process as well. If there is a particularly difficult problem that needs digital repair, a digital artist can access the frames needed from the server, make the repair, and send it back to the server, without interfering with the color-correction process. Once complete and back on-line the colorist can color correct the fix as well.

Feature projects will take at least 3 days to master depending upon who is supervising the color correction and how time-consuming the project is. When the color is finalized the project is again saved to a data file and viewed for quality control.

When the final fixes and color are approved, the project is saved to D5, DVD, DLT, DST, etc. depending upon the available formats at the transfer facility and the delivery requirements. This is then delivered to the digital projection company who encrypts the master with anti-piracy protection. The new master will then be loaded into a digital projector and tested before it is sent to the theatre for screening. Additional copies are created, as needed, encrypted, and shipped to theatres for release.

The mastered feature will be stored similar to videotape but as data in all of it's various forms, raw data, color-corrected, digital repairs, and final masters. It is important to keep records of where these assets are located, so that they can be recalled to make additional materials when needed and you don't have to call all over town looking for your elements.

The transfer process for D-Cinema is very similar to video mastering; however, the technical aspects vary from projection system to projection system. So get your digital projection distributor involved and make sure you have all the elements needed prior to starting this process. Once finished keep detailed notes as to where any masters or digital projection copies may be stored.

As of this writing, the digital projection industry is still shaking out which projector models will become industry standards. And, the projectors themselves are getting better very fast. There are not any published technical specifications to use when mastering for digital projection—although there will be shortly. For the most part, you'll have to rely on the expertise of the facility where your work is being done to help guide you to a successful delivery.

Planning Ahead

It is important when arranging a film to tape color correction to know if any other versions of your project will need to be created that will require separate laydown from film to tape (at least until this *one master* system is in full swing). These can include a PAL version for foreign delivery, letterbox or pan and scan versions, or 16:9. Any of these other versions will require a separate pass of your film on the telecine.

Telecine Drift

Drift refers to small changes that occur in telecine settings and tube burn patterns that happen slowly. Over time, telecine drift can affect reproduction of your original color-correction settings. On the telecine, your film travels over a photo multiplier (light source or tube). The intensity of light coming from this tube determines what color-correction settings the colorist programs to get the desired look for the picture.

As the telecine tube burns, the intensity and consistency of the light being emitted changes. If you program color corrections for a show and then come back a few days later with the same source material, you can recall those color corrections and relay the show and it will look exactly the same. Therefore, if you put your film back on the telecine after the tube has burned for some length of time, the color-correction settings are going to change because the light being emitted has changed. This is called "drift." It could take weeks or even months to develop—depending upon how many hours of "burn" the tube is subjected to. Therefore, it is best to lay down any other film to tape versions as quickly as possible after the original transfer. If some drift has occurred between laydowns, it is possible for the colorist to still reference the original corrections, but adjustments will be required, which will add time to your session.

Color Correcting Tape to Tape

When color correcting using the tape-to-tape method, the final color correction is done after the on-line is completed and after all opticals, effects, and stock shots are in place. Sound may or may not have been laid to your picture at this time. Whether your videotape element has sound or not is unimportant, as the tape-to-tape process involves altering picture only.

Do not title before you do your tape-to-tape color correction. This saves the colorist from the almost impossible task of having to color correct around the titles—without altering the colors of the letters.

The tape-to-tape color correction process works exactly like film-to-tape color correction, except that your source is videotape instead of cut film. The corrections are stored in a computer linked to the timecode of your source. The source is then played at real time through the color corrector and a second tape is created—usually called the color-corrected master (CCM) or the color timed master (CTM). If you are working in an analog system, or with analog tape, then the CCM or CTM is essentially a dub. If you are working in the digital realm, the CCM or CTM is a digital clone.

The tape-to-tape colorist will probably want a computer disk that can be loaded into the color-correction computer. This disk will contain a video-only of the final on-line EDL. While not absolutely necessary, this list saves the colorist from having to "notch" or mark each cut manually, thus avoiding delays caused by having to manually mark each correction point. The source master (probably your on-line or edited master) becomes the playback source for the color correction. Vertical interval timecode may need to be present on the playback source for the color-correction system to be able to read the timecode. Ask the facility that will be color correcting your show for their specifications. This is especially important if the playback source was created at a location other than the color-correction facility.

Dirt Fixes

Dirt fixes can also be addressed at this phase of the completion process. Many facilities have the ability to run film or videotape through a dirt removal system to electronically "clean up" small dirt and hairs.

This may not be the final answer to dirt and hair problems on your videotape. But it can be very effective for cleaning all but the larger pieces, greatly reducing the time spent in an on-line bay or graphics bay doing dirt fixes. This method will also prove much more cost-effective than doing all the fixes in an on-line or graphics bay. This is assuming you are not introducing any rejectable problems with the introduction of the electronic clean up. Even though it is less expensive up front, we still stress our opinion that it is more prudent to introduce DVNR, noise reduction, etc. in a separate pass.

Noise Reduction/Picture Enhancement

There may be instances when your picture needs electronic help to reduce grain, minor focus problems, or improve overall dirt fixes. Many facilities are equipped to address these issues.

None of the available methods should be used unless necessary, as they all carry the possibility of introducing undesirable artifacts. These undesirables can take the form of trailing, smearing, and grain. Using a dirt-removal box must be evaluated on a project-by-project basis. Pictures with lots of sharp edges may see these edges seem to "dance" if the levels are too high on the dirt-removal box. Pictures with lots of fast camera movements, object movements, or bright flashes may see trails and smearing. Or, the system might mistakenly interpret something in your picture as an unwanted anomaly and eliminate it completely. Some shows have segments that will lend themselves very nicely to electronic dirt removal and other segments of the same program that will tolerate no amount of electronic clean up without creating artifacts.

Starry, Starry Night

This is a true story. The names have been changed to protect the foolish. One of the authors worked on a TV movie that had many visual effects. These effects were very expensive to create. One recurring effect was a star field used to make the night sky look as if it was filled with millions of twinkling lights. As agreed, the picture was run through an electronic dirt-removal box during the laydown of the color-corrected version. The tape then went back to the effects house for titling, at which time the effects supervisor nearly had heart failure. Most of those lovely and very expensive stars that he had so painstakingly created were gone. During the laydown, the dirt-removal box had mistaken those stars for specks of dirt, and it had done a very thorough job of deleting them as the color-corrected master was being created.

Fortunately, because this process does not affect the playback source, the facility was able to easily create a new color-corrected master. The show was then taken into an edit suite for dirt fixes. This was one case where large segments of a program could not be subjected to the lowest setting on the dirt-removal system.

Just remember: if your material isn't perfect, make sure the imperfections are worse than the possible downside of the cure. There are no miracles, honey, but technology is pretty incredible. If you do need a miracle, only the depth of your pocketbook may limit your options.

Video In, Film Out

As you know, there are several ways to approach the making of a film and television product. Those with some money can afford to shoot film and finish on video.

Those with even more money, or maybe more money and a theatrical release, can afford to shoot film and finish film. Then there are those who don't have any use for film at any point in their process, so they are content to shoot video and finish on video (be it high or standard definition). But what about those poor soles that need a film finish but only have a video budget—or less? How are they going to shoot a movie and finish it in a form that people can at least view? The answer: They are going to shoot their movie on videotape and then cross their fingers for funding for a "film-out" finish.

Now, I suppose we should take a breath here and respond to those out there saying, "Hey, wait a minute. I chose *video to film* for artistic reasons." Okay, there are going to be some of you. And, as the technologies continue to evolve, video shooting becomes more cost-effective in the higher resolutions, and film-out becomes more affordable, maybe more will join this small, yet determined group. But for right here, right now, the biggest reason most people shoot on video and finish on film is money! It is a cheaper way to get your movie shot so you can show it to potential investors or distributors who hopefully will pony up the resources to do this film-out thing.

So, What Is This Film-Out Thing?

Well, on a practical level, it starts as an inexpensive way to shoot your movie. When you shoot on videotape, you initially avoid the costs of film stock, laboratory processing, negative cutting, sound mixing, and renting an expensive camera package. Video packages are much less expensive to rent than film packages (unless you decide to go high definition) and stock is affordable. The editing part for both your picture and sound can be done on a desktop computer.

Let's pretend you survived shooting your movie and the video postproduction process. A studio, desperate for a big hit to drag its stock out of the toilet sees your movie and makes you an offer you can't refuse. (Good place to start, huh?)

If you shot on film and finished your project on a digital format only (could be video, could be data) and you now need to deliver a film element you have two choices: 1) go back, cut your negative (please tell us you generated a negative cut list) reproducing all the effects, titles, opticals, etc. on film; or 2) have your finished digital movie "output to film." Other terms used to identify this process are "record out to film" or "film-out." We're going to use film-out here a lot because it is so many less words to type and when you're writing a book, this becomes important. (Sorry, we digress.) We should mention here that 3/4″ videotape is not going to cut it. So don't finish your movie on 3/4″ and expect to create an acceptable film element. Betacam SP is borderline with digital Betacam, D1, or an HD format being your best choices. You'll color correct and dirt fix your videotape master just like any other videotape finish. Then you'll take your final videotape master or data files and trot off to your film-out facility. And, believe it or not, you'll have a few to choose from.

Most "film-out" facilities can output from several different source data formats. However, each facility may differ in what type of data files they can read, so do your homework. You'll probably have to choose your facility based on the software you are using instead of tailoring your software options to a facility. What source element you deliver to the facility will be determined by the type of software you are working with (for data files) or what type of final videotape master you created (when working with videotape).

Understanding Data Resolution

When you enter the world of film-out, everyone is going to start talking to you in terms like 2K, 4K, 307,200 pixels, etc. It is important for you to know what they are talking about so you can order exactly what you need and only have to go through this really expensive process just once.

To reproduce the quality of a 35 mm film frame, you need an image with 5000 × 3760 pixels. When NTSC video is copied to film about 307,200 pixels are copied to a medium that can hold about 19 million pixels per frame. Film frames stored as computer image files come in three common pixel dimensions—2K, 3K, or 4K (the "K" stands for "kilo" and is a thousand [1000]). A 2K image has 2000 pixels, a 3K image has 3000 pixels, and so on. Working in 3K or 4K most closely matches the human visual threshold of about 2500 × 2500 pixels (in a square picture). Your scanning might be done at 4K, the highest resolution available. However, most film-outs are done at 2K because of reduced costs and data requirements at half the output time. Many would argue this makes financial sense because there is little visual difference for most people between 2K and 4K. Some would counter argue that once again money wins out over art.

Film-Out Specifications

There are a few details the facility will need from you when you are ordering your film-out. They will need to know:

- The original format you will be delivering.
- If a data file, they'll need to know the size also.
- The runtime of your project will be important, so they know how much storage space you will need.
- If you are not outputting an entire feature from beginning to end, but only outputting negative pieces, have you added the additional frames you'll need for negative assembly?
- What aspect ratio is going in and what aspect ratio needs to come out?
- Do you have a separate sound element that will need to be married to the print you receive? And, who will be responsible for syncing that sound?

A sample specification sheet (Figure 9.1) follows this section to help you gather the necessary information before speaking with the film-out lab.

Prior to outputting your project, the facility will do a test to make sure the output will meet your expectations and that you have done everything right technically with your source material. Depending on their schedule and your needs, the test could take from overnight to several days.

There are several variables that might affect the look of your film-out project. First of all, the equipment and lighting used in production will have an affect. Pans and camera moves may look different once transferred to a different frame rate. Once it is determined the outcome will be acceptable, the facility will then output the entire project to a negative film stock. Be sure to find out if the price you have been quoted includes your negative also. Some facilities only quote prices for prints.

The film-out negative is simply exposed negative and will need to be processed and printed. The first print will be a check print to check for overall quality. Then you will need to go through at least some color correction. The process will not be as extensive as when you time original cut negative because the digital master has color correction built-in and during the testing phase the facility should have also made some adjustments. Once color balance has been finalized, the sound track will be lined up and a final answer print will be made. We recommend that when you shoot your movie, record your sound to a separate audio element as you would in a normal film shoot. Then you can go through regular audio postproduction and produce a higher quality audio track than you would if you just recorded to your video source audio tracks. You are now ready to make your IP, dupes, and theatrical prints.

Three Film-Out Processes

There are three types of film-out processes. They are 1) the Film Recorder, 2) the Electron Beam Recorder, and 3) the Kinescope.

The Film Recorder

The film recorders that reproduce the highest resolution (2K or 4K) offer two basic technologies. There are the film cameras that shoot high-resolution black-and-white video screens through red, green, and blue filters. And red, green, and blue micro-lasers that scan an image on the film's surface. The facility takes your final video-tape master and digitizes it into their computer. The images are then fed a frame at a time into the film-recording machine. The recorder captures each frame and creates a film negative. At several dollars a frame, these systems are on the more expensive side of your choices.

Electron Beam Recorder

The electron beam recording system fires electrons directly onto unexposed black-and-white film. Three passes are made, one each for red, green, and blue. The three separate exposures are then printed through red, green, and blue filters on an optical printer to produce a color negative. This process is not too widely used but can be more cost effective if you stay in the standard definition format.

Kinescope

This is another method of shooting your image off a video monitor. The kinescopes drop selected fields and produce a 24-fps film element, thus eliminating the visible roll bars that occur when filming TV screens.

So as you're going along shooting your motion picture on videotape and people constantly ask you, "Hey, what about the film part?" Just put your fingers in your ears, roll your eyes, and repeat "lalalalalala" over and over. Your masterpiece will be so compelling when completed that *someone* will insist on paying for the film-out process—no question! Come on, this is Hollywood. It happens all the time.

Figure 9.1 Film-Out Specification Form

Film-Out Specifications

Date_____   Project Title_____

Production Company_____   Contact_____

                                                        Ph _____ Alternate Ph#_____

Source Material:
___ 1 Gig Jazz ___2 Gig Jazz ___Zip ____CD-ROM ___Floppy ___Other
___ DLT 4000 (UNIX-based) Retrieval Command _____
___ Exabyte (UNIX-based) Retrieval Command _____
___ DTF 1 (UNIX-based) Retrieval Command _____

File Type:
___ Cineon ___ SGI.rgb (16 bit) ___ SGI.rgb (8 bit) ___ Targa ___ Tiff ___ Call regarding others

File Size:
___ 2K (2048x1536) ___ 2K (2048x1556) ___ 1.85 2K (2048x1107)
___ 4K (4096x3072) ___ 4K (4096x3112) ___ 1.85 (1828x988)
___ 5 perf 65mm 4k (4096x1796) ___8 perf 65mm 4k (4096x2930) ___15 perf 65mm (4096x3002)
Other: _____Horizontal _____Vertical

Image Alignment: **Scope:**
___ Centered ___Academy Centered   ___Anamorphic ___Anamorphic (unsqueezed)

Comments:

Record Format

35mm Academy center: ___ 1:33 ___ 1:66 ___ 1:85 ___Scope

35mm Full aperture center: ___ full ____ 1:78 ___Super 35 common center ___Super 35 common top

___ 65mm 5 perf ___ 65mm 8 perf ___ 65mm 15 perf

Negative Film Stock

___ 5245 ___5244 ___5369

Laboratory Instructions

___Daylight Rush ___Develop Only   _____# of Positive prints ordered

___Interpositive ___Registered I.P. ___Schmitzer I.P.

Special Notes or Requests:

Sound for Film Out

Whether you shoot your project on film, standard definition NTSC or PAL video, or in high definition video, there are a few things you need to straighten out before you say goodbye to your sound facility. Once the project goes through the "magic film-out" and becomes a film element, it might not sync up unless a few precautions are taken. Your sound facility will need to know some basics:

- What format will you be delivering to the sound facility—DAT, DA88, or MO?
- How is the sound master configured—what audio is on which channels?
- How will the film out be formatted—1000′ or 2000′ reels?
- How was the film/sound originally recorded and at what speed?
- Who is going to sync the tracks?

2 Pop

It is imperative that the sound facility adds what is called a *2 pop* at the head of the track. This is a tone that corresponds to the visual countdown on your film leader on the number "2" (counting backwards from 10). The 2 pop will sound confirming your track is in sync with your picture. Without a 2 pop, it is nearly impossible to sync your project.

Finally we strongly suggested that you take the check print of the film-out and project it against your sound master before making any optical tracks or video laybacks. This seemingly small last minute double check will save you money and embarrassment. Otherwise, you may find out in the screening room with the executives that your track is out of sync.

Formatting

Formatting for Network Delivery

Several aspects of postproduction can be accomplished during a formatting session. The format is designed to finish a videotape to meet the distributor's requirements about how the program is laid out on the tape.

One or more of the following reasons to format can apply to your show. If none apply, then you don't need to schedule a separate format session. This means you are able to accomplish the "formatting" of your show in the off-line bay and have it carried through in the on-line session. The videotape master that comes out of your on-line already meets your distributor's format delivery requirement.

The following are some reasons to format:

1. To incorporate special head formatting (i.e., duration of bars/tone, slate, etc.).
2. To incorporate commercial blacks into program.
3. To pull up (or shorten) blacks between acts to a specified length. (This usually varies from a few frames to several seconds.)
4. To varispeed the program to lengthen or shorten the current run time.
5. To integrate recaps or trailers into program.
6. To close caption and/or V-Chip encode.

Formatting can be incorporated into the on-line by including placement and duration of commercial blacks as part of the edit list. This way your show is on-lined with the appropriate act lengths and commercial breaks/blacks. It can also be done in a separate formatting session.

If you cut your show "to the required delivery length," (also called cutting to time) then you can usually format as part of your on-line. However, this works only if you do not need to varispeed or close-caption to meet the final run time requirement. If your show is not cut to time, then you may need to varispeed.

The basic rule of thumb for varispeeding is that the networks will accept one minute per hour (either slower or faster) without requiring that you adjust the audio pitch. A pitch stabilizer keeps your audio from sounding too high (like chipmunks) or too low (talking in slow motion) when you varispeed, depending on whether you are making your show shorter or longer. If your show is just a few seconds under or over, talk with the network before you varispeed. They are often willing to allow some leeway if you are just a few seconds either way.

If you do need to varispeed your show, this is often done in a format session in an edit bay. If your show is delivered closed-captioned and/or V-Chip encoded, be sure to do this once the show has been varisped. You will not be able to close caption a varisped master (the timecode will be different and will not match your captioning—unless you make a cassette for the captioning company after you varispeed), nor will you be able to varispeed an already-captioned master.

The Format Session

The following are usually included in the format session:

- Formatting of the head of the tape according to delivery requirements. Usually, although not always, program starts at 01:00:00:00. However, what is on the tape prior to the hour mark can differ. For example, one cable network currently requires formatting to start at 00:56:00:00 with various lengths of black, bars, and slate making up the time until 01:00:00:00.

- Editing any logos to the show's head or tail if they were not added as part of the on-line session. For example, the network logo may go only on the air master.
- Closed-captioning. There are several companies that create closed-captioning information. Also see the separate "Closed-Captioning" section in this chapter for more details. Closed-captioning slaves to timecode. When a show is locked and on-lined, a 3/4″ cassette is made to the particular captioning company's specifications.

In closed-captioning, the 3/4″ captioning cassette is sent to the captioning company. Using the 3/4″ tape, along with a copy of the script, they put into type all spoken words, voice-overs, description of effects, and song lyrics. The information is then sent via modem over telephone lines or delivered on a computer disk to a decoding/encoding device at the postproduction facility.

Be sure to check, and let the captioning company know, whether your postproduction facility needs a computer disk or is able to receive via modem. If the information is being transmitted by phone lines, the caption company will also need the telephone number that is connected to the captioning device at the postproduction house.

The captioning information is triggered by the timecode on the master. It is then recorded into the vertical interval (line 21) of the air master when it is made. Because vertical interval is part of the picture information, a new closed-captioned tape must be created. Captioning cannot be encoded onto an existing videotape. Closed-captioning is discussed in more detail later on in this chapter.

Another delivery issue is type of timecode. Many shows are now being on-lined and completed in nondrop-frame timecode (NDFTC). All networks and cable stations, without exception, require air masters to be delivered in drop-frame timecode (DFTC). This type of timecode provides an accurate run time to within one second. NDFTC and DFTC differ in running time. DFTC adds 3 seconds and 18 frames each hour (1 second and 9 frames each half-hour) over NDFTC.

Nondrop-frame timecode must be converted to reflect actual program length. This is important for two reasons. First, if your show is cut in NDFTC, do the conversion to DFTC to make sure you know your show's exact length. Second, you will need to make your air master and delivery cassettes in DFTC. This conversion is done in the format session, if there is one. If not, it is done when your air master and delivery dubs are actually created in your postproduction facility's machine room. They simply play back your NDFTC master to a tape machine that is generating DFTC. If your calculations have been done properly, your tape will come out exactly to the second using this method.

Along with your air master and the corresponding completed format sheet, you will be required to deliver a series of additional cassettes to the network. This may include a protection copy of the master and several 3/4″ and VHS cassettes.

Formatting for Foreign Delivery

Whether foreign distribution formatting will need to be done in an edit bay will be determined by your distributor's individual specifications. If the delivery requirements call for blacks to be pulled to exactly ten frames, you should do this in an edit bay rather than relying on someone in your duplication department to do this from one machine to another. Remember, music often "rings out" into a commercial black a few frames after the picture has faded out. Be careful not to upcut the music when pulling up commercial blacks. Make sure to start counting the ten frames after the music ring-out is completed.

You must also include textless material at the tail of your foreign delivery master. These are picture backgrounds for all shots in your show that have titles over them. Foreign markets need these shots so they can replace the words in their own language. Occasionally a company will require that the textless be provided on a separate reel, but usually they want it to start 30 to 60 seconds after the end of the program. Titles for which you must provide textless shots include the main title, opening credits, end credits, bumpers, and any parts in the body of the show that have text—such as locales and legends. Textless material is created in the titling session. For more information on textless material, see the "Titling" section in this chapter.

Credits and Titling

Credits are the actual listings acknowledging who did what in a program. They include everyone who is getting a screen acknowledgment for the part they played in making your show.

In episodics and sitcoms, the names that are built as part of the main title and that stay the same from week to week are referred to as the main title credits. Credits displayed over the show opening are called opening credits, and those shown at the end of the show are called the end credits. The text that is used throughout the show to identify a place or date is called the locale.

Credits

When you work for a large studio, the credits will usually be provided to you. If you are working for an independent, you may have to figure them out for yourself. This is a very important task. If they are incorrect or incomplete, you or the producer can be held legally responsible and may be fined.

Tips for Creating Credits

Creating credits for a show can be tedious and even nerve rattling with the potential for expensive legal ramifications if it is not done properly. Here are a few tips to help you through the process:

1. Always get a copy of the signed contract of every actor and crew member. The producer or production manager will have the contracts. Read the contracts and highlight the credit provisions.
2. Request a credit list and order of credits from the casting company. The deals were made through them and they will know the legal agreements.
3. Ask the production manager for any company deals that require credits, and ask the producer if there are any extra or nonstandard credit deals.
4. Secure legal verbiage from your lawyers regarding copyright and fictitious-persons wording.

Put all of these together and then pull out the "credit section" located in your distributor's delivery requirements.

Sometimes distributors do not allow certain departments in the main title, or they won't acknowledge these departments at all. After going over the credits and making your adjustments, give the first draft to your producer. After the producer's adjustments are completed, recheck all the spellings against the contracts and then distribute the credit list for approval to casting, legal, the producer, the director, and the editor. After the credits have been approved internally, send them to the distributor for approval.

The delivery package usually includes a list of those who need to sign off on credits before they can be considered approved. You will probably end up creating more than one draft of credits before they are finally approved. Be sure to date and number each page (1 of 13, 2 of 13, etc.) of each version of the credits so you always know you have the complete and final version when you go in for titling.

When all the adjustments have been made, confirm the number of main title cards with the editor and submit the approved final copy to the lab for opticals or to the titling person at the postproduction facility to pre-enter your copy.

Credits for Features

Feature productions are generally larger than television productions. They shoot longer, have larger crews, larger budgets, and even shoot a larger aspect ratio than most programs created for television. Keeping in line with these "larger" items, feature films usually have much larger, more elaborate main title treatments and much longer end credits. Some movie title treatments are being worked on before production even starts. The elaborate and distinctive titles from the James Bond movie series come to mind.

We're seeing a trend with some filmmakers who feel that a grand artistic title display detracts from the tone or introduction to a film's beginning. They have begun to down play all the credits in the interest of directing your complete attention to the movie itself. These filmmakers save all the credits, sometimes even saving the main title of the movie, for the very end of the movie. This is the opposite of some early filmmaking where all of the credits are seen in the movie's opening titles and the end of the movie is simply followed by a card that reads "The End."

Regardless where your movie titles appear, the order in which the individual credits can appear is predetermined. As in television, the unions rule how and when their members are acknowledged and their rules must be adhered to. The guidelines for features and television shows are very similar in order, wording, and on screen duration of the credits. The end credits for features, however, will be much more extensive and every crewmember for every shooting location will be listed. All music and clip licenses will be listed as well as company logos and legal, copyright, and ownership information. Compiling the list of credits for a feature can be an enormous undertaking. Your first hope is that a studio legal person will take on most of the legwork and supply you with an already approved list. Anyone who has ever worked on a low budget film knows that many times credits are extended in lieu of payment, or in exchange for reduced payment. These credit lists can be seemingly unending and there probably won't be any studio person to help you. Be sure executives and legal people sign off on a hard copy and all the appropriate guilds give their approval as well. Every guild has a website that lists the credit provisions and provides forms and procedures for your convenience. Ignorance is not bliss, and in this case it can be costly.

Credits for MOW or Pilot

When making an MOW or pilot, the credit order is fairly standard. Some contracts will require certain actor credits to appear on the screen before the show's main title card is shown. These are called "above the title" credits. A traditional credit lineup will look like this:

Opening Credits

> Actors (above the main title by special contractual obligation only)
> Main Title
> Actors
> Composer
> Editor
> Art Director
> Director of Photography
> Producer(s)
> Executive Producer(s)
> Writer(s)
> Director

Instead of being included in the opening credits, the executive producer(s) may elect to take the coveted last fade at the end of the show before final commercial break position. Only the director or the executive producer(s) can use this credit position. In rare instances, a short credit roll is approved that includes producers and associate producers.

End Credits

> Unit Production Manager
> First Assistant Director
> Second Assistant Director
> Actors and roles played (lead players usually appear first)
> Crew Members (job performed, then name)
> Service Providers (lab, sound house, prop providers, etc.)
> Legal Disclaimer (get the verbiage from your lawyer)
> Copyright Notice (get the verbiage from your lawyer)
> Logos

Later in this chapter we have listed some additional guidelines and union rules for dealing with credits and union members.

Credits for Episodics

A permanent main title sequence is created that includes the regular actors, the main title, and sometimes the creator. This main title sequence is used for each episode. Each episode will have new opening credits listing guest stars, writer, and director. A traditional credit lineup will look like this:

Opening Credits

> Actors (above the main title by special contractual obligation only)
> Main Title
> Actors
> Composer
> Editor
> Art Director
> Director of Photography
> Producer(s)
> Executive Producer(s)
> Writer(s)
> Director

Instead of being included in the opening credits, the executive producer(s) may elect to take the coveted last fade at the end of the show before final commercial-break position. This credit position can be used only by either the director or the executive producer(s). In rare instances, a short credit roll that includes producers and associate producers is approved.

New end credits will also be created each week to include new actors and crew members.

End Credits

> Unit Production Manager
> First Assistant Director
> Second Assistant Director
> Actors and roles played (lead players usually appear first)
> Crew Members (job performed, then name)
> Service Providers (lab, sound house, prop providers, etc.)
> Legal Disclaimer (get the verbiage from your lawyer)
> Copyright Notice (get the verbiage from your lawyer)
> Logos

Many end credits are contractually regulated by the following:

- Contract requirements
- Casting company deals
- Producer requirements
- Production manager deals/requirements
- Legal jargon
- Production company logo requirements
- Network/foreign logo requirements

Union Rules Regarding Credits

The blanket rule for all of the above procedures is that regardless of what is negotiated, the unions—SAG, DGA, WGA, etc.—rule. All of their guidelines are written in their basic agreements and are traditionally not negotiable. For detailed explanations of each union's guidelines, contact the unions individually and ask to speak to the person in charge of either feature or television credits.

For convenience, here are some simple guidelines outlined by these organizations:

The director can be either the last card in the main title or the last card before the final commercial break. If the director is the last card in the main title, then the writer is the second-to-last card in the main title. If the director is the last card before the final commercial break, then the writer is the next card, which is the first card in the end credits. The writer's card must be on-screen a minimum of 2 seconds, or the same length of time as the producer's or director's card—whichever is longer. The unit production manager and the first and second assistant directors, respectively, share a card. This card is placed in the most prominent technical position in the end credits. The production executives are considered technical and should appear after the unit production manager/first and second assistant director card. A major TV producer tested this rule and lost. This was very expensive for the production company. So, putting the unit production manager/first and second assistant director card first in the end credits will guarantee you've fulfilled this critical requirement. Of course, the exception to the rule is that the director of photography (cinematographer), the art director, and the editor credits can be placed ahead of the unit production manager in the technical (end) credits.

The rules for actors, on the other hand, are less mandated. SAG has very few rules for actor credit placement; therefore, the actor has to make his deal up front in his contract. Any contractual obligations that follow the rules must, of course, be honored. There can be no more than six actor credits per card in the end credits, and the screen time for each card can be no less than 2 1/2 seconds.

After successfully obtaining all of your in-house and network credit approvals, you must submit them to the WGA and DGA for approval.

WGA (Writer's Guild of America):

Get a tentative writer's credit form from the WGA (see Figure 9.2). Fill it out and make two copies. File one copy and have the original hand-delivered to the WGA with a cover letter. Be sure to get a signed receipt from the WGA that they have received the form. Also, the WGA requires that you send the writer two final drafts of the script and a copy of the "notice of tentative writing credits" form with a cover letter.

Figure 9.2 Notice of Tentative Writing Credits—Television

Date_____

TO: Writers Guild of America, West, Inc. 7000 West Third Street, Los Angeles, CA 90048, or to
     Writers Guild of America, East, Inc. 555 West 57th St., New York, NY 10019
     AND
     Participating Writers

NAMES OF PARTICIPATING WRITERS   **ADDRESSES**_____

_____   _____
_____   _____
_____   _____
_____   _____

Title of Episode_____Production #_____
(If pilot or MOW or other special or unit program, indicate network and length)

Series Title_____

Producing Company_____

Executive Producer_____

Producer_____   Associate Producer_____

Director_____   Story Editor_____
                                         (or Consultant)
Other Production Executives, if Participating Writers_____

Writing Credits on this episode are tentatively determined as follows:

ON SCREEN:

Source material credit ON THIS EPISODE (on separate card, unless otherwise indicated) if any:

Continuing source material or Created By credit APPEARING ON ALL EPISODES OR SERIES
(on separate card):

Revised final script was sent to participating writers on_____

The above tentative credits will become final unless a protest is communicated to the undersigned
no later than 6:00 p.m. on   _____   _____
                                                      (Company)

                                                      By_____

The WGA and the writer have seven business days to respond. If you have not heard from either in this time period, you may assume you have fulfilled your legal obligations and are free to proceed. The WGA does not send written approval.

Should there be a dispute before the seven business days have expired, the WGA will arbitrate between the producer and the writer. If the writer is a producer on the project, the WGA considers this an automatic arbitration. If there should be an arbitration, you will need to immediately send the WGA another copy of the tentative writer credit form, the original script, the final script, and any written information required by the arbitrator.

This can be a time-consuming process and underlines how important it is to do the credit approvals early on.

DGA (Director's Guild of America)

The DGA will accept a fax of your credits with a cover letter requesting approval. If the credits are approved, you'll receive a return fax of your cover letter stamped "Approved" with the approval date and the authorizing person's initials.

SAG (Screen Actor's Guild)

To date, SAG does not require prior credit approval. It is considered a courtesy, however, to also send a copy of the credits to SAG for their approval.

Armed with your officially approved, technically correct credits, go ahead and calculate the duration of each card in the end credits. (Actual placement of the opening credits sometimes falls to the editor or the producer, although, often the associate producer has this responsibility.) The network and other distributors will have predetermined the run time of the show's end credits. Remember not to violate the predetermined lengths discussed above. If you find, when calculating credits, that you are over the time allotted, you may want to call your distribution contact to see if they will allow any exceptions. If there's a good argument for bending the rules, it may be allowed. This doesn't happen often, so don't try their patience by trying this every week. Usually, by doing your job and being prepared, you can avoid this situation.

Choosing a Font

Okay, now here's the fun part! Well, it's more fun than sending credit copies to the DGA and SAG or begging producers to sign off on credits so you can deliver on time. Sometimes in this business you have to broaden your definition of fun.

Ask the titling facility to provide samples of the available font types, and submit these to your producer. If asked, most facilities are happy to lay to tape the opening title and an opening and end credit in several fonts for the executives to view. This may help them visualize how their copy will look in the different fonts. It is sometimes easier to choose when you see your actual titles on the screen. Put forth the effort to have the producers narrow down the font types before asking the postproduction house to put samples to videotape. Most houses will work with you as much as possible in choosing a font style, but try not to take advantage of the situation. Of course, as an associate producer you may not have any control over the actions (or inactions) of the producer and the production company executives. But the facility will appreciate your efforts in any case.

Once the type style has been chosen, let the lab or title artist know. If the show is a tape-finish with tape-to-tape color correction scheduled, be sure to title *after* the color correction. Otherwise, you will end up changing the color of the titles.

In the case of film titles, the editor will order the opticals, approve them, and cut them into the work print for the negative cutter.

The graphics person assigned to create the opticals or type the titles will need to know which size to make the credits. Generally the opening credits are all 100% of title. The end credits vary with the more prominent cards being 100% of title and multiple cards being 80%. The legal disclaimer is as large as needed to fit in the space allowed.

Mine Is Bigger

A trick for deciding the size of the main title is to take the longest name in the opening credits and use this as the size for the rest of the opening credits. There are rules to follow that determine the relative size of titles and credits. Be sure to check your contracts for size guidelines. Traditionally, no credit can be larger than the main title. Other limitations will be stated in the contracts.

A final note on credits. Even though everyone and their brother (industry nepotism gives a scary reality to this cliché) has approved these credits, try to find the time to personally check each one for spelling. A good trick is to use the actor's signature on the contract. A further check is to count all the speaking parts and make sure you have a credit for each. Ninety-nine percent of the time, speaking parts get a credit.

Red Alert

Please take the following as a warning and not as a hard and fast rule. We recommend that when choosing a color for your video titles or drop shadows, you avoid the color red. It does not reproduce as well as other colors, and it sometimes shifts. Visually, it may appear to smear on lesser formats such as 3/4″ or VHS.

Titling

In film, this is when you order your opticals and have them cut into your negative. Film opticals, which include fades, dissolves, scene transitions, titles, and other effects, are created on film at a laboratory or optical house. When the opticals are shot, an internegative is created. This then becomes part of your cut negative.

For videotape titles, graphics technology is one of the most rapidly changing aspects of postproduction. Graphics equipment has become much more affordable and flexible, so some facilities now use equipment that makes titling much easier, less time consuming, more creative, and more accurate. Fancy movements can often be accomplished on the same equipment that you use to create your simple text credits.

In some cases, you can give the postproduction house a computer-disk copy of the data file in which your original credit list was typed in the production office. This copy has already been approved by all, and spelling has been checked. You can simply save your credit data file to a text file on a 3.5″ floppy disk or CD-ROM and deliver this to your titling facility. This eliminates the need for them to retype the information, thus avoiding names being misspelled or left off completely due to human error.

Titling in 16:9

When you are delivering a 4:3 master that originated from a 16:9 master, you must create the 4:3 master before you title. Then you will have to title each version separately. Be sure your titling facility is aware that you are creating these two different versions so they can be prepared to do this for you. This could require some engineering effort at the facility, so be sure to give them plenty of notice.

Title Parts

Your titles are made up of the following components, although not necessarily in this order:

- Main Title
- Actors
- Executives
- Service Providers
- Disclaimers
- Copyright Notice

To create the credits that make up your titles, see the "Credit" section in this chapter.

Titling Requirements

For your titling session you will need to have done the following:

1. Approved title copy;
2. Chosen a font style, color, and size;

3. Spotted the place where each title will appear on the screen and determined how long it will be on the screen and whether it will fade or cut on and off; and
4. Designed a main title. For a series, this is usually a prebuilt separate element that includes your regular stars and is inserted into your show each week. This main title sets the tone for the show and becomes the show's signature.

On videotape, your titles will be laid into the "title safe" area of the picture. This is an area inside the "picture- or action-safe" zone that will be seen on all television sets, regardless of their size. Figure 9.3 shows these areas.

Figure 9.3 TV Safe/Title Safe Action

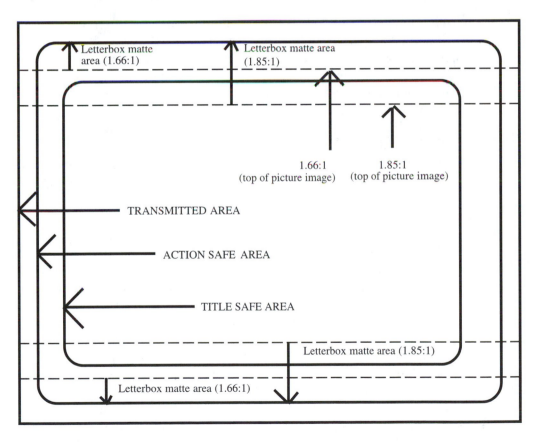

Textless—It's Not a State

Check your delivery requirements to see if you need to deliver textless material. These are the backgrounds that your titles will be placed over. Traditionally, textless material will be tacked onto the tail of your titled videotape master. This is done for two reasons:

1. If you are required to deliver textless materials, the distributor rarely wants a separate tape to keep track of.
2. You will always know where your textless material is and always have it to use whenever you are working with your master to do fixes or create different versions.

If your show has many locales throughout it, thus, a lot of textless footage, it may not fit at the tail of your master. In this case you will have no choice but to put it on a separate reel or create an entirely textless master. You may want to make a note at the tail of your master that textless exists on a separate tape. For a program that has more than one part (an MOW may have two parts or a mini-series may have four or more parts), the textless material is usually put at the tail of the last part only. For a mini-series that is shown over two nights or more, the textless goes at the tail of each part that contains end credits. If there is textless material at the tail of your master or one part of your master, be sure to indicate "with textless" or "textless at tail" on the label to avoid confusion later.

Be the Hero

We strongly urge you to create textless elements, even if they are not part of the delivery requirements. The following incident explains why. Once one of the authors worked on a pilot presentation. This is a shortened version of a pilot that is often made to save money to "present" to a broadcast entity to see if they are interested in spending the money to make a full-length pilot episode. This method is most often used with hour-long dramas. Because it was a pilot presentation and there were only partial credits laid down, the production company did not think they would need textless material. Fortunately, we decided to go ahead and tack the backgrounds to the end of the show. This proved a prudent move. Just hours before the presentation was delivered for the network screening, the production company had to change the credits. Had there been no textless material to lay new credits over, the company would have either incurred a lot of money re-on-lining those shots (without titles) or been unable to make the change. As it turned out, we were able to quickly make their changes *and* the screening.

Titles and Captions

People don't often think about the relationship between titling and closed-captioning. But when decoded, captions (now called open captions) appear across the lower third of the screen. This is also where opening credits are often placed. This means the captions appear over the credits, and neither will be readable on the screen.

If you provide the captioning company with the timecodes of the start and end of your opening credits and where on the screen they appear, they will place the captioning higher on the screen during these times. This way the credits and decoded captions will be clearly readable.

Varispeed

Varispeeding a show means changing the program's run time—making it either shorter or longer—on the master delivered to the distributor.

When to Varispeed

Varispeed can be used on tape-finish projects only. It is used when your program length is too long or too short and you don't want to edit any additional material into or out of the program. The film and sound elements or the videotape master are played back at a faster speed than normal and recorded at that speed onto videotape. This process does not affect the record-machine timecode. The record videotape still runs at 30 fps, but the picture and sound were physically sped up or slowed down by the playback machine.

There is a formula for determining varispeed rates, but advanced telecine and editorial equipment can usually figure the varispeed for you. Basically, you're dividing the run time you have by the run time you need and the difference is calculated as a percentage. The equipment is then sped up or slowed down by that percentage. You can varispeed individual film reels or acts, or you can set an overall varispeed for the entire program.

A good rule of thumb is not to varispeed the opening titles or end credits if you don't have to. If you do varispeed the credits, be careful that you are not violating your delivery requirements by making the credits longer or shorter than allowed by the network or distributor.

One minute per hour (3.5%) is generally the maximum (or minimum) acceptable varispeed rate. In other words, for every full program hour you can make the show one minute longer or one minute shorter without worrying about noticeably affecting the audio or having the tape rejected by the network. It is important to remember that an hour-long TV show is actually less than an hour of program run time. If you need to take out or add more than a minute of time per hour of program, you may have to use a lexicon (pitch corrector) so the audio won't sound sped up or slowed down.

You can also elect to varispeed only specific acts or parts of acts if you are only slightly altering your run time. You can then varispeed areas without music or with little dialogue, thus reducing the possibility that someone will notice any pitch changes in voices or music.

It is possible to varispeed tape-to-tape on certain videotape machines. For example, a 1″ with a Zeus or a digital Betacam equipped with the proper boards can varispeed tape-to-tape without going through an edit controller.

Varispeed and the Foreigner

Delivering a varisped foreign master is rarely acceptable to the foreign client. Sometimes if you are delivering a videotape master that has English composite stereo on channels 1 and 2 and full stereo music and effects on channels 3 and 4, you might get away with delivering a varisped master to foreign distributors. But, the foreign client will never be able to easily match any other sound track to the varisped master. Their audio will run at normal speed, while your picture will vary in its speed rates. If the foreign clients plans to add their own music and effects or to dub the speaking parts in another language, the new sound will fall out of sync and will need to be hand synced throughout the program.

In nearly all instances, it is best to deliver to the foreign markets a program played at normal speed—even if it means creating a new master. Knowing your delivery requirements ahead of time can help you plan for this more cost-effectively.

Summary

Varispeeding can be a way to meet your distributor's program-length requirement without editing out program material. Varispeeding should be used with caution to avoid pitch changes in people's voices and music.

If your show's length is just a few seconds shorter or longer than the distributor has specified, be sure to check with your contact at the distribution company to see if they will agree to the slight change in program length in lieu of accepting a varisped master. Often this is the case.

Finally, do not arbitrarily use varispeed. Make sure the master will be acceptable to your distributor. And never varispeed a foreign delivery master unless you have prior approval from the foreign client.

Closed-Captioning

Closed captions are the dialogue, song lyrics, and effects typed out and then encoded into the picture's vertical interval. The actual captioning is the signal that contains text information incorporated into video that can be viewed on your television when run through a decoder.

It's Not Just for the Hearing-Challenged

Originally, programs were closed-captioned solely for the deaf and hard-of-hearing. Persons with these disabilities could purchase a signal decoder. The picture signal ran through this device which decoded certain lines in the vertical interval, making the information on the audio track visible as written words on the screen.

Due to a federal law that went into effect in 1993 mandating captioning decoder chips in all new television sets that are 13″ or larger, modern-day television sets come standard with the ability to read captions.

Closed-captioning on your show is not a legal requirement, but it is a delivery requirement of most networks and cable stations. Even some home-video and foreign distributors are requesting that their masters be delivered with closed-captioning.

The production company is expected to pay all costs for captioning, although in some instances the network does help cover the costs. This may be especially true if the network requests last-minute changes after the captioning has already been completed.

Technically speaking, "captioning" is the recreation of the words, lyrics, and effects of a program's audio track, along with action descriptions, onto a computer disk. This is done at a captioning agency.

Captioning Needs

To caption your show, the captioning company will require a script and a 3/4″ video-tape with timecode matching your locked, on-lined master. Therefore, try not to deliver a closed-captioning work tape before the show has been on-lined.

The exception to the above statement, of course, is if the show is very dialogue-heavy and there is an unusually short turnaround between on-line and delivery. The captioning agency will need to make last minute adjustments to the captioning, but at least they will have a head start on entering the information.

Be sure to provide the captioning company with your postproduction schedule as early as possible so they can add you to their schedule. And if your schedule changes or episodes air out of numerical sequence, please remember to let the captioning company know. This is especially true of sitcoms and episodics, which generally deliver weekly and are on a very tight schedule.

The captioning company will provide you with specifications for their 3/4″ tape. These generally include audio combined onto channel 1, timecode on channel 2 that matches your master videotape timecode, and nothing on channel 3 (this is also called the address track). If your captioning company of choice does request timecode on channel 3, be sure it is made to match the timecode of your videotape master (and channel 2). They will also want a visual timecode window, usually upper left in the picture.

Sample Caption Cassette Specifications

Written out, the specifications look something like this:

Closed Caption Cassette Specifications

One-3/4″ with:
    Ch 1: Comp
    Ch 2: Timecode (matching master)
    Ch 3: Blank
    Visible timecode upper left (matching master)

Captioning Your Master

Once captioning is completed, the captioning company will either deliver a computer disk or modem the information to the postproduction facility scheduled to do the actual captioning of the delivery tapes.

If the information is being sent via modem, it is a good idea to let the postproduction facility know when the captioning will be sent. You want to make sure their modem is set to "receive" and is not in use at the time the information is being transmitted.

"Encoding" describes the process of laying the captions onto a videotape. The term "closed" refers to the signal being encoded into the vertical interval. Captioning is embedded into line 21 of the vertical interval. The term "open captions" refers to captioning that you can read on the screen.

Because it lives in the vertical interval in the picture area, the captioning information is recorded into a new videotape created from the original master, either in a format session or during dubbing. This captioned-formatted tape is usually called the "air master" or "delivery master."

Once the postproduction house has the captioning information, they include the captioner in the duplication path when the delivery tapes are made. The captioning locks to the timecode and the system does the rest.

Captioning vs. Titling

One thing to consider when captioning your program is where the captioning physically appears on the TV screen when decoded in relationship to where your credits are placed. When decoded, captions appear across the lower third of the screen. This is often where opening credits are placed. This means the captions may appear over the credits, and neither may be readable on the screen.

If you provide the captioning company with the timecodes of the beginning and end of your opening credits, they will place the captioning higher on the screen during these times. Better yet, if time permits, have the work cassette that goes to the captioning company made after you title your show. They will then have a visual reference of your title placement and can place their captions so that when decoded they will not overlap with the credits. The drawback is that television delivery schedules don't always allow enough time for this method. If a tight delivery prevents you from providing a captioning work cassette with titles, give the caption company approximate timecodes where you expect to place your credits and tell them where on the screen the credits will appear (i.e., upper third, center, lower third). They will do their best to avoid overlapping.

Summary

Nearly all domestic, and some foreign, distributors require programs to be delivered with encoded captions. Planning ahead will help ensure that everyone who sees your show is able to read the credits and the accompanying captioning.

Captioning companies archive each show's captioning information for an extended period of time. Therefore, should you need to make changes that affect the captioning, or should you have to remake your delivery master for some reason, the captioning company can resend the information to the postproduction house.

As the number of home TV sets with built-in caption decoders grows, captioning becomes an issue for an even larger audience.

Subtitles

Most of us are familiar with what subtitles look like. They are used when a foreign language is being spoken on screen to tell the viewer what is being said in their language. They manifest as one or more lines across the bottom of the screen and are timed with the actor speaking.

Subtitles are usually done with white letters, but sometimes they are done in yellow letters. White letters can be hard to read if the pictures in the movie behind them are very light.

Film subtitles are created one of two ways. They are shot on high contrast film stock and are married to picture in the same way opticals are. But, instead of being created in sections as fades, dissolves, etc. usually are, they are usually run the length of the movie during printing. In the other method, the text is literally etched onto the print's emulsion side. The emulsion is scraped away in these areas and the subtitles appear when light goes through from the projector. A deviation from that may be a movie where there are only a few scenes with subtitles—instead of the entire movie being subtitled.

Videotape subtitles are generated electronically, like titles. They are inserted into the picture at predetermined timecodes. This can either be done in an edit bay, or more commonly just like captions are created and encoded. In fact, subtitles are often referred to as "open captions."

There is an art to creating subtitles. There are rules to how many words are in a line, how many lines appear on the screen at once, the duration, and punctuations used. Be sure to have your subtitled movie done by an experienced professional subtitling company, and not just a company that does captioning.

Be mindful about the differences in subtitle placements between full frame and letterbox images. If you are subtitling both, you'll have to have the subtitles reformatted for one or the other. If you use full frame subtitling for a letterbox movie, the subtitles will appear somewhere in the letterbox. If you use letterbox subtitles for a full frame movie, the subtitles will appear high up into the picture.

V-Chip

V-Chip encoding is the process of encrypting information into a video signal that will allow you to block a program from being viewable on TV sets equipped with a V-Chip decoder.

Some networks started limited broadcast with V-Chip in mid-1996. In 1998, the FCC officially approved the ratings symbols. Broadcast and cable industries are airing these ratings on a voluntary basis to alert parents to programming that contains sexual, violent, or other adult material. The move was "encouraged" by the FCC as part of the Telecommunications Act of 1996.

By July 1, 1999, half of all new model TVs with screens 13″ or larger were required to have V-Chip decoders. By January 1, 2000, all sets were required to contain the decoders. All of the major television manufacturers complied.

The guideline icon is displayed for 15 seconds at the beginning of each program. It is visible in the upper left-hand corner of the screen. The symbol is encoded with the same technology used to encode closed-captioning. Closed captions are placed in the vertical interval on Line 21, Field 1. V-Chip is placed on Line 21, Field 2. In many cases, facilities with the encoding capability are using the same piece of equipment to encode both the captioning and V-Chip, so that the insertion is happening simultaneously.

All of the rules for caption encoding apply to V-Chip encoding, including the varispeed issues.

Video Descriptions

The FCC has ruled that beginning April 1, 2002, the four major networks' broadcasts must include video descriptions a minimum of 50 hours a quarter in the top 25 markets. The rollout for wider broadcasts is still being worked on.

Video descriptions are to the visually-impaired what closed captions are to the hearing-impaired. They are spoken descriptions of what is going on in the picture that may not be readily apparent from the dialogue or music, but important to the story's plot.

It appears that the networks will bear the financial responsibility for creating these audio tracks. Special writers are hired to write the descriptions and actors to record them. The descriptions are placed in the natural pauses in dialogue and do not get recorded over any dialogue.

This new, and sort of sudden requirement, by the FCC has left a few unanswered questions. Some of the problems yet to be ironed out include:

1) How to cover these extra costs.
2) How to incorporate the current 5-day turnaround needed to create the video description tracks into current postproduction schedules.
3) How to overcome stations having to chose between their third channel (on stereo shows) being either a SAP channel (generally Spanish) or taking the video description audio as the third channel.

Although this book will be in the hands of our publishers prior to April 1, 2002, by the time the book hits the streets some of these issues may have been decided.

One of the perks of DVD has been the ability to include a similar audio track where the director, actors, etc. in a movie will talk about the movie while the video portion plays. While this audio commentary track usually takes on a more "free" style in the writing and recording, the concepts can be the same.

Fox Broadcasting (FBC) aired *Star Wars: Episode One—The Phantom Menace* with a video description track. What feedback they received from viewers was very positive.

As-Broadcast Scripts

An As-Broadcast Script is a transcription of a program exactly as it aired on television or was shown in a theatre.

"Why not use the production script," you ask? Production scripts are often close approximations to what really ends up in the final mix. The reason for this is that dialogue lines and even songs or song lyrics can change once a program is locked and goes into ADR—and maybe even after the final mix has already started.

This happens because once a show is put together, complete with the "final" audio track, the producers or executives may feel or realize that some dialogue, for example, doesn't work as well as originally thought. Or, maybe they realize that more exposition or explanation is required for the audience to understand a plot point or character's action. Sometimes audience testing will show an unfavorable reaction to a scene and the producers make a change to correct that reaction.

There may be a song mixed in and the last minute clearance cannot be obtained and another song must be substituted. This may happen so close to air or release that the change is made "on the fly," quickly mixed in to meet the delivery deadline and not incorporated into the script. These kinds of last minute changes are especially common in television series.

Another example of a time when the script is incorrect is when movies are then cut down or re-edited for television viewing. There are rules each network, cable channel, and airlines have for words and actions that cannot be shown on television. These are called Standards and Practices (S&P). To conform to S&P guidelines, language, violence, or sexual content may be edited out. Then, the script needs to be redone to accurately reflect those changes.

When a program is cut down to make its runtime shorter for syndication, a new script may need to be created so the captioning can be updated.

These are all called As-Broadcast Scripts. These final scripts are used by the caption companies to create the closed captions and foreign language dubbers to create foreign language tracks or foreign language subtitling.

Should your job include providing these accurate, revised transcriptions for any of these purposes, you will need to plan for the creation of these scripts. They take time (often several days), which will need to be factored into your delivery schedule and will cost additional dollars, which will have to be factored into your postproduction budget. There are script creation companies, or transcription companies, that specialize in this service.

Quality Control

Usually shortened to just "QC," quality control is the process by which a print or videotape is scrutinized to make sure it passes technical muster prior to delivery.

Either the postproduction house's QC department does this and it is billed to the client on an hourly basis, or the client will perform an independent check for quality. If there is a studio involved, they may also insist on a separate quality check, particularly in the case of release prints.

For film, you will need to book a screening room and a projectionist. The exception is that some laboratories take responsibility for checking the prints they make in which case you will just need to check with your executives to see if they want to sit in on the QC session. For release prints, the IP is checked and a sampling of release prints that are struck from the IP are also evaluated for both picture and audio quality. All special wetgate prints, such as screening prints and premiere prints, are checked.

Two Types of Quality Control

"Spot QC" means the tape is checked for basic setup and general specifications. This type of QC will check at least vertical interval timecode (VITC), horizontal and vertical blanking, front porch, chrominance and luminance levels, and audio track configurations and levels. The setup for bars and tone are verified and the tape is checked randomly at several spots throughout the program. This is sometimes referred to as a three-point or five-point QC, referring to the number of random spots on the tape that is checked.

One hundred percent QC means that the tape is checked for basic setup and general specifications and that the entire program is watched very carefully. If there is audio on more than two channels, the tape is checked once through for picture and channels 1 and 2, then again for the additional channels.

The Quality-Control Form

Figure 9.4 shows a typical QC report used when a 100% QC is ordered. If you are aware of any special specifications required to be checked for the program, be sure to provide this information to the company performing the QC. These special requirements may include the audio configuration, the vertical interval information, textless requirements, and head-of-tape formatting.

Figure 9.4 A Sample Videotape Quality Control Report

Company Name:
Program Title:
Episode Title: Episode #:
WO#:   PO#:   Run time: Part_____ of _____
Pass/Fail   Summary:
Format: Standard: Version:
Timecode: Aspect Ratio: QC Initials:

Full QC: Video____Ch1____Ch2____Ch3____Ch4____Cue____
Spot QC: Video____Ch1____Ch2____Ch3____Ch4____Cue____

QC Date: Revised Date: Videotape Record Date:
QC VTR: Revised by: Videotape Record VTR:
Record Facility: Subtitles: Slate:

Horizontal Blanking: Front Porch: Channel Conditions:
VITC: RF Envelope: Sync/Burst:
Closed Captions: Tracking: Vertical Blanking:
VITS: VIRS:
Luminance Avg.:   Luminance Peak: Chroma Peak:

	Levels		Tones			
Audio Track Content:	Avg.	Peak	100 Hz	1K	10K	Dolby
Ch1:						
Ch2:						
Ch3:						
Ch4:						
Cue:						
Audio Phase/Tone:	Audio Phase/Program:		Noise Reduction			

Comments:

_____

_____

This form is usually followed by a page of specific problems rated from acceptable to unacceptable and listed at particular timecodes. If it can be determined in the QC, it will be noted whether the problem is film-, video-, or audio-related.

Quality Control Costs

The costs for QC are usually billed by the hour. A 1-hour program with stereo audio on channels 1 and 2 and stereo M&E on channels 3 and 4 will require two passes. Between 2 1/2 and 3 hours will be required to 100% QC this tape. It will take about 15 to 30 minutes to spot-check this tape.

The accelerated schedules of TV does not always allow time to have a QC performed prior to network delivery. The network or cable company will do their own in-house quality check and come back to you with any fixes they want done.

QC is approached differently for foreign delivery. Often production companies will pay for a 100% QC prior to foreign delivery—especially for 1-, 2-, and 4-hour programs and cartoons.

Foreign Risks

After taking delivery of a videotape, the foreign distributor will usually order an independent quality check, either in-house or by hiring an outside company. The delivery master must pass this 100% QC on that tape before they accept delivery and provide payment. This QC is very thorough and extremely detailed. The foreign distributor will deliver to many different countries—each with varying rules for acceptance. Foreign distributors want to do all they can to assure that their clients will not have a technical reason for rejecting the program. After the foreign distributor has accepted delivery and made payment, they become financially responsible should any of their clients demand technical fixes in the future.

It is also prudent for you to insist on a 100% QC if you are shipping your program out of the country. This offers you some recourse or protection against liability if the tape arrives at your foreign client and that client claims the tape arrived damaged. With a 100% QC you have the word of a third party that the videotape was shipped without any physical damage and that any subsequent problems must have happened either during shipment or after the tape was received. This may not release you from having to replace the damaged tape, but it places some of the responsibility with the receiving end.

Who Is Responsible?

When you deliver your final videotape air master to a local network or cable company and the tape has physical damage, the postproduction facility will often provide a replacement tape on good faith, free of charge. But, if the tape has been shipped to another country and you did not order a QC prior to shipment, your postproduction house may not accept liability.

If you create both an NTSC and a PAL version of your master, you should budget to QC both masters.

Standards Conversion

Historically, international distributors have received either film (usually in the form of an IP or a print) or videotape transferred directly from finished film. However, now in television postproduction, negative is not always cut (or it is cut and vaulted). Often the only finished master is on videotape. This change has forced foreign distributors to begin accepting a videotape master for product shot on videotape or shot on film and posted electronically. In this case a down conversion (from high definition) or a standards conversion is the only method available for serving the international markets.

The down conversion process from high definition to standard definition may involve inserting 3:2 sequencing and assigning NTSC or PAL characteristics from the high def master. The NTSC-to-PAL (or vice versa) standards conversion is the process of changing the number of lines that make up the picture and possibly the frame rate as well.

As you've probably guessed, there are several types of standards conversions. Within the different types, there are also variables. The variables address the specific needs of the client that you are servicing. So, to determine what type of conversion is appropriate for you to use, there are several questions that need to be answered first.

NTSC (National Television Systems Committee) is named after the committee that established the color transmission system used in the United States, Canada, and Japan. It also refers to the system of 525 lines of information scanned at approximately 30 frames per second, the broadcast standard for North America (including Canada and Mexico) and Japan.

PAL (Phase Alternation Line) differs from NTSC in that it uses 625 lines of information and a 25-frames-per-second frame rate. PAL is the broadcast standard for many countries throughout the world.

These two systems are also what are referred to as "interlace." The horizontal lines that move from left to right and build from top to bottom of the screen make up the picture that you see. To produce the image on your television, these lines start at the top and travel across from left to right, filling in every other line, then when they come to the bottom of the screen, go back to the top and fill in all of the alternating lines. The odd lines are filled in first, then the even, thus, an interlace pattern is formed to make the picture you see on your television.

The Source Material

- Are you starting with a high definition or standard definition master?
- Is the material film-based, videotape based, or a mixture of the two?
- If high definition, what type of high definition master is it (720p, 1080I, 24p, etc.)?
- If standard definition, what standard is it (NTSC or PAL)?
- Is your master already a standards conversion?
- Does the master have an unbroken 3:2 sequence and is it field one dominant?

Your Delivery Requirement

- Are you delivering a high definition or standard definition element?
- If high definition, what resolution and frame rate are you to deliver?
- If standard definition, what standard do you need to deliver (NTSC or PAL)?
- Are you to deliver a field-based or frame-based conversion?
- Does the 3:2 need to be consecutive or be field one dominant?

It is important to answer these questions to know how to proceed and what to order.

Starting with a High Definition Master

Starting with a high definition (HD) master means that unless you are going to deliver a high definition tape, you will need to do a down conversion.

It is good to know the resolution and frame rate of your high definition source. In the currently available formats, 720 and 1080 lines of resolution are considered high definition (these are active lines of video), while 480 is not high definition. 480p is a progressive format and can be encoded for digital broadcast, but it does not fulfill the FCC high definition requirements. You might also know the frame rate of your master and whether or not it is interlace or progressive. Nowadays, you'll be able to find a facility that can convert any HD standard to any other HD standard. They are not all straight one-to-one conversions; that is why it is helpful for the facility to know your source information so they know how the work has to be completed and about how long it will take.

Delivering a standard definition (NTSC or PAL) element from a HD source will require a down conversion. Basically, you are taking something where a high number of lines make up the picture and creating something that has fewer lines making up the picture. You'll also be going to an interlace format if your HD master is progressive (such as 1080/24p).

Starting with a Standard Definition/Film-Based Source

If your source master is a standard definition master and you are delivering a standard definition master, the process can still be complicated because there are so many variables to consider.

The first item you want clear up is that your source is not already a standards conversion. There are a couple of reasons for this. Most notably, it is almost impossible to make a good conversion from a converted tape. This makes sense if you think about it. If your material was film-based originally, you've had to deal with the 3:2 pulldown. Therefore, in the initial conversion a machine had to determine where to either insert the additional video frames or delete them. Now you're asking a machine to do the opposite and there will be no guarantee that the same fields/frames will be affected, meaning you're going to end up with a tape full of interpolation and stutter movements. Sometimes you can perform a low-end or field based conversion on an already converted tape. However, the end result will still be inferior and these types of conversions are generally not accepted here in the United States or abroad. So, it is a good rule of thumb not to standards convert an already converted tape. Always insist on starting with a tape in its originally mastered standard.

Once you determine that you are not starting with a standards converted tape, you now need to decide what type of conversion is called for. If your master was made from film, then you will need to do a frame-based conversion. This will ensure that either the 3:2 will be properly inserted (if going from PAL to NTSC) or converted to 2:2 (if going from NTSC to PAL).

Delivering standard definition product that was originally produced as NTSC 525 lines in the United States, to any country other than Japan, Canada, and Mexico (which are also NTSC/525) requires that the video be upconverted to a PAL 625-lines signal.

There are several kinds of frame-based methods of standards conversions. DEFT and TK 3:2 are two popular ones. There are also several proprietary systems developed by individual facilities.

The DEFT (Digital Electronic Film Transfer) and TK 3:2, plus the handful of proprietary systems are used only when the material for the show that you are converting originated on film. These standards conversions can be used to go from NTSC to PAL. (There is also a reverse TK 3:2 process available to convert from PAL to NTSC.)

Primarily, these systems overcome the phenomenon of motion artifacts, or "motion judder." This movement was commonplace with earlier technologies and traditional field-based conversion systems and is unacceptable to most foreign concerns. There is a 4% runtime change when the frame-based conversion methods are used. That is due to the fact that when going from NTSC to PAL you are removing fields to eliminate the 3:2 (PAL is 2:2—two fields for each video frame), thus, there are less fields that make up the picture and the picture is shorter (by 4%). Going from PAL to NTSC, fields are inserted to create the 3:2 sequencing. Thus, there are now more fields that make up the picture than there were and the show now runs longer (again, 4%).

DEFT and TK 3:2 and the other high-end conversions are acceptable to the most critical foreign markets. They are also more expensive than some other conversion processes that are available. To QC these conversions, a highly trained person scrutinizes each scene to assure that all motion artifacts have been removed from the converted video.

Starting with a Standard Definition/Video-Based Source

Product that 1) originated on video; 2) has undergone time compression; 3) has program made up mostly of digital graphics or animation; or 4) includes a significant mixture of material that originated on film and video, is handled differently in the conversion process. The biggest difference is that because this material did not originate on film, there is no 3:2 sequence to mess with. Video is video is video. Only material transferred from film to videotape has 3:2. It is the result of putting 24-fps film onto 30-fps video; it just doesn't divide evenly. However, when something is shot on video, two fields for each video frame are recorded, it is much more straightforward. Therefore, when converting either from NTSC to PAL, or vice versa, all the conversion is concerned with is changing the lines of resolution and frame rate. It's a one for one process—or field for field, thus, the name "field-based" conversion. It also means that the runtime between NTSC and PAL will not change because you are not adding or subtracting fields.

Using Field-Based Conversions on Film-Originated Videotape

Technically speaking you can use a field-based converter on film-originated videotape. This just means that you do not correct for the 3:2. The most common time this option might be chosen is if you just need an inexpensive conversion from NTSC to PAL or PAL to NTSC to be used for viewing purposes. Otherwise, it is very unusual that a foreign client will accept this type of conversion. The only other time this might be acceptable is if maintaining the original program runtime is more important than the quality of the conversion.

The field-based conversion systems have always been plagued with various motion artifacts. A phase correlation process is usually used to successfully limit (or eliminate) the amount of picture judder (stutter) and movement. In the past this process has been difficult to perfect due to its complexity. However, recent advances in circuitry and digital hardware have made the process more widely available. The higher-end versions of these systems offer motion clean-up at edits and scene changes (called *clean cuts*).

Field Dominance

The last item we need to discuss regarding conversions is field one dominant masters. One thing that happens in the editing process is that edits are made solely for creative and artistic results. Consideration for "technically" what is happening at an edit point is not usually an issue. Well, not issues for the creative team, that is. But, there can be problems for certain delivery requirements down the road.

It seems very clear that the creative folks are not going to change the way they do their business. It then becomes incumbent on facilities to figure out how to create the materials needed down the road by their clients from what we will describe as politely as possible, *less than perfect masters*.

Specifically, we're talking about where in the video frame an edit is placed. Remembering that interlaced video frames are made up of two fields (the even lines and the odd lines), it follows that there is a 50% chance that the editor will edit on the odd lines (field one). There is an equal chance that the edit will fall on the even lines (field two). When an edit falls on field one, everyone is happy because we have an entire video frame to work with. However, when the edit falls on field two the editor is still happy, but those of us trying to work with this material down the road, are not. This is because we now have only half of a video frame and it really makes things tricky when converting material to another standard or when trying to encode the material for digital transmission. In both cases, the machine will falter when it comes to the broken sequence. This can cause some machines to stop and some to make wrong choices. Either way, it isn't good. You are so smart by now from reading this book that you already know that this is a phenomenon found only in interlace video and is not an issue for product that is posted in the progressive format. We mention it here only for those who came in during the middle. It also makes it difficult to access dubbed versions of programs that were NTSC and converted to PAL with a frame-based corrector. Ideally, if the programs stayed field one dominant, you could take the PAL converted master with the foreign language tracks and using a high end converter try and reconvert back to NTSC. Otherwise, a low end or 4-field converter will have to be used which will definitely introduce unwanted conversion artifacts throughout. For this reason, tracks are usually accessed and then a layback has to be done to an NTSC version, which costs both time and money.

We've already established that the answer is not to expect the creative team to change where it edits, albeit the most practical answer and one that will forever frustrate the engineers of our world that it is not an option. The answer then is to "correct" the field dominance somewhere in the mastering process. Right now that is done at one of several junctures in the postproduction path. Should you be delivering a standard definition master for digital broadcast, either you or the entity receiving the material will need to do this. If not, it will probably fall to the international folks to take care of. Right now, some studios and international distributors have taken it upon themselves to do this—knowing it will someday soon be a requirement, and some have not.

DVD PAL

The DVD PAL specification determines that all program material must be field one dominant. This is because in the Pause/Freeze mode the player assumes the field one dominance and combines field one and field two to make a "frozen" image. If the program is field two dominant, the machine will inadvertently combine field two from one frame and field one from the next frame and the freeze will not be a clear image but a partial image combined from two separate frames of information. This will cause the image to flicker back and forth between the two images.

Negative Cut/Negative Conform

Negative cutting is a concern only if negative is going to be cut—either for a film-finish, or later, to satisfy some delivery requirement.

Once your picture has been locked, the negative is physically cut and assembled according to your EDL (also called the negative cut list). This process matches back (conforms) your original negative to your final version of the show (either videotape cut or work print). The original negative contains numbers along one edge that serve as a reference for the negative cutter. These edge or key numbers are either originally gathered as part of the dailies film to tape transfer or printed through onto the work-print stock from the negative. The negative cutter matches back the edge numbers in the cut list to the original negative.

When you know you are going to need a negative cutter, it is best to choose one as early as possible—preferably before you start shooting. All the information the negative cutter will need comes off film, so it is helpful if you can include your negative cutter's requirements from the beginning of the postproduction process.

LokBox Cassette

These days, some negative cutters cut with the aid of a hard-lock synchronizer called a LokBox. To use a LokBox, the negative cutter will need a 3/4" cassette made to very definite specifications. Be sure to get those specifications from your negative cutter as early as possible. Traditionally, those specs include a 3/4" cassette made from either the off-line output of the locked picture or the final edited master. The 3/4" will need a visible window continuously displaying the key numbers, vertical interval timecode information (VITC) on specified lines, and no address-track timecode. The LokBox system synchronizes film to videotape. To maintain the sync relationship, the videotape must have VITC recorded on it. The synchronizer houses a built-in VITC reader. The reader locks to the VITC forcing the tape machine to stay with the film. The film is the demanding master, and the videotape follows like an obedient slave.

Some negative cutters use a pair of scissors to cut the negative, and then tape the splices together. This cut negative is then sent to a film laboratory with a negative assembly department to be hot-spliced together. Hot splicing creates a permanent bond that will pass through the film printing machines or telecine transfer without breaking apart.

If you are making a true film-finish show, complete with film print dailies, the negative cutting requirements are pretty basic. If any of the postproduction process is being done electronically, you will need to remember that film information (edge numbers/foot and frames) must come from the film. If you do a film to tape dailies transfer without gathering this information at the time of the transfer, the only way to recapture this information after the fact is to retransfer the film. This will add an additional expense that will be difficult to hide! This mistake is huge. It will not impress your producer and is definitely one of those "oops!" situations that could be a career-breaker.

It's only fair to mention here that there is technically one other way to retrieve key number if this is not done at the time of the dailies transfer. This is a very time-consuming process whereby the film is put back up on the telecine and the key numbers are recorded at each clap of the slate for the takes used in the final locked picture. The timecode on your original dailies is converted and feet and frames can be calculated.

Wrap-Up

As you can now appreciate because you made it to the end of this very long and information-intensive chapter, a lot goes into completing your film or video project.

Don't be intimidated by the number of steps covered in this chapter, our advice is consistent. Read your delivery requirements early, question anything you do not understand, and constantly update your postproduction schedule so you can keep track of where you are. As technology changes almost faster than we can keep up with from project to project, your film laboratory, sound house, and postproduction facilities will play a bigger and bigger role in helping you successfully finish your show. They won't be able to do that, however, if you don't ask them for help when you need it. They often have more up-to-date knowledge and experience because they are completing many different types of shows on a daily basis. That hands-on type of experience can be invaluable when trying to understand *how* and *why* things work. And they have continual access to the equipment manufacturers who are creating this technology.

10 Delivery

Contrary to what we may wish to happen, when it is time to deliver your product, the great antennaed stork does not swoop down, gather up all the precious elements you've nurtured through the postproduction process, and magically deliver them into the distributor's crib. You must get them there.

A Long Labor

Delivery begins with dailies (usually in the form of cassettes of dailies footage) and progresses in stages throughout the completion of your show. Delivery is completed only when you have fulfilled all of the delivery requirements and the distributor has accepted the elements. Make sure you get signed confirmation that the appropriate persons have received all the items listed in your delivery requirements. This is an important suggestion, as items have a way of getting lost, and if you cannot produce a signed receipt for all of the elements you delivered and things come up missing later, the onus will be on you to track them down.

Get the Delivery Agreement

At the start of your work on a picture, make sure you get a copy of the agreement that clearly outlines the delivery requirements for each of your distributors. These requirements tell you exactly which steps in the postproduction process you must complete.

To your producers, successful delivery is the most critical step in the postproduction process. Each day that passes beyond the delivery due date can translate into dollars lost by the production company. Distributors will not make the final payment until all of their delivery requirements have been met.

Makin' a List and Checkin' It Twice

In general, TV shows are delivered to a network or cable company, the foreign distributor, and the production company. Read through your individual network/domestic, foreign, and production company delivery requirements and make yourself one big checklist. The items on your checklist will vary depending on which distributors you are responsible to. It could be a lengthy list, and unlike the list St. Nick makes, naughty or nice, they will get what they want.

Large budget features are delivered to studios, international distributors, home video distributors, or specific territorial sales agents. Independent movies without a distributor will need to anticipate delivery requirements for theatrical release, video mastering, etc. Part of that will include dealing with contracts outlining the legal rights and requirements related to the project.

Combining all the material requirements serves two purposes. First, it keeps you organized, and let's face it, if you are not organized the show is in lots of trouble.

Second, you will find that some of these requirements overlap, allowing you to plan ahead and meet some of the criteria in more cost-effective ways. In fact, if your domestic and foreign distributors are one and the same, you may find that many items do overlap, helping you see that this part of your job may be less daunting than you originally thought.

Later in this chapter, you will find that each set of delivery requirements, network/domestic, foreign, and production company, is covered in detail.

Know Who Gets What

Delivery, of course, does not count if you do not deliver to the correct person in the correct department. Make sure you know who is expecting your materials. Neither your daily contact nor the person who sent the requirements may be the same person who gets the final product. When you determine who the appropriate persons are to receive the materials, call prior to the delivery date and introduce yourself. Confirm the delivery date with them. Let them know how you plan to get the materials to them, and determine if there are any special instructions. For example, will your delivery person need a drive-on (permission to enter the property)? Do their offices close at a certain time?

Accompany any materials with two copies of the delivery letter and have the appropriate person sign one of the copies upon receipt. Make sure the delivery company returns the signed delivery letter to you so you can add it to your files. We have found that wording the delivery letter as close as possible to the wording of the delivery requirements helps avoid confusion.

Figure 10.1 shows a sample delivery letter:

Figure 10.1 Sample Delivery Letter

Two Girls Production Company
2222 2nd Street 2nd floor
Hollywood, CA 90000
213-555-1212

September 27, 2001

Mr. Nick Rooty
Foreign Distributor Grande
5000 Galaxy Drive
Galaxy, CA 90002
RE: The Two Girls "Kiss 'N Tell"/Delivery

Dear Nick:
Per the Foreign Distributor Grande delivery requirements dated 1/1/01 for the above named movie of the week, please find accompanying this letter the following materials:

     1-Editor's Lined Script
     1-Camera and Sound Reports on Dailies
     1-Editor's Code Book
     1-Footage Worksheet
     All dubbing cue sheets for dialogue, music, sound effects, and foley
     1-Dialogue and cutting continuity script
     1-Closed caption disk
     1–24 track of the original score
     1–24 track stereo master of the complete picture
     1–35 mm four-track print master
     1-super 35 mm silent timed answer print
     1–35 mm print and negative of the textless backgrounds
     1-D2 NTSC master of the complete picture

If you have any questions or need any additional information, please don't hesitate to give me a call at the number listed above.

Sincerely,

One of the Two Girls

TG/og

cc: Producer
      Accounting
      Legal

The sample delivery letter in Figure 10.1 does not cover all of the items on our sample delivery list, just those that Mr. Rooty is scheduled to receive. If there is a point person you have been working with at the distributor regarding the general delivery of elements, make sure that person also receives a copy of this letter.

Network/Domestic Delivery

Each network and cable station has a pre-established set of delivery requirements. These requirements are usually part of a "delivery packet." Make sure the network sends this packet of information to you at the start of production. If you do not receive it, call your network contact, which will put you in touch with the appropriate department.

With the advent of high definition, and in anticipation of broadcasting in the 16 × 9 aspect ratio, networks have added additional delivery requirements. Hopefully you have read the network delivery list prior to setting up the dailies transfers and final mastering and will be able to deliver all the appropriate masters required. (See "Television Dailies" in the "Dailies" chapter for more details.)

A specialized department at the distribution company handles each step of the TV postproduction process. The number of different departments/people you will need to interface with usually depends on the size of the distributor. Creating a road map of who's who and what each person receives will help you.

Network Resources

Networks have a lot more in-house resources than some smaller cable stations and other distributors. Production stills are a good example. Networks will sometimes provide their own photographer on a shared-cost arrangement with the production company. The network therefore provides its own stills and you have access to all of the photographs, including gallery shots, for your foreign distribution requirement.

Even if the network retains the foreign distribution rights, it may be to your benefit to use the network's photographer. It insures that they will accept the quality and content of the stills. In addition, you won't have to hire a photographer.

Other packages available from a network may include duplication, formatting, and closed-captioning work. This may save you money in the long run, and, if they do the work, they generally have to accept it or make it right at their own expense.

These resources are not always available from a small distributor. For example, photographs, you may still be required to deliver publicity stills, but you must provide them at your own expense and using your own personnel. Don't hire your brother-in-law to take pictures unless he is a professional photographer. Professional stills are required. You will need to budget to pay the photographer's fees for several days of work.

Network Meetings

Some of the networks hold meetings prior to the start of production. In attendance will be the producer(s), postproduction supervisor, promotion department, publicity department, delivery folks, attorneys, photo department, and network executives.

These meetings can be useful for several reasons. You have a chance to meet the people you are going to be dealing with for the next several months. A timetable is established for each phase of the project. All expectations and "no-nos" are established up front. Any special needs, such as on-set interviews and specific promotional elements, can be arranged at this initial meeting.

One of the first departments you will work with is the promotions department. Sometimes this is combined with the publicity department, sometimes not. They will need materials to work with early on. Then there is the publicity department, which may have separate requirements. It sort of snowballs from there. Various executives will want copies of the show through its different stages of completion—dailies, producer's cut, rough cut, on-line, color correction and titling, etc.

Feeding the Promotions Department

The promotions department will want the cleanest copy of the rough cut or on-line master as soon as it is available for release. They will require split tracks (preferably separate dialogue, music, and effects tracks). This is much easier to accomplish now that digital formats are so commonplace. They have four audio channels, thus, allowing the promotions department to receive all of the tracks separately. After it is complete, they will also want an audiotape of the score.

In situations where an episodic or sitcom is not going to be completed in time for the promotions department to get their advertising on the air, they may elect to come in on their own dime and edit together some promotional material to broadcast. To promote an MOW with a tight postproduction schedule, they may ask for a partial or temp copy of the off-line of the show, go into the postproduction facility and cut something together from the masters, and pull something from that to air.

Network Delivery Packet

At the beginning of production you will receive a delivery packet from the network. This packet will include 1) a cover sheet, 2) a rate card, 3) a format sheet, 4) delivery requirements, 5) credit guidelines, 6) standards and practices guidelines, 7) music cue-sheet instructions, 8) broadcast technical specifications, and 9) film and TV diagrams.

Cover Sheet

The cover sheet will welcome you to the network folds, wish you the best of luck on the project, and offer assistance should you need it along the way.

Rate Card

If the network offers duplication as a service, a rate card will be included in their packet. These rates will cover multiple copies in various formats. Prices will vary by program length and number of copies ordered. They may also offer closed-caption encoding services. You will never be required by the network to utilize any of their duplication services. On the other hand, the prices may be very attractive, and it can be a convenient option.

Format Sheet

The format sheet will have the network IDs, commercials, etc., already filled in. There will be blank spaces wherever the information is to be completed by you. This sheet outlines exactly how your show is to be laid out for network delivery. It tells you where to put the commercial blacks when you format. It also gives a space to fill in the run time of each act. You will be required to provide timings for each section of program and commercial blacks at specified lengths and intervals. There will also be a requirement regarding program run time and main title and credit lengths. This is the length the show must be when you deliver.

The format sheet the network provides in your delivery packet will be appropriate to the show you are delivering. If yours is a half-hour sitcom, your format sheet will be specifically for a half-hour sitcom. If you are delivering a 2-hour MOW, then the format sheet will reflect that. Figures 10.2 and 10.3 are sample format sheets for a half-hour sitcom and a two-hour MOW. The *how's* of completing these forms are detailed in the chapter on "Completion." Basically, the format sheet should be a paper account of the layout of your entire program, including cold open, main title, each act, and commercial blacks.

Figure 10.2 Sample Format Sheet for Half-Hour Program

NETWORK: _____
PROGRAM/TITLE: _____
EPISODE #: _____   EPISODE TITLE: _____

DIRECTOR: _____   EDITOR: _____
AIR DATE: _____

FORMAT ITEM	IN	OUT	LENGTH
MAIN TITLE W/CREDITS (MAX :30)	01:00:00:00	01:00:31:00	00:00:31:00
ACT I	01:00:31:00	01:05:40:15	00:05:09:15
BLACK	01:05:40:15	01:05:50:15	00:00:10:00
ACT II	01:05:50:15	01:10:36:06	00:04:45:21
BUMPER (MAX :03)	01:10:36:06	01:10:39:03	00:00:02:27
BLACK	01:10:39:03	01:10:49:03	00:00:10:00
ACT III	01:10:49:03	01:22:04:15	00:11:15:10
BLACK	01:22:04:15	01:22:14:15	00:00:10:00
TAG/CREDITS	01:22:14:15	01:22:35:00	00:00:20:15
EXECUTIVE PRODUCER LOGO	01:22:35:00	01:22:38:00	00:00:03:00
NETWORK LOGO	01:22:38:00	01:22:41:00	00:00:03:00

FORMAT ITEM	LENGTH
SHOW TIME	
(INCL. COLD OPEN, MAIN TITLE,	
ACT 1,11,111, BUMPER	
TAG,CREDITS, and LOGOS)	00:22:11:00
SHOW TIME PER NETWORK	00:22:11:00
FORMAT BLACKS	00:00:30:00
TOTAL RUNNING TIME	00:22:41:00

TEXTLESS STARTS AT _____	INT'L TEXTLESS MATERIAL	TIMECODE
	MAIN TITLE	01:25:00:00
	ACT I	01:25:31:00
	ACT II	
	END CREDITS	01:26:40:00

COMPLETED BY _____ DATE _____ DELIVERY DATE _____

Figure 10.3 Sample Format Sheet for Two-Hour Movie-of-the-Week

NETWORK: _____   AIR DATE: _____
PROGRAM/TITLE: _____
EPISODE #: _____   EPISODE TITLE: _____
DIRECTOR: _____   EDITOR: _____

Network ID/Movie Opening	:35
Act I (incl. Main Title)	18:25
1st Commercial Position (1)	2:34
Corporate Promo	:45
Act II	9:52
2nd Commercial Position (2)	2:34
Network Title Card (w/Announce)	:05
Promo (Promo Swap)	:31
First Station Break	2:04
Network ID	:05
Act III	10:14
3rd Commercial Position (3)	2:04
Network Title Card (w/Announce)	:05
Local Affiliate Swap Position	:31
Second Station Break	1:34
Network ID	:05

--END OF REEL 1--

Act IV	19:05
4th Commercial Position (4)	3:05
In-Show Promo	:41
Act V	7:06
5th Commercial Position (5)	2:35
Network Title Card (w/Announce)	:05
Promo	:41
Third Station Break	1:49
Network ID	:05
Act VI	15:29
6th Commercial Position (6)	2:34
In-Show Promo	:41
Station Break	1:34
Act VII	10:14
In-Show Promo	:11
7th Commercial Position (7)	:31
Movie Trailer	:31
Credits	:60

Network Elements	**28:35**
Program Content Time (91:25)	**1:31:25**
	2:00:00

The run times you will need to complete this sheet can be calculated during your format session. If you off-line with the appropriate blacks built into your show, then you can also get this information from your assistant editor. Be sure to keep a copy of this format sheet in your paperwork and box it up with your other important papers. If you keep any videotapes with this same formatting, keep a copy of the format sheet in the tape box for easy reference.

Sometimes you can procure a small variance in the required run time of the program you deliver. This is usually granted to avoid a varispeed. But do not change the delivery run time without talking with your network contact. This must be approved prior to final delivery.

Delivery Requirements

The delivery requirements will come next. (Promotional and publicity requirements may also be listed here, or they may come as a separate section in the delivery packet.)

You will find listed here dailies requirements, master videotape format, rough-cut materials, credits, timing sheets, music cue-sheet requirements, and the names and telephone numbers of all the people who are to receive these materials. Confused by any of the items listed in this portion of your delivery packet? For crying out loud, call somebody! Make sure you understand each item completely.

Network delivery requirements outline the final delivery format (D2, D3, digital Betacam, etc.) along with the audio and video technical specifications. Even though these technical broadcast specifications are used industrywide, provide them to the facility doing your on-line, color correction, and delivery dubs, to avoid misunderstandings down the road. The delivery requirements will also outline any other special requirements (closed-captioning, VITC, etc.).

Along with videotapes and format sheets, delivery will include most, if not all, of the items on the checklist below. In this checklist, we have endeavored to include anything you might have to account for to satisfy your distributors' particular requirements. Remember that your list may be shorter than our list. If you are delivering both film elements and finished videotape, your delivery list will be longer than if your program was shot on videotape and videotape is all you're delivering.

The Network Final Delivery Checklist

This checklist is derived from items in actual network delivery packets. Dailies and rough-cut materials are not included here, as they have been handled earlier in the process. This list covers only those items included in the final delivery requirements, and remember your list may differ from this list, depending on your distributor.

Air Cassettes:

- (2) Standard Definition videotapes with drop frame timecode on the address track, closed captioned, and formatted to network delivery requirements. Do not use long-play stock (over 90 minutes in length). And, possibly, (1) HDCam high definition videotape formatted to network delivery requirements.
- (1) 3/4″ tape with channel 1 composite audio, channel 2 with timecode. Visible timecode in the upper part of picture and matching timecode on the address track (if the network is doing the captioning).

Screening Cassettes:

- (5) 3/4″ tapes with commercial blacks shortened to 2 seconds and stereo audio.
- (1) Betacam SP formatted the same as the 3/4″ tapes above.

Promotional Cassettes:

- (1) Digital Betacam with channel 1 dialogue, channel 2 effects, and channels 3 and 4 with stereo music. Timecode on the address track and textless at the tail of the program.
- (1) VHS with visible timecode matching the above D2.
- (1) 1/4″ audiotape of the theme music.
- (1) 1″ tape of the main title with the main title music and any appropriate fade-ups and fade-outs.

Other Stuff:

- (1) Act-by-act timing sheet.
- (6) Music cue sheets (also send a copy to BMI and ASCAP).
- (1) Printout of the final main and end credits.

In addition, your production company will have a series of cassettes they will require when the network delivery is completed. Some distributors will offer package deals if you hire them to make all of your delivery tapes. This is something else to check into when setting up with your vendors.

Credit Guidelines

If your cover letter does not specify the run time your show must be when delivered, you will find this information in a footnote or rule sheet. The rule sheet tells you to the second how long your program must run and where the act breaks must occur. You will also be told who is and who is not allowed to have screen credits and the person(s) at the network who must have final credit approval. Logo rules and screen placement will also be spelled out.

A special rule sheet on credits may be included. This will contain more detailed information on credit trade-outs (companies' compensation for allowing their products to be shot), length and legal limitations, and information about delivering your credits on floppy disk instead of paper copies.

Standards and Practices Guidelines

Some networks will include a standards and practices rule sheet from their legal department. This will outline the rules regarding profanity, nudity, product placement, and credit trade-outs. These guides follow FCC regulations and help the network establish, prior to delivery, responsibility for any editing required after delivery to meet these guidelines. Some producers will still keep a certain amount of profanity, violence, and nudity in a program and leave the onus with the network to demand they be removed.

It is not your job to determine what does or does not stay in a project—only to make sure your producer receives the guidelines.

Music Cue Sheet Instructions

Next may come the music cue-sheet examples. Give a copy to your music supervisor. These are standard forms, and your music supervisor will know how to fill them in for you. You are responsible for sending the final copies to ASCAP and BMI, the network, and any other entity that requires them. Take time to look over the forms to make sure all of the blanks are filled in.

Technical Broadcast Specifications

The network's technical broadcast specifications will come next. This is a rather large text of technical and engineering requirements. These vary little from network to network. To cover yourself, be sure to pass along a copy to your postproduction facility as soon as you receive them. If you look carefully, you will see that these also specify timecode requirements, blanking placements, audio and video levels, tape head formatting, etc.

Sometimes the networks will include information vital to you. So try to read them carefully, questioning any item you think may apply to what you are doing.

Framing Guidelines

Finally, there will be a film aperture and TV safe-area diagrams. These are standard TV measurements. Most postproduction houses have the ability to call up a prebuilt safe-area template on screen for you to use when titling or in determining if something in the picture will be picture-safe or outside the normal viewing area.

Making Use of the Delivery Packet

As soon as you get your delivery packet, make a copy of the delivery materials list. Use it as your master delivery list, noting in the margins when each element is delivered and to whom. Create a giant delivery list combining all departments' delivery requirement lists to catch any overlaps and economize your ordering of elements and work. This eliminates having to spend money to go back and create forgotten or missed elements because another pass is required. You can also consolidate or even speed up delivery by creating your various elements in an orderly and economical fashion. This may mean earlier payment for your producer.

Combining all of the requirements of the delivery packet for videotape, the following is a comprehensive list incorporating all the distributor's requirements. Again, this list will vary based on what your individual distributors demand.

Network Videotape Delivery List

- (4) D2 videotapes: (2) air masters with sweetened stereo audio, (1) promotional copy with dialogue only, (1) foreign master with separate stereo composite and music and effects tracks.
- (8) 3/4″ cassettes: (6) network copies ([1]-matching air master and [5] with shortened blacks), (1) production company library copy, (1) for the DP (if a contractual obligation).
- (1) Betacam SP for the network.
- (12) VHS viewing cassettes: (5) network, (1) production company library copy, (5) production company executives, (1) actor (if contractual); all made with shortened blacks.

International or Foreign Delivery

With the advent of high definition, and in anticipation of broadcasting in the 16×9 aspect ratio, foreign distributors have also added additional delivery requirements. Hopefully you have received and read the international delivery list prior to setting up the dailies transfers and final mastering and will be able to deliver all the appropriate masters required. (See "Television Dailies" in the "Dailies" chapter for more details.)

As with network delivery, the foreign distributor will provide a detailed set of delivery requirements. See "Foreign Delivery Checklist" later in this chapter.

Granting Access

If the foreign distributor has purchased all the rights to your show, your delivery materials list will be quite extensive. We culled the following list from a very large and very active distributor. If, however, the distributor purchased rights for only a specified length of time, the original negative and dailies trims and outs and other elements will remain the property of the executive producers. These materials will be sent to a vault or other holding area and must be inventoried and cataloged for the owner's files. An access letter (see Figure 10.4) will be sent to the company that is holding the materials specifying who may access them and under what conditions. Be sure it is typed on the appropriate letterhead.

Figure 10.4 Sample Access Letter

December 3, 2001

Hollywood Film Laboratory
2222 Hireme Lane
Hollywood, CA 90027
RE: "Charging at Windmills"

Dear Ladies/Gentlemen:

You have previously received from us, as a bailment, the following material (collectively "Materials") relating to the above entitled motion picture.

Ten (10) reels of 35 mm negative action
Ten (10) reels of 35 mm optical sound track negative

This letter will serve as authorization for you to grant full and complete access to any and all of the Materials to Laughing Pictures Entertainment, Inc., or any of its representatives or designees.

This authority will remain in effect unless revoked in writing by the undersigned.

Cora L. Filter
Cora L. Filter
President

cc: John Flush/HFL
        Horace Wrangler/LPE
        Jean Pocket/The Lawyers

Foreign Delivery Checklist

The following checklist will assist the distributor in securing or defending the rights to the picture and marketing the picture, as well as outline his financial obligations to the picture's participants, crew, and other licensees.

- (8) Cast and crew lists. The production coordinator can help you obtain these at the end of production.
- (19) Paper copies of the final main and end credits and a 3.5″ disk or CD-ROM of those credits.
- (8) Copies of the final script. This will also come from the production coordinator.
- (4) Sets of all the production reports. These, again, will come from the production coordinator. It may seem a lot to ask of one person, but if you arrange this with them ahead of time, they will be glad to run extra copies of whatever you need.
- (1) Editor's lined script. The foreign distributor will use this to find trims and outs. Often the foreign distributor will use this to reedit for length, foreign content, or even promotions.
- (1) Set of dailies camera and sound reports; also used for tracking trims and reediting.
- (1) Footage worksheet or timing sheet, or an act-by-act footage count if negative was cut.
- (1) Set of dubbing cue sheets covering music, dialogue, effects, and foley. These are road maps for all of the individual sound locations on the original and 24-track elements.
- (1) Dialogue continuity script. This is a list of all of the dialogue in the final version and the timecode at which it starts. It may also contain small descriptions of selected scenes and a footage count to locate these. Viewing a videotape with visible timecode creates the continuity, and a script comes back to you as a typed report. The continuity person usually charges by the reel or by the picture length. Foreign utilizes this for looping.
- (1) Closed-captioning disk (if available).
- (1) Original multitrack audio element of the entire score. Your music editor will provide this when the dub is completed.
- (1) Original multitrack audio master of your sound, music, dialogue, effects, and foley.
- (1) 35 mm 4-track print master. This is a mag of your final mixed sound. Foreign uses this to create masters with whatever audio configurations they need. Be certain that the effects and music tracks are a "full foreign fill." This means that all the sound effects originally part of the dialogue are on the music and effects tracks. This way no effects are lost when a foreign lan-

guage is substituted for the current dialogue track. Your foreign fill should be created as soon after the domestic mix is completed as possible—preferably the next day. Your sound facility can complete the foreign fill for a two-hour MOW in about 1 day.

- (1) Negative and print of alternative version of writing credit (when you are providing both a video and a feature version). If the credit reads Teleplay, this refers to the "video version." The feature version should read "Screenplay by." If the credit reads "Written by," no separate element is required.
- (1) 35mm negative and print of all textless backgrounds, including titles, credits, bumpers, subtitles, etc. Your optical department will make this upon request.
- (1) Original D1 or digital Betacam standard definition fully color-corrected master.
- (1) HDCam high definition fully color-corrected master. Aspect ratios: 4:3 and 16:9 in both letterbox and full frame. Sometimes the distributor will want to supervise this telecine or tape-to-tape color correction. However, any additional costs this incurs will be added to your bill. We advise that you are also present if foreign insists on supervising.
- (1) 35mm original cut negative (OCN). This must be complete with titles and opticals. Some distributors will even ask for super 35mm. Know this going in so that you can use the proper framing for shooting principal photography. The distributor will use this for striking new prints or transferring to videotape. Some distributors will have vaults to store this film in. Others will just want access letters sent to the facility storing the negative. This will be determined by who has final ownership of the picture.
- (1) Fully-timed interpositive
- (1) One light internegative
- (1) Composite check print mounted on reels and packed for shipping.
- All original trims and outs, opticals, title tests and trims, including those trims and outs used for a foreign version. These can be used for recuts and sometimes for promotions. Get these from your lab/negative cutter/editor. In the case of *Star Wars,* George Lucas kept all the optical elements in his personal vault, and 20 years later he used them to restore the film to its original condition.
- All telecine masters, logos, and edit decision lists (EDLs). Get the EDL from your editor.
- All production audio. You will retrieve these from the sound-effects company. Your distributor may have a vault or they may be vaulted with the company that did the audio transfers. An access letter to that facility may be all that is required.
- (1) 3/4″ off-line cassette of the final cut with timecode corresponding to the final negative cut list. This can be the same cassette generated by your assis-

tant editor to be used as a reference in the on-line. If you did not on-line, this cassette can be the final locked version output from your off-line system.

- All film interpositive materials and count sheets for title cards, mattes, overlays, opticals for titles, bumpers, and opticals. Also any video-generated material for the above. Used for generating any new title treatments and restoring opticals.

- (1) Copy of all literary material acquired or written for the picture, which includes one copy of each script draft (each draft version is identified by a change in paper color, and the version number will be on the cover page) labeled with the writer's name and the date. A list of all of the public-domain materials used in the picture, including literary, dramatic, and musical, and those that provided the services to clear the rights to use the public-domain material, must be provided. This will help the distributor's legal department in securing or defending the rights of the picture.

- (1) Copy of each contract and/or license for the use of screen credits in print advertising and paid advertising obligations. These contracts detail who gets credit and under what circumstances. If you have the contracts, you can supply this information. If not, get the information from your legal department.

- All writing credit documentation. This includes the notice of tentative writing credit, any arbitration material, and final received-by signatures. These will be in your files.

- A schedule or report of the following information, to be used to compute residual payments when the picture is replayed, shown in foreign theaters, or sold in the home video market, or if the musical sound track is sold. All of these details come from your accounting department or your legal department. Traditionally, the accounting department has the information, so start there. This information must include: a) production dates and locations (these can also be obtained from the production coordinator's call sheets or production reports); b) a list of all actors—including loop group players. Make sure the social security number, guaranteed days, days actually worked, salary, loan out or gross participation, and SAG status are included for each person affected; c) names of director, first and second assistant directors, and the unit production manager, along with their social security numbers, guaranteed days, days worked, etc.; d) a list of the writers and all of their pertinent information; e) total dollar amount for salaries below the line and any IATSE labor; f) list of any other individuals entitled to gross or participation moneys; and g) a list of all individuals or companies that require credit in paid advertisements.

- (6) Copies of the music cue sheets and the cover sheet indicating who else you provided with cue sheets.

- All composer agreements, sync licenses, master record licenses, and artists' licenses (singers). Any music licenses you have—including needle drop licenses. These can all come from the legal department.
- The original written score. This will come from your music supervisor. If there is no written score, a memo to this effect from the music composer will suffice.
- If musicians were hired, include a copy of the AFM report, social security numbers for the musicians, and their salaries and AFM status. Your accounting department will have this information. If you did not use AFM musicians, a memo to this effect from the composer will suffice.
- All accounting records, including checks, vendor files, bank reconciliations, and payroll records from pre-production through postproduction. Your accounting department will provide these materials. Also have them prepare an inventory and include a copy inside the boxes with the records and a copy taped to the outside.
- (20) Black-and-white still photographs titled and captioned with each actor's real and character names. If the main actors retain still photography approval, begin early so that their approval does not hold up this process. The stills come from your photographer and it is your responsibility to label each shot.
- (100) Color transparencies labeled as copy information. Transparencies, also known as slides, come from your photographer.
- (1) 8 × 10 main art color transparency. This will be made from your main title card and it can be purchased from the optical house or department.
- (1) Billing block outlining credit requirements, paid advertisement requirements, and photo approval. Obtain this from the legal department.
- Biographies on actors, director, producers, and writers. These come from the manager or agents and sometimes, in the case of producers, directly from the person. Start early and have them faxed to you. It will take some time to collect all of these. Requesting them at the time your looping session starts usually works. This material helps the distributor market the picture.
- A 1- to 3-page synopsis of the picture. This is a marketing tool. Often the promotional departments will have something you can use. Or, you may have to write something yourself and get producer approval for publication.
- Reviews—you can try to collect these yourself or get them from the network. Often the picture is delivered in such a rush that these are not available.
- (1) Cast and crew list with the name of the characters and the actors' real names and the crew members' titles next to their names. This comes from your production coordinator.
- Internegative or interpositive—some distributors will want you to provide these or have the negative available to make these to avoid overuse of the original cut negative.

If you created your project on video or data and recorded out to film, your delivery items might also include:

- Original color-corrected video master
- Original data file used for film recording
- Access to negative (from film out) may also be called an optical dupe

If this is a theatrical release you will also need to create an IP for future release prints. These items are in addition to any textless, sound, or accounting and legal documents previously listed.

If you are delivering for digital cinema release, you will deliver a D5 high definition master with 5.1 audio or a separate audio element as specified.

Remember that the number of delivery items you will be required to provide depends on who has picture ownership. If the producers sold the picture outright to the foreign distributor, the distributor will want every element and legal document made. If the ownership remains with the producers, only access to the original negative and sound, delivery of internegatives or videotape masters, and the usual legal paperwork and photographs will be required. These will be outlined in the distributor's obligations and materials for promotional use.

Foreign Formatting

Again, whether foreign distribution formatting will need to be done in an edit bay will be determined by the individual specifications. If the delivery requirements call for blacks to be pulled up to exactly ten frames, you should do this in an edit bay rather than relying on someone in your duplication department to do this machine to machine. Again, be careful not to upcut the music. Make sure to start counting the ten frames after the music ring-out is completed.

You must also include textless material at the tail of your foreign delivery master. Occasionally a company will require that the textless are provided on a separate reel, but usually they want it to start 30 or 60 seconds after the end of program. Textless material must be provided for all parts of the program that have text. This includes the main title, opening credits, end credits, bumpers, and any parts in the body of the show that have text—such as locales and legends. Textless material is formatted in the titling session. For more information on textless material, see the "Titling" section in the "Completion" chapter.

Detailed information regarding formatting your program for foreign delivery is located in the "Completion" chapter.

Foreign distributors will also require separate music and effects (M&E) audio channels if they are available. Most modern-day videotape delivery formats have four channels of audio so the M&E tracks can be included on the delivery master in stereo without losing the English composite track.

Remember that there may be additional delivery elements for foreign distribution that are not required by the networks. As noted earlier, these can include trailers, slides, music cue sheets, continuity scripts, and separate audio elements. Don't wait until you are ready to deliver to compile your foreign delivery requirements. Your company won't be paid until they deliver all of the required elements. Going back to recreate elements can be expensive and hold up delivery and incoming moneys.

Details that seemed so minor compared to all the postproduction emergencies you were handling with levelheaded authority can surface at the eleventh hour and catch you. Many companies have specific box-size (the size of the box you pack their elements in for delivery) and box-labeling requirements. Check these out ahead of time. If possible, get them in writing so you can pass the information on if someone else will be physically packing the materials into boxes.

Production Company Delivery

Compared to the networks and foreign distributors, the production company delivery requirements will seem like a walk in the park.

Most production companies will have very simple requirements. Often it will be all of your notes and files documenting delivery and files of contracts and videotapes for the producers'/executives' personal use. If the picture is sold in total to the distributor there will be very little film or videotape material to retain, as the producer will not have the right to reproduce the picture for anything other than a record of the accomplishment.

If, however, the producer retains ownership of the project, you should make a road map showing where all the remaining materials live. There will be negative at the lab, sound at the transfer house, and trims, outs, and master videotape materials in storage. Some producers keep very little of the trims or videotape on-line and off-line material, so confer with them and find out their requirements.

Cast/Crew Cassette Copies

Often cast and crew members asking for cassette copies of the show will approach you. Sometimes there is a contractual obligation to provide these cassettes. You should have a list of these obligations when you make all of the final materials. However, if this is not a contractual requirement, check with your producer before allowing a copy of the show to be borrowed or made. Unauthorized copies could cause a legal problem, and the producer could be sued. Ask the legal department to make a 1-page agreement for the requesting party to sign before receiving a videocassette copy. Usually they just want the footage to add to their work reel.

Technical Requirements for Cassettes

Production companies don't usually care to have their library and viewing tapes closed captioned (but be sure to double-check this . . . there's always an exception to every rule). If your show was formatted in on-line with long commercial breaks, you may want to make these cassettes with the blacks shortened. This can be done machine-to-machine instead of in an edit bay. The charge should be your regular duplication cost plus a small machine-edit charge. If you are going to need a lot of pulled-blacks cassettes it may help to create a pulled-blacks submaster to avoid picture glitches on the cassettes. You can use a low-cost tape stock, such as 1″, for this intermediary step.

Production Company Delivery Checklist

The production company's delivery requirements will depend primarily on whether the producers retain the rights or the rights are sold to another distributor.

Regardless of who retains the rights, the production executives and possibly the cinematographer, the director, and some of the cast are going to want copies for their personal libraries and reels.

The relative simplicity of production company delivery expectations compared to the rigmarole that domestic and foreign distributors put you through should not negate the value of a checklist. In the heat of the delivery moment, things can get harried, and a forgotten executive could do more to hurt your reputation on the job than admitting you cross-dress!

When the Producer Sells the Rights

When the producer has relinquished all rights to the picture, the production company delivery list will be very short. This order will consist of one or more 3/4″ copies and several 1/2″ copies. Be sure to poll everyone before you put this order in with the duplication facility. Check into any possible contractual agreements with stars or crew members who have been promised cassettes. Some companies split up who makes these cassettes. The more prominent members of the production company may get cassettes made by the duplication facility, because the quality is usually better. They may then order a Betacam SP or 3/4″ for making any additional cassettes in the office.

The cassettes made at a professional tape house will be of a higher quality because they will make them from a better source tape and their equipment is presumably commercial grade with regular maintenance. However, the cassettes made in your office can be made virtually for the cost of the stock, thus lessening the burden on your probably already overburdened budget.

If the production company wants viewing cassettes made for their executives and staff, or if they request a playback source for making their own copies, they will want these tapes to have shortened or pulled blacks. This means that the formatting and blacks between acts that were put in for the air master delivery are taken out. Executives are notorious for not having the patience to sit through a 10-second black between acts. They will usually want the blacks no more than 5 seconds or even 2 seconds in length.

It Rings True

A word of caution when making a pulled-blacks videotape: be very careful that the facility does not up-cut (cut off) any music ring-out. If an executive views a cassette you've had made for their library and the music is cut off, you will have a really hard time convincing that person that it is not that way the on the air copy is. You'll probably have to order a new cassette (at the facility's expense, of course).

When the Producer Retains the Rights

Low budget independent features (Indies) are often complete and have screened around the globe before the executive producer has realized one penny of profit. They may have screened in film festivals and film markets for months looking for a suitable buyer. Many important details can be forgotten due to the extended amount of time that may elapse between the completion of an Indie project and it's purchase. For example, a distributor may want to add or change a title over action, which means you will have to find all the textless and texted materials needed to create the original titles in a timely manor. The elements might be at the optical house where the titles were made, they may be at the laboratory, or they may be at the negative cutters. An hour of phone calls later you will realize how important it is to keep track of your elements.

Try to keep all of your masters together. Keep the negative at the film lab and video at the video facility if you do not have access to an appropriate centralized vault. It will also help to make textless backgrounds and other material required by distributors. Keeping your paperwork organized and in legal and accounting order will save you from scrambling when the big sale hits. Be aware that sometimes distributors will want creative changes. It may be due to bad language; reference to a product, person, or thing; or just to tailor the project to their audience. If you have made all your delivery masters prior to the sale you will now have to edit those masters. Choose carefully which materials get made and only make the elements you need as sales tools prior to that big sale.

When the producer retains ownership of the negative, your production company checklist will look something like the following:

- (1) Cut or uncut negative of the entire show. This is usually stored at a vaulting facility.

- (1) Interpositive of the full feature.
- All film interpositive materials and count sheets for title cards, mattes, overlays, opticals for titles, bumpers, and opticals. Also any video-generated material for the above. Used for generating any new title treatments and restoring opticals.
- (1) Multitrack audio masters of the entire show including any filled music and effects tracks. This is usually stored at a vaulting facility.
- (1) D1 or digital Betacam master with textless at the tail, dialogue, music, and effects split out onto separate tracks. Delivered in 4:3 and 16:9 full frame and letterbox. This is usually stored at a vaulting facility or with a duplication facility.
- Positive and negative trims and outs stored at a vaulting facility. These boxes should be inventoried and numbered. One copy of the inventory should be inside the box, and one should be taped on the outside of the box.
- All editorial paperwork boxed and labeled with an inventory inside and one on the outside. Included in this material will be a lined script, act-by-act timing sheets, opticals orders, negative cut list, EDLs, etc.
- The postproduction supervisor or associate producer's paperwork boxed and labeled with an inventory inside and one on the outside.

The above material will allow your show to be formatted to meet future needs.

If the producer is retaining all rights, there may be additional items on the delivery requirements. In fact, these delivery requirements could follow the foreign checklist very closely.

Taking Stock

Some production companies that produce several shows a year choose to make or save a little money by bartering or selling their trims and outs to stock houses.

Establishing shots and crowd scenes and any potential stock location shots or specialty shots may be of interest to a stock house. If the producer retains the rights to the show, there may be an arrangement that can be worked out with a stock house. The stock house receives a videocassette of the show and all the film trims and outs. They pull out the negative they want and the rest goes into storage with the rest of the program elements. Then, whenever the stock house rents or sells any of the shots, the production company will receive a percentage of the fee. In addition, should the producer want to use any of these shots again, they will be available at a discount, or possibly at no charge. This is a way for the producer to receive extra income from the production.

Executive Quality

Most importantly (after meeting the delivery deadline, that is), the production company executives are going to want high-quality 3/4″ or VHS copies from the final color-corrected, sweetened (stereo) digital master. Determine how many you need and whether you should have individual names typed on the cassette labels. You also need to know when they expect to receive their tapes. If you deliver to the network on Friday night, you may need to messenger tapes to the production company executives' homes, or they may be willing to wait until Monday morning to receive their copies.

Delivering

Once you have created all of the required elements and gathered all necessary paper-work, you are ready to deliver. Make sure you double-check everything, label each item as instructed, and box and inventory as required. Proper labeling may save your neck and will certainly make it easier to distinguish what is what if you have multiple versions of your project. Video master labels need to include:

- Production company name
- The final title of the show and a.k.a. if needed
- The date the element was made
- Run time
- Whether tape is subtitled or captioned
- If the tape contains textless title backgrounds and where they begin
- Note if this tape one of multiples, e.g., Tape 2 of 2
- Aspect ratio
- Type of conversion (if applicable)
- Purchase order number
- Channel configuration
- Language

When boxing up elements be sure to include on the outside of the box and on the inventory inside the box:

- Production company name
- Final show title and a.k.a. if needed
- Boxes must be labeled and inventoried. Each box label needs to include: box number, e.g., Box 26 of 50.

Be sure to place a master inventory sheet on top of box one and inside each box prior to sealing.

With this done your office will begin to resemble a warehouse, with boxes stacked high. Get rid of everything as soon as you can. When all the items are delivered and have been accepted at their respective destinations, you are no longer responsible for their safety. Accompany elements with a detailed delivery letter stating what materials are being delivered, when, and where. Again, utilize the wording from the delivery requirements. This makes the distributor more comfortable that what is delivered matches what was requested. Be sure to send your foreign or network point person a copy of this letter if their material is being delivered somewhere else.

Put your delivery instructions in writing for those responsible for the actual delivery. Also, require that a signature be obtained (written and legibly printed) whenever any element is delivered. Make sure you retain all of these "received-by" signatures in your files. These will prove that the materials were delivered and put the onus on someone else for locating lost or misplaced items. As an extra precaution, take time to call the receiving facility or contact person to let them know what materials are coming and when.

Delivery is a great relief. It's the reward for all the work you've done to get your show on the air. Don't botch the moment with some careless faux pas. And remember, get all the appropriate signatures as you move along the postproduction path. This way, if there is a mistake that doesn't come out until your program has been broadcast, you will have some company with you in the doghouse.

11   Legal

Lawyers are our friends, and they are here to protect us and look out for our best interest (and I have some swamp land to sell you . . .). No, seriously, attorneys are an important part of any movie or TV project. And, it is important to know when they need to be consulted and the most cost-effective way to work with them. We are going to guide you in this area.

Some of the suggestions in this chapter may save you from expensive and embarrassing legal hassles. Some are just common sense and "cover yourself" kinds of stuff. But, it's good sometimes to be reminded about the legal ramifications and the responsibilities that go with the job.

Sooner or later one or more lawyers will be involved in some phase of your project's postproduction process. These lawyers will have the power to second-guess each decision you make to your personal frustration and possible embarrassment. Their involvement will either help you or slow down the process to a crawl. Because of this, it is important to understand how to work with attorneys and get the most out of what they can do to help you. It is our experience that trying to work around the attorneys often backfires. And, if it comes down to them or you . . . guess who almost always has the last say.

Worthwhile Advice

When you have access to an attorney, consult with that attorney for approval on all contracts and license agreements. This is particularly important whenever there is unclear language in contracts, licenses, or delivery requirements.

As you go through the various steps in the postproduction process, protect yourself by getting everything you can in writing—especially regarding services performed. Then back yourself with a memo in case there is any question on anything you or someone else agreed to. Whenever appropriate—or maybe whenever you can—get all signed agreements and releases faxed or mailed back to you.

While some of what is in access letters and laboratory agreements is considered "technical information" about which lawyers are ignorant, these documents have serious legal ramifications. It is important to have someone in your legal department look over the wording of these documents before they are signed. For many documents, it may also be appropriate that they be signed by someone with "ultimate authority."

To achieve timely and worthwhile results, agreements must be reviewed legally early in the process. After you have committed to using certain stock-footage, for example, or awarded work to a particular facility, you or your attorneys will have little leverage to change what you do not like. And, if you really do not like what can no longer be changed, you may be faced with expensive and embarrassing replacement costs.

On a final note, it is a good idea to check with your attorneys before making payments on deals that remain "in negotiation."

Five Reasons to Check with the Lawyers

To help you determine which steps of postproduction may have legal ramifications, we've broken this chapter down into five easy pieces.

Stock Footage

Before purchasing stock footage (or music, for that matter), get a blank contract from the vendor(s) with whom you are negotiating. If you have a legal department at your disposal, send a copy of the blank contract for their review. Chances are they will want to change some of the wording. Often standard agreements do not grant the rights they purport to. You will need to ask the vendor to approve the new language and have it incorporated into your license agreement before the deal is signed. This saves you the difficulty of having to go back after the fact to try to rearrange the rules.

Although many of the details of stock footage are taken care of in postproduction, the availability of such footage can be a determining factor in planning the shooting schedule and budgeting. Therefore, sometimes research on available stock footage is done during pre-production. The production executives will need to decide if there is suitable footage available for a certain location that can be incorporated into their story. If not, they will need to shoot at the location to get exactly the footage they need. If appropriate, check with the production coordinator to see if any research was done for stock shots prior to shooting.

There are many stock-footage houses around. Prices are pretty consistent from house to house. Final costs will depend on the extent of the rights that are granted and how many feet of a certain clip you are planning to use. Based on your descriptions, stock houses will provide a print or videotape of the various shots available. Look at the clips with your editors and producers and determine which ones you will purchase the rights to.

Music

If you are working on a show for a large production company or studio, they will employ a music coordinator to secure bids and finalize licenses. We strongly recommend this whenever possible. The best coordinators are typically more knowledgeable than attorneys about this area.

The decision about which rights to clear, questions regarding financing, licensing, and insurance are, at least in part, beyond the authority of the postproduction supervisor. Direct these questions to a higher authority. Do not take the risk that a unilateral decision on your part will put your production company in breach of contract with its distributors.

Even though you may not be making the final decision, there is groundwork you will need to complete before the producers will have enough information to make a decision:

1. Determine the foreign distributor's requirements regarding music rights and clearances;
2. Determine the producer's expectations regarding the feel and length of the piece, along with cost limitations; and
3. Determine if you need the rights to the lyrics (sync) or the recording (master). If your actor is going to sing the song, you want the sync. If you are going to hear the song from a jukebox, you want the master.

To receive a bid on licensing a piece of music, call BMI and ASCAP. These are not unions, but rather watchdog societies that track all music used or played over the air. They also track royalties. Ask for their index department to find out who holds the copyright(s) for the song(s) you are interested in. You may find that several publishers own the rights or that a publisher holds the rights in the United States but not in other countries. You will probably need to obtain the rights for worldwide distribution, so be thorough. Call whoever the copyright holder is and ask for a cost. Most likely, you'll need to submit your request in writing and include the following:

1. What the music will be used for (feature, MOW, etc.).
2. How much of the music you are planning to use (the entire piece, a certain number of bars, etc.).
3. The scene in which the music will be used.

Fax the request. It may take several days to get the quote back. Not all music can be purchased for perpetuity, world distribution, or all media (many have five-year options). Let an attorney guide you on this; it can get complicated. The publisher may inquire regarding video buy-outs and whether the show will appear on TV or as a feature. Music clearances are not something you can learn in a day. With the help of an attorney, sometimes deals can be structured in a way so that someone other than the producer, such as the distributor, bears part of the costs.

The actual music license may take weeks to finish and execute. You may end up using the song long before all of the paperwork has been completed. That is why it is crucial to have legal or music coordinator assistance. In lieu of an attorney, a music coordinator may be willing to assure you and your insurers that the music has been "cleared" pending completion of the paperwork.

Copyright protection laws used to be very complicated and vary widely from country to country. In the past few decades, the basics have become standardized as a result of international copyright treaties. Our attorneys recommend that your legal department handle all copyright issues, and be involved in all discussion regarding copyrights and chain of title. Chain of title refers to the history of title transfers and rights for a property.

Products

Products are physical items for which use must be licensed that are featured in a show. Some examples would be a Smashing Pumpkins T-shirt, a Gorman painting, a name brand on a food label, or an actual magazine cover. To obtain a license to use these items you will need to find out the product owner, then:

1. Call the company and determine who negotiates the use of their product in a TV show.
2. Explain how you to plan to use the product (cable, broadcast series, feature, etc.).
3. Find out how to get permission to use the product (not all companies charge a fee).
4. Provide them with a scene description and when is the scheduled airdate.

They will want this information in writing. Fax it. When the copyright holder grants permission, whether or not there is a fee involved, be sure the response is in writing and includes all media, worldwide rights, and perpetuity.

If a fee is involved, present the quote to the producer(s). If they agree on the fee and the terms of the license, confirm this with the copyright holder via fax. Make sure you receive the copyright holder's signature of agreement before sending payment. Have an attorney review the agreement before it is signed.

Some companies may request screen credit in lieu of payment or for a reduced fee. This decision is for the network and the producer(s) to make. Do not agree to any screen credit without prior approval. Be aware that federal regulations and network broadcast standards and practices (BSP) require the disclosure of any deals in which a producer accepts "consideration" (e.g., a product discount, free airfare, or free product use) in return for inclusion of a product in a production. The disclosure rules are complicated; to cover yourself it is best to disclose everything to the person you report to or the network and let them decide how to handle the situation.

An item containing a photograph of a person, such as on a movie poster or magazine cover will generally require permission from the person in the picture as well as the photographer and/or the copyright holder. If the photograph is of an actor he or she will usually want payment for use. Be sure you have obtained the rights of all parties involved or received legal assurance that such rights need not be obtained.

References

This involves any mention of a person, place, or thing in the body of a show. If the reference is casual, nonderogatory, and not a featured story point, you are clear to use the reference in dialogue. However, if the reference shows a person or product in a derogatory way, you could be looking at a lawsuit. Furthermore, even if something is legally okay, it may violate standards and practices, embarrass a network, or lead to a series of letters from the named person's or element's representatives. Be careful—when in doubt let someone higher up make the call.

References can get tricky when you're talking about inferences. Say you have a scene in a bar and the bartender is making references to how great Elvis songs are. In the background Elvis-style music is playing, but it is not actually Elvis Presley singing. This may mislead the audience to believe that it is Elvis music they are hearing: therefore, permission from his estate may be required. When you think you are in a potentially gray area, it is always best to consult your attorney.

Film Clips

Use of a film clip for playback on a TV on the set, or in a movie theater, requires special handling. First, you will need to secure the rights to use the clip; second, you may need to do a film transfer, rent a special type of projector, or arrange special lighting.

There are two ways to approach obtaining film clips. First, there are several firms that will grant rights to films, sporting events, newsreels, cartoons, and old TV shows for a set fee. The film libraries will have catalogues for you to choose from.

If you are looking for a certain film, such as *Star Wars*, you must contact the copyright holder and go through the channels outlined above to obtain the rights. Normally the costs are extreme. Part of this cost is to cover the actors, who must be paid a residual every time the clip is seen. Another part of the cost goes to pay the composer of any music included in the clip. There may also be others attached to use of a clip. The person providing the license will also provide a list of those who must be compensated, and this compensation is usually included in the cost of the license.

As with music and stock footage, begin the clip licensing process as early on as possible. Determine costs and legalities and then discuss them with your producer.

Disclaimers

A disclaimer is another legal tool that affects all television programs. Disclaimers are pretty standard, and your company should have one already created for you to use.

The disclaimer usually goes at the very end of the end credits, just before the logos appear. There is no hard and fast rule about how long the disclaimer must remain on the screen. Below is a sample of a disclaimer used in a TV program. Occasionally the foreign distributor will have some input into the wording of your disclaimer. It is best to always have your legal department determine the wording of your disclaimer.

Sample Disclaimer

The characters and events depicted in this motion picture are fictional. Any similarities to actual persons, living or dead, are purely coincidental.
This motion picture is protected by the copyright laws of The United States of America and other countries. Any unauthorized duplication, copying, or use of all or part of this motion picture may result in civil liabilities and/or criminal prosecution in accordance with applicable laws.
(c) 1991 (place company name here)
All Rights Reserved. Country of first publication: United States of America.
(place company name here) is the author of this motion picture for purposes of the Berne Convention and all national laws giving effect thereto.

Disclaimers like the one above are designed to protect the show's copyright holder or distributor from infringement and other legal battles stemming from any misuse of this protected material.

Is It Clear?

Keep in mind that obtaining stock footage and music—especially music—clearances can be very time-consuming and costly. Before you go through the steps, make sure that your producer really wants to pursue use of the material and that you're not jumping to the whim of the editor. If you cannot cut around or substitute and your producer gives the go-ahead, then proceed.

Stock footage clearances, music clearances, product use and placement, references or inferences, and film clip clearances are the primary areas in which you will find you need legal advice. Other areas covered in previous chapters, such as finalizing titles and credits and obtaining main title use clearance, will also require input from your legal department.

Often, common sense will be your best defense against legal trouble. If there is any doubt about anything you are doing, consult your legal department. Remember to get signatures on all agreements and releases and keep hard copies in your files.

Just remember that anytime a decision is being made that involves signing a contract or agreement, it is probably a good idea to run it by your legal staff. Contracts are binding and it is important to ensure that what is being agreed to will not be a decision that could turn costly or result in some type of legal action down the road. Long after you complete a project and move on, the details of that project will live on.

12   Acquisition

Acquisition . . . the act of acquiring or gaining something.

What Is an Acquisition Title?

An *acquisition title* is a feature film, TV show, documentary, etc. that is purchased by a studio, network, or distribution company for the purpose of distribution. This may be brand new product or even an older library of movies or TV series. Sometimes this is referred to as the "back-end" (the product is being "picked up" for distribution after it has been created). Often the license fees paid for the distribution rights represent a sizeable amount of money for the producer, so it is very important that all delivery requirements are met. This can get complicated because there will probably be multiple "distributors" for product and there will be differences in their delivery requirements.

There are many outlets for distribution of entertainment product, and within those areas there are varying degrees of license rights. These include domestic free TV, international free TV, domestic pay TV (cable or satellite pay-per-view channels), international pay TV, video-on-demand (hotels/airlines), and home video/DVD. There are also others, such as the military, Internet, streaming video, etc.

Within these categories, you may have wide-ranging rights or very limited rights regarding the territories to which you can distribute and for how long. For example, "all media, worldwide, in perpetuity" means the distributor has full rights to distribute the acquired title anywhere in the world. The title can be distributed via any medium from the date of the contract until the end of time. Buying only free TV in France and Germany implies a very different thing. Because these two scenarios are so different, the materials needed to service all media worldwide and free TV in France and Germany can vary a lot.

With all of the variable markets and legal limitations, it is important to create product of the highest technical quality that will be acceptable in all distribution scenarios. We're going to help you do just that.

What If You're Just a Little Guy

So, you are an independent filmmaker, making a movie and you hope to sell the distribution rights to a major motion picture studio. The rights you sell will determine the materials you will need to provide. If you are lucky enough to know who the distributor is before you complete work on your project, your job is easier. You can request a list of delivery requirements and technical specifications up-front. This makes it possible to prepare the necessary materials as you go, which will be more efficient and cost effective for you.

However, this is not always the situation. There is a good chance that you will make your independent film then shop it at festivals and distribution conventions looking for a company or companies to pick up the distribution.

Determining Delivery Elements

When you can't get specific delivery requirements and technical specifications ahead of time, you'll have to do your homework to determine what is normally expected. Be aware that in addition to the picture elements there are legal documents the licensor will need before final payment is made.

In the "Delivery" chapter of this book, we have provided a very comprehensive list of delivery elements that you may be required to provide as part of your distribution contract. You may also be able to get various studios or distribution companies to give you sample delivery requirements to use as a guide. Also, if you are working with a production company that has made other projects sold as acquisitions, they may have old delivery requirements in their files that you can reference. And, of course, remember to use the lists provided in the "Delivery" chapter of this book. If there are elements listed and you don't know what they are, ask. If they are not explained in this book and they are film-related, call a film lab. If they are not explained in this book and they are video-related, call a postproduction facility. If they are contracts or legal documents, call your attorney.

Some simple questions should help you at least weed out the items you won't need to deliver. For example:

- Did you shoot film or videotape?
- Are you planning on doing a film-finish?
- Is there a large amount of subtitling that would cause you to create both a texted and textless version?

- Are you planning on doing a videotape finish?
- What audio format are you mixing to?

If you shot on videotape, you won't have many of the film items to deliver, such as trims and outs. However, if you did shoot on video and plan to do a film-out, then there are film elements in the list that you can make. If all of your audio was recorded and mixed in the digital realm, then you won't have any mag material readily available for delivery. You'll have other audio master material such as DA88s, which may be just fine. And so on.

Technical Acceptance

So now you've determined what physical elements you are going to create. Of course, just delivery of physical elements and legal documents does not mean your work is done. You need to know that your product is "technically" acceptable. If you are not savvy technically, you will need to rely on someone else to help you know that your product will pass a technical inspection. Hopefully, your film laboratory or video facility has had experience with the type of project you are doing so they will be able to offer dependable and accurate technical guidance. This brings up a really good point that we should sway over to for a moment.

As an independent filmmaker or even a small production company, you may not have a lot of experience working with various facilities on a variety of projects. Therefore, when looking for a postproduction facility, film laboratory, or sound house, there are some basic questions you should ask before placing your work in their hands. And, while money drives many of our decisions in this business, it is also important to pick the "appropriate" facility for your work. It doesn't help you if you go with the cheapest facility and then have to go back and spend money fixing items or trying to make elements after the fact.

- You need to question facilities about the types of work they specialize in.
- Are they a feature house specializing in film-finish projects?
- Do they focus primarily on long form television, such as MOWs?
- Do they focus on TV sitcoms?
- What type of clients do they have? Are they large studios or does the facility cater to the smaller independents?
- Are their shows mostly for domestic delivery or are they experienced in deliveries to international markets?
- Do they have an in-house QC department?
- Can they provide multiple services or will you need to move your materials to another facility during the process?
- How many other projects will your facility rep be handling besides yours?

It is important to choose a facility that specializes in your type of project. This is especially important if you are going to need help from your facility to guide your show through the process. You don't want to find yourself trying to get a MOW completed amongst a bunch of TV series trying to meet harried airdates. In this situation you simply won't find yourself a priority.

It is nice to work at a facility with clients who are working on projects similar to yours. It is a good networking opportunity for you, and a great way to get advice and suggestions from those working on similar shows. An important tool for learning, aside from doing something yourself, is to learn from others. We always recommend not reinventing the wheel, if you don't have to.

Sometimes facilities get so wrapped up in servicing their large studio clients, that the smaller client can get a bit lost. Smaller facilities with a more independent client base are usually poised to provide more personalized service as they have to rely more heavily on repeat business than some of the larger facilities that have a much bigger client pool to draw from.

Postproduction facilities that specialize in TV sitcoms and other TV programming with weekly airdates always work on a very tight schedule. Usually the shows have preferred editors, colorists, etc., and have booked them well in advance of the season. These clients pay top dollar to ensure that they will be able to complete their shows in time for delivery and air—no matter what delays they run into. That means bumping other sessions and possibly working a lot of overtime well into the night. If you are trying to complete a show that is not working against looming broadcast dates, at a facility that is on this schedule, good luck. You might very well find yourself bumped or delayed or moved to another colorist or editor. The other issue with TV-oriented facilities is they often don't have QC departments, or ones that are geared to recognize issues that are common problems for foreign clients. In a situation where you are depending on the facility to know what problems to look for in your materials, this will be disastrous for you. If they don't have a formal QC department at all, then you are faced with moving your materials elsewhere for the quality control check. This is inconvenient on two fronts. First, moving your materials around is never convenient, it makes tracking more difficult, the possibility for damage or loss is greater, and it can be costly if you end up relying on messengers to deliver items. Secondly, it can result in finger pointing. If facilities disagree on the severity of problems and where/how they occurred, you'll have to play referee and make some unpleasant decisions. When one facility does the work and then QCs the work, it makes them responsible for the entire project. Then, if you have any rejections from clients down the road, you have a place to go to air your grievances and one place to go for restitution.

The same argument applies to moving your materials from facility to facility to have different steps completed. There is always the danger that a problem will be introduced and it might be difficult to ascertain where the problem originated. Also, facilities don't like to work on other houses' masters, just for this reason. They might be blamed for something that was done prior to them receiving the materials, but that may be hard to prove.

You also want to be careful about going with a facility where each rep handles a heavy workload. In this situation, the fires will get the most attention because the person is juggling multiple projects and cannot possibly focus on every detail of each. For a seasoned client, this may not be such an issue. But if you are new and not aware of all of the potential areas of trouble, you could get lost in the shuffle and important issues may not be addressed until they too become fires.

The bottom line is that you need to do some research when choosing a facility. Don't only request a bid on a project but ask some of the tough questions. Try to make sure you will receive the service and attention you are going to need to get through your project properly.

A good rule if you don't have technical specifications from your distributor at the time you are posting your project, is to follow the Society of Producers and Television Engineers (SMPTE) broadcast specifications. The absolute rule of thumb is do not post your project without some sort of technical guidelines. This SMPTE guide will provide you with industry acceptable technical specifications with regard to video and sound record levels and record parameters—whether you are creating a project for theatrical release, U.S. or foreign TV broadcast, DVD release, etc. SMPTE information is available for both high definition and standard definition. SMPTE can be contacted through their website, www.SMPTE.com. Also, most facilities follow SMPTE specifications already.

This is another good point we should talk about. When you're creating a show for television broadcast, one of the responsibilities of your telecine colorist, on-line editor, tape to tape colorist, etc. is to ensure that your program does not exceed acceptable video (brightness) and chrominance (color) level limits. While editing or color correcting, the operator should be watching the various scopes and alert you to any problems you may be causing.

So, if in the color correction session your colorist tells you that you are exceeding those limits, heed this warning and back off. You will save yourself many headaches down the road. Delivering a program well out of legally acceptable limits will certainly result in rejection by one or more of your distributors.

Other Common Causes for Rejection

There are also items that are common causes for rejection that are often the result of small budget projects trying to cut costs and save money. The phrase penny-wise, pound-foolish comes to mind. Be careful when cutting corners not to cut quality. Below are several common areas for rejection:

- Missing sound effects
- Production sound problems

- Film dirt/damage problems
- Artifacting
- Recut negative
- Film weave in camera

Missing Sound Effects

We'll discuss two sound effects problems. The first concerns the effects that are mixed with the dialogue track to create composite (dialogue/music/effects) stereo tracks. Second are the effects that need to be recreated to create your separate fully filled foreign music and effects (M&E) track.

Distributors intending to sell your film in the same language in which the film was originally shot (example: U.S. distribution for an English language film) may or may not be concerned about how complete your separate music and effects track is. This is because they shouldn't need to do any audio remixing. Don't, however, rule out the possibility that they might still require this element as part of delivery. They could, for example, use the M&E track for cutting promos or creating trailers or TV spots.

Chances are you already plan to sell your show internationally and have already created a foreign M&E track. If, however, you only think you'll have a domestic sale, don't rule out the possibility that you might still need to fill your M&Es for a domestic delivery.

In either case, don't scrimp on the effects. Missing effects, whether they are mixed with the original language track or generated for a separate M&E track, will be flagged. It is a whole lot easier and cost-effective to only mix once. Going back in to add effects then remix and relay your sound track(s) is both time consuming and costly, and can eat into the producer's profits significantly.

Production Sound Problems

Production sound problems can be a heartbreaker for a producer. No one wants to hear that dialogue shot on location that should be fine, is not. Do be aware that if there are audio problems on the set, the producer will have to make a judgement call about how much dialogue replacement and/or clean-up work will be done. Once mixed with your music and effects, any production audio problems not fixed are then married to your track and it will be much more costly to go back after the fact to do fixes. Depending on the severity of the problems, they can be cause for rejection.

Film Dirt/Film Damage

While international clients may be more lenient with this issue than some domestic distributors, you have to fix any major or distracting dirt and damage. Many distributors are sophisticated enough to know what tools are available to do this work.

Just realize that should you decide not to do fixes, yet the clients insist they be done once you've delivered, any costs incurred for this work will probably be deducted from the license fee you are to be paid.

Electronic Video Dirt/Damage Clean-Up

Often referred to as dirt fixes, paintbox, DRS, and DVNR, the artifacts that can be introduced from these processes may be the most common reason for rejection of videotape delivery materials. One must be very careful when utilizing the tools available for clean up of dirt and damage. Paintbox/DRS fixes are a little more user friendly in terms of controlling any artifacts they may introduce. If careful, the operator should be able to insert these fixes into your master materials without introducing any new problems or side effects.

However, as we keep warning, you may want to go ahead and make a clone (copy) of your master and introduce any fixes into the clone—preserving for yourself a pristine master.

DVNR can be another matter. The operator cleaning up your picture with DVNR is utilizing an electronic process to cover up or mask small imperfections in your picture (such as film dirt, simple scratches, film damage or marks, etc.) overall. This process can be very useful as a preliminary clean-up tool to get rid of the small particles of dirt and damage before going into a more expensive and time consuming paintbox session.

This overall dirt clean up is not a substitute for going in and doing paintbox work, if needed. As we describe earlier in this book, in the "Completion" chapter, inappropriate use of this process can easily cause problems more severe than the ones you are trying to fix. This phenomenon is referred to "artifacting."

The very best advice we can offer in this area is to **always** keep a clean master. This means, if you are doing a film-to-tape transfer of your movie and you plan to use DVNR or noise reduction to clean up some dirt or reduce some graininess, do NOT do it in the film transfer process. Transfer your film to tape "clean." Then going tape-to-tape, do the dirt cleanup or other processes you feel the movie needs. You'll have a small additional charge for this method. But, you will always have a clean master to deliver, if you need it. We can't tell you just how many movies we've rejected over the years for unacceptable artifacting that was caused by these processes. And, in so many of those cases the licensor did not have a clean master to send us. In each of those cases, either the deal was cancelled or a retransfer took place at the licensor's expense.

Recut Negative

As we advised in earlier chapters, do not start your negative cut until you have a locked picture. Recutting your negative will cause a jump in your shot at the recut and sometimes film stretching and splice or glue marks. If you find you will need to do a major recut of your film, consider making an interpositive element and/or duplicate negative (dupe neg) to avoid chopping up your original negative again and losing frames by resplicing.

Camera Problems

While, strictly speaking, they do not fall under the area of postproduction, production problems can plague a show right through distribution.

One of us recently worked on a movie that was shot in a very distant country. Much of the movie had been shot before dailies were received, processed, and seen. It turned out that one camera had a weave problem that was quite severe. The movie was rejected by a major studio for acquisition due to this problem. However, it turns out there is a piece of equipment just available that can minimize, and in many cases, fix picture stabilization problems. By electronic process, it isolates the unwanted camera movement and stabilizes the picture. Of course, the fix is not cheap. And, the cost to do these fixes was deducted from the license fee paid to the distributor. It did, however, save the sale to the studio.

Camera problems can manifest in many other ways. There can be scratches from debris inside the camera; there can be physical damage such as perf tears from a bad magazine; etc. Many of these can be fixed or reduced with electronic devices. Just remember, as we always preach, be careful not to introduce something worse than the problem when trying to fix the problem.

Textless

Textless material is an important delivery element and an item best planned for early on in postproduction, rather than addressed at the last minute.

You already know that textless is the picture material backgrounds over which text is placed. Main and end credit textless is pretty standard, but don't forget about text within your show. All locales, legends, subtitling, etc. will need to be accounted for in your textless materials. Also, do you have graphics with text built-in? Often, that will have to be built with and without the text.

Other Delivery Items

There are many paperwork items and legal documents that will have to be delivered. Many of these will be prepared by others in the company or a service outside the company that is contracted to do so. You should be aware of what these documents are and if they've been created and/or delivered already. Production companies have a bad habit of disbanding once a project is completed and most everyone is off the payroll. Don't get stuck with last minute items that you didn't anticipate. Items such as chain-of-title, errors & omissions insurance, a script, music cue sheets, marketing, and publicity materials will all be on the list.

Be sure you know what is delivered to whom. The same person receiving the videotape or film elements may not be the same person receiving the E&O insurance documents. For more tips on successful and proper delivery, turn to the "Delivery" chapter in this book.

Rejected Delivery Materials

Realize that rejections are not abnormal in the acquisition world. Both of us have seen only a handful of titles delivered without rejection. The reasons for rejection will range from small (e.g., missing textless background), too much bigger (e.g., having to remaster your movie). If your project is rejected, be sure to get the following information from the licensee making the rejection:

1. The specific written rejection(s) with exact locations of the problems on your material.
2. A letter stating that the materials will be accepted once the fixes are completed to the licensee's satisfaction.
3. A written acceptance by the licensee once the fixes are completed.

Written Rejection Report

For discussion, let's say you delivered a digital Betacam NTSC master of a feature to a prospective licensee. The licensee performs a technical evaluation of the material you have delivered. Upon inspection, it is determined that the material is not acceptable as delivered and fixes will need to be made.

The first thing you're going to ask for when the licensee informs you of the rejection, is a written rejection report. This report should detail very specifically what the problems are and the exact location (in this case because we're talking about a videotape delivery, this means the exact timecodes) of the problems.

This is the only way you are going to know that you and the licensee are talking about exactly the same spot on the tape. Once armed with this information, you will move to the next step.

Conditions of Acceptance

Before sinking a lot of money into meeting the licensee's demands regarding fixes, be sure you know that doing these fixes to the licensee's satisfaction will guarantee acceptance. When sending you the rejection report in writing, there should be a sentence that states the materials will be accepted once the fixes are satisfactorily completed. Otherwise, you could end up going back and forth with the client as they find new problems each time you redeliver.

Acceptance

Once your materials have been accepted, you should receive notification of such from the licensee's legal department with a note as to when final payment will be made.

Fixing Rejections

The first thing you'll do is confirm that the problems really do exist as claimed by the licensee. Some aspects of evaluations are subjective and prone to human interpretation. For example, someone might hear footsteps on gravel off camera and mistake them for an audio distortion. You always have to have the rejected areas checked by a technical person that you trust. This may be someone on staff who is familiar with the show or maybe a facility you've worked with. The best scenario might be to go back to the facility that did the work and see what they say. Others might think you won't get an honest answer and a neutral third party is a better choice. You will need to make that decision.

So, you've taken the material and your written rejection report somewhere and confirmed the problem exists, now what? Now you need to determine the following:

1. Is the problem bad enough to require a fix?
2. What is the cost for the fix and is the cost justified?
3. How much time will be needed to make the fix. Is there a contractual due time in which fixes must be completed?
4. When fixes are completed do you need to deliver a whole new element, fix the originally delivered materials, or just provide short pieces with the fix that the licensee can insert into the existing materials?

Is a Fix Required?

Take your master and the written rejection report and go to your facility to look at the problem. This accomplishes two things: 1) you will start to understand what certain problems look like, how to fix them, and how they are caused; and 2) you can determine with the facility if the complaint is legitimate and how to proceed with fixes.

Should you determine the complaint is not valid, send a written response to the licensee explaining what you found. Hopefully, that will end the issue and the materials will be accepted. If the complaint is legitimate, you need to start fixes.

How Much Will the Fix Cost?

The best scenario when doing fixes is to discover the problem is the facility's fault and the fix is done at no expense to you. Barring that good fortune, you will need to negotiate the cost of the fix with your lab. If this is going to be very expensive, like a new telecine transfer, you might speak with the licensee. If they are a studio or large distribution company, they may be able to get better pricing. If so, they may agree to do the work and just deduct the cost from the license fee. Be sure to get a copy of the invoice for your records.

How Long Will the Fix Take to Complete?

If the fix will happen relatively quickly, just get it done and redeliver. If the fix is more complicated, let the licensee know when it will be completed. Again, it is always best to communicate in writing, as there are legal contracts in place regarding payment upon acceptance.

You also need to check the license agreement to see if there are time constraints as to how long you have to deliver acceptable materials and if there are time limits for doing fixes. Often if the license period is short, these timetables will be a part of the agreement so the licensor can ensure proper time to exploit the product before the license period ends.

What Needs to Be Redelivered?

Ascertain how to do the fix and determine it is something you are going to take on. Then you can figure out 1) if the elements need to be completely redelivered, 2) if you can just fix the material you originally delivered and redeliver that, or 3) if you can deliver the fix on a separate element.

Redelivering all the elements again can be costly. However if you did fixes that were extensive and throughout most of the show, you probably cannot avoid this. But, if you just fixed a spot or two, maybe the licensee will return the materials and allow you to insert your fixes and redeliver, since this often benefits both parties. First, it is more cost effective for you and it means the distributor doesn't have to re-evaluate the entire materials again—which will be costly for the distributor. This way, they can just spot check and sign off on the fixed area.

Often if the rejection is a result of a missing element, such as textless materials, the licensee will be happy to take this material on a separate short element. Then they just have to add that material to the tail of the originally delivered materials and check to make sure everything is complete. As with the previous scenario, this saves you and the licensee money.

Once the licensee has approved the materials and delivery is considered complete, the producer can collect the final funds owed.

Acquired Libraries

If your company is acquiring the library from another company, ensuring that all materials are accounted for and acceptable can be a very tricky and time-consuming proposition. This is especially true if the library is large, old, or made up of multiple items, such as many years of a TV series.

Hopefully, the selling company has good records of what is being purchased. In this scenario, you may just be faced with spot checking appropriate samples of the product to ensure that what was promised is what was delivered. Unfortunately, too often this is not the case and then things become complicated. You will have to pull together the materials and organize them to ascertain what you have. Then you will have to start the technical evaluation process. Usually the best way to do this, as it can take a very long time to complete this project, is to try and figure out which titles have the best chance of being distributed first. This might go faster if you include the head of your sales force in this project. They should have a pretty good feel for what titles will be most desirable to your clients, so start there. Generate an inventory as you go along so that you can account for the materials and document the work you've done, as it is completed.

In Summary

Burgeoning distribution opportunities with the increase in theatre screens, the growth of cable, satellite, and foreign markets has generated a very real shortage of product. Distribution is a very good business to be in these days if you can offer product that is desirable and in acceptable shape. The key to this is to do things right when you are creating or cleaning up this product. You would expect this large increase in sales would result in nearly limitless budgets. However, this is not the case so you will need to be savvy about negotiating with labs to do the work necessary. You have an advantage if you are creating something from scratch. You can do things right from the start and not have to try and fix the mistakes of others. If you don't have the funds to complete your new project properly, then think about a cost-effective way to have product to shop around to those who do have the money to complete the project properly. And, as we always stress, pick a facility that can show they know what they are doing and then listen to their advice.

13 The Future

As the saying goes, "If I could predict the future I'd be a rich woman."

Even though we don't know for certain how every aspect of our business will shake out over the next few years, we've asked around, questioned some folks and have formed a couple of opinions of our own that we'd like to share with you here.

A Little Background

In the last 5 years the world has seen the largest advances in technology probably since the space program in the 1960's. Communication is faster and better (well, faster anyway), we can feel like Dick Tracy talking into our wristwatches, and access people and information with direct connections and Internet access from anywhere on the planet. Medical research has found a way to manufacturer some organs, remove wrinkles without surgery, and promises that cloning will empower us to live longer, healthier lives. Technology has created smaller phones, computers, and everything digital. These breakthroughs have touched our everyday lives, so much so that we rely on technology today that was not even available in the early 1990's. We no longer marvel at e-mail and the Internet, but get irritated when downloading takes too long.

So how does all this new technologies-talk relate to the age-old art of film-making? "Film" is important to so many industries, including medicine, the military, and space. Improvements made in film stocks and processes also benefit filmmakers. Motion picture film has been around for more than 80 years. And in all that time the basic principals haven't changed. We still measure by the same film standards and resolution today that we did then. Film has to be exposed through a camera aperture, developed, printed, and projected. However, many of the film stocks and chemicals used in processing have changed. Some of these changes have been good for our environment and resulted in new and interesting visual results. Film's ability to capture light and information in very high resolution, and its archival quality, remain the benchmark for all new mediums developed.

It's Videotape—Run for Your Lives

Videotape seemingly appeared overnight and many predicted almost immediate extinction of film. Boy, were those guys wrong. They couldn't predict the future either. Videotape did not end film's reign, but opened new doors of possibility for film and may have even enhanced the role of film in creating entertainment. Granted, videotape has a solid footing in many areas previously owned by film. But even so, film is still the only medium proved to last a hundred years. So, is the extinction of film really in danger of happening this time? Will film be replaced by a new digital format? Will "going to the movies" be nothing more than viewing a high grade DVD on a giant screen? And if not, why? There are some very compelling arguments for this scenario. George Lucas has said that he may never shoot on film again. For the theatrical distributor what market will they have left if there is no film? Of course, Lucas never said he wouldn't make film from the video he shot.

One big disadvantage of using a video format to acquire original images is the reduced options for future uses. Once an image is limited by a video standard, the resolution and aspect ratio of that image is permanent.

We get to see *I Love Lucy* because the episodes were shot on film. But, we'll never see again the first two years of *The Tonight Show*, which were recorded on tape. And, we believe that until there is a medium that proves to be as resilient and versatile as film, and programs don't disappear but through human error, that film will continue to have a major place in the entertainment industry.

Oh, Digital Cinema

In 1997, there were approximately 31,000 movie screens in the United States. As of 2001, only 19 had made a permanent equipment commitment to be able to project via digital projection. Currently, there are only 34 digital cinemas worldwide. The new technology is not exactly shutting down film production on a massive scale. It has advantages, such as pristine viewing every time, no dirt, no scratches, and no poorly printed prints. The digital disks have room for more sound tracks, alternate languages, commentaries, and other sound elements.

Shipping costs and logistics are dramatically reduced when sending disks via freight or satellite. A 2-hour movie's film reels weigh about 50 lbs. while a disk weighs several ounces and fits in a much smaller box. Manufacturing costs are also greatly reduced. It's as you may have guessed, significantly less expensive to make a few thousand DVDs than a few thousand release prints. Estimates are that with digital projection, studios will see savings in the tens of millions of dollars in distribution costs. Ultimately, the manufacturing and shipping costs issue is probably what will drive this technology to success.

The advantages seem pretty clear and economically sound. Of course, there are the issues of how to make a smooth transition and of resolution. There are still tons more picture information in a frame of film than a frame of video—even high definition video. (See "Digital TV and High Definition" chapter for more details.) So there is the artistic argument for film which will be hard for video to overcome in some circles. But are these circles responsible for getting butts in chairs? And if so, will the same butts sit in those chairs to watch a pristine, albeit less detailed, video projected movie? Hmmm . . . we think they might.

Getting It Going

In 2002, the manufactures of digital content and equipment have agreed to install 250 digital screens into existing movie theaters. In exchange, exhibitors have promised to pay a flat fee per screening to the equipment manufacturers. This will help pave the way for exhibitors to become players in the digital cinema market without the equipment expense, which can be in excess of $150,000 per screen.

On the other hand, should there be a technology breakthrough that out performs the current digital cinema model, we could see a whole new generation of projectors and postproduction requirements spring up. We don't believe that digital cinema will lose out to film as a distribution and exhibition medium. The cost savings and efficiencies will prove too compelling. The distributors will drive the manufacturers and a solution will be forthcoming that allows the market to move forward.

Anti-Piracy

Although projector installation and screen upgrades are major expenses, they aren't the only issues in the D-Cinema discussion. Anti-piracy (theft) is high on the minds of motion picture distributors. Means of fingerprinting or identifying the origin and manufacture date of each disk is currently available. But how to prevent the theft and black market copies is another issue. Trying to stop someone from going into a theatre with a video camera and pirating your movie by shooting the screen is one thing. It is an impossible problem, whose end result is a very poor quality video recording. And there is a market for this type of pirated product. But, what this new system means is there will be a pristine digital copy of your movie in existence even before it opens in theatres. And theft of a disk will mean DVD quality available on the black market before the theatrical release.

Manufacturers are working to make theft at least difficult, and hopefully impossible. Ideas such as encoding a password needed to play the disk, limiting the number of plays a disk will make, or even requiring machine hook up to a remote computer which will "unlock" the disk for use by the theatre. As long as there are hackers and small digital cameras there will be piracy in the current theatrical world. One of the key issues with digital cinema is to figure out how to make it theft proof.

The good news is that this is a worldwide problem. It is in both domestic and international filmmakers, distributors, and exhibitors best interests to at least reduce this problem of piracy—especially when you are speaking of satelliting a new motion picture around the world for first run, or shipping pristine digital disks to distant locations. The folks working on this problem encompass a very large and powerful group of companies and individuals, all with a large financial nut at stake, and all working toward the same goal.

Who's Driving the D-Cinema Movement?

So it comes up again, will digital cinema and high definition video finally beat film into extinction? This is one current dilemma—digital vs. film, and which will survive? The short answer is there are still too many opinions and no straight answers to give you a yes or no. We don't know what scientific breakthrough will happen in the next few years and how it will influence the way we create entertainment. We do know what some major corporations are banking their technology on and that they are teaming up to shape the new face of the entertainment world.

Several companies have designed and manufactured digital projectors. One such manufacturer has teamed up with a motion picture studio, a film laboratory, and a communications company. Their goal is to perfect the technology and methods for sending digital motion picture material to theatres anywhere in the world via satellite transmission. At the same time, another digital projection manufacturer has teamed up with a major distribution company to develop yet another distribution method. Their focus is distributing digital motion pictures via a DVD type disk that will be returned by the theatres to the original distributor for reuse.

Why would these companies invest so much money and time in order to advance motion picture postproduction? One of the biggest expenses of motion picture distribution is creating theatrical prints. Each print is made one at a time. Trailers for upcoming movies are added manually to the beginning of each print and then they are packed and shipped usually to thousands of theatres—all in a very short span of time. Once these prints are delivered for the movie opening and first run, they are then returned to the distributor and stored or bicycled to alternate theatres. For movies made in the United States and sent for release abroad, the foreign distributor will replace the domestic sound track with a foreign track made just for that specific language. This is an additional financial burden.

Digital projection will eliminate the need for film prints for at least the theatres projecting digitally. Offering multiple sound tracks will become a significantly less expensive and labor intensive process. Making film prints is also expensive. Having the option of either satelliting movies to multiple locations or distribution via less expensive disks will take much of the guesswork out of printing too few or too many prints, and eliminate wasted costs when too many prints are ordered

A big motivator was put into place when the government required broadcasters to provide only high definition transmissions by 2006. This has done its share to push digital technology forward. Whether or not the broadcasters will be able to make all the necessary changes by this date remains to be seen. (See the "Digital TV and High Definition" chapter.) One thing for sure is that many consumers will be unwilling to go out and spend thousands of dollars on a new TV, so, they will still own analog TV sets for sometime to come—making the dramatic switch to digital seem nearly impossible.

The high definition technology has brought us high definition video cameras and better tape stock. These improvements have closed the gap somewhat between the video and film worlds. We already see low budget filmmakers and product made for television or video distribution adopting the high def format. However, for theatrical release the filmmaker must eventually come back to film and the TV show might consider generating a film archival element. Entertainment is a business and in the United States a significant part of our economy. Changes in the way feature films are produced, put through postproduction, and ultimately projected will be based on the better, faster, and (listed last only out of good taste) cheaper theories. D-Cinema already exists on a very small scale in larger markets. If research finds that overall digital projection will save the distributors' money as expected, and is acceptable to viewers, producers, and studios, distributors will find a way to achieve worldwide digital cinema distribution.

Will High Def and Digital Transmission/Projection Catch On?

High definition video, both shooting and posting, has a very good chance of gaining a stronghold in the television market. (And the FCC mandate doesn't hurt the cause.) The format is starting to impact the low budget and independent, and even high budget, markets. The overall price to shoot and post in high def is less than that of 35 mm film and equal to shooting and posting 16 mm film in most cases. The quality is very good and acceptable to foreign markets making it a good future choice for the home entertainment and television markets, while maintaining the option to film out for a future film finish.

Satellite distribution to digital projection screens will also open up other areas of entertainment besides exhibition of feature films. Live broadcast via satellite will be a natural extension for theatre owners. Events such as concerts, professional boxing, New Year's Eve in Times Square, etc. can be satellited to theatres. Exhibitors can now offer large venues for pay-per-view screenings. This will change the way we look at and use theatres. The expanded markets for theatres will give exhibitors more power over what movies are screened and what venues are publicly available. Studios may be faced with exhibitors cutting their losses on a particular feature with poor ticket sales in exchange for a higher rate of sales on a sports or concert venue. Satellite capture and digital projection has the potential to create a much broader market for the theatre owners.

Fiber optics and dedicated servers have made huge gains in sending large amounts of complex data to off-site. Pictures, sound, and text can be successfully sent and retrieved in frame accurate form either around the corner or across the country, and beyond. This innovation makes it possible to send detailed dailies files to editors or directors on location. You can download dailies on your desktop and begin editing immediately—even without digitizing if you are receiving formatted files from your transfer facility. As a studio executive you will be able to watch dailies off a dedicated server somewhere on the studio lot, even in your own office. Gone will be dailies tapes cluttering up your office or the mad rush to ship them off to the executives. Right now this is still about money and time. Until delivery systems become more affordable or there are more high-resolution options, this is going to remain an expensive way to deliver dailies to clients. However, if your client can justify the money, then there is technology available.

Universal Mastering

The obvious next extension of high definition telecine and data transfers is creation of one master or data file that will service any need, present or future, that you may have for your project.

A universal master, also known as a *digital intermediate*, is created by scanning each film frame's entire exposed area. The images are color corrected. While still data, any fixes or overall changes can be made—such as dirt and scratch fixes, credit fixes, color correction fixes, etc. The scanned image is stored as data on any number of available disk formats, hard drive, or laid off to videotape. Later, whatever aspect ratio is required can be recouped just as from film. As many copies can be made as needed without any resolution degradation, because you are working in a fully digital realm of ones and zeros.

This method, when truly perfected, will be cost effective in so many ways. If the image is stored in 24p, the material is easily recorded out to any standard. Because the data holds the originally photographed aspect ratio, any aspect ratio can be created from the data file—just as from film. You save money in QC, paintbox, audio laybacks, duplication, and the physical storage of all versions in all formats.

Eventually, this information will be accessible from a desktop computer so you can view portions of your project from your office and order manipulations and request delivery materials for your clients to whatever their specs may be.

Digital Asset Management

The idea of housing content as digital information is very exciting. Manufacturers and producers of content are focusing very heavily on the services that will be available as this process refines. Postproduction facilities and film laboratories see this as the next level of servicing for their clients.

One of the initial and potentially most appealing uses for Digital Asset Management is the management of library services at the major studios and larger distribution companies. This refers to storage and access of studio and distribution companies' product. This product will take many forms. Marketing and promotional materials such as one sheets, electronic press kits (EPKs), and trailers can be much more efficiently stored and distributed when available in a digital format.

Distribution of digital dailies, which we touched on earlier, will also benefit and become much more widely available as the technology advances and costs go down.

Imagine being able to access your vault database, click on a particular trailer or movie, and view the entire element from your desktop—and not in a jerky sub-VHS quality—and then drag and drop that trailer or movie to a client. The facility managing your data will then distribute exactly what you've selected, in the required format to your client. Initially, this will probably mean generating videotape. But, very soon it may place broadcast quality material on a server that your client can access immediately.

Once movie theatres are able to receive regular delivery of features for exhibition, trailers can be distributed just as easily. What a great marketing tool for studios to have the flexibility to change what trailers are being paired with their movies by day, by market, and by specific location—all with the simple click of a mouse.

There should also be a "green" advantage. Shipping prints requires trucking or flying of materials to their various locations. A satellite feed will reduce the amount of resources required to move these materials.

A Summary and a Chart

So, there it is, one click distribution beamed into your desktop. No matter what you're buying or selling, it will get there fast. This is exciting and confusing. There is new technology to grasp and new ways to create content that need to be learned and nurtured. Will it all happen? We think so, and probably better than we anticipate. But relax and don't panic. Like all new technologies, progress will start out slow, giving us the opportunity to grasp the new concepts and changes. Will there still be a need for associate producers and postproduction supervisors? Yes, someone will still need to schedule and manage the workflow and put out fires. Will the job be much different? Technically, yes, but the basics will be essentially the same.

To help show you how we see the flow of postproduction in the not-so-distant future we are wrapping up this section with one of our handy charts.

Figure 13.1 Possible Production Workflow Chart

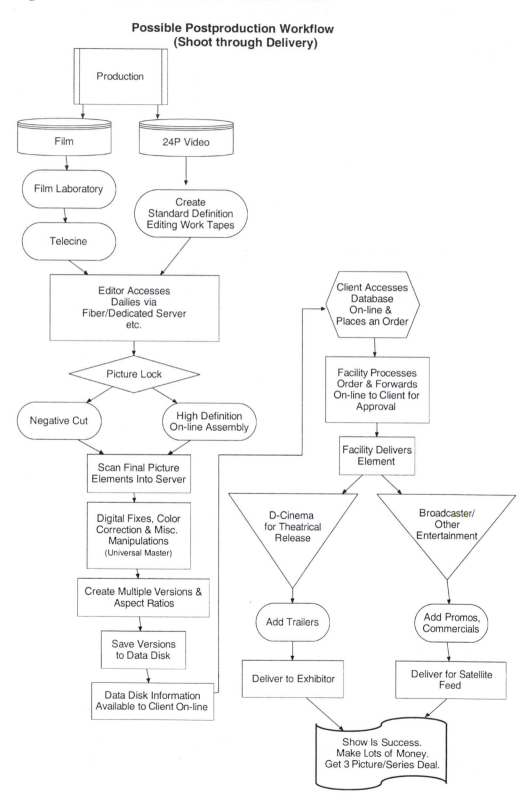

Possible Postproduction Workflow
(Shoot through Delivery)

Sound Improvements

Speaking of "green" or environmental advantages in the future, there will be some changes in sound application that will be good for the earth. While we are still distributing film prints to most theatres, it would be environmentally and economically beneficial to reduce waste in the application of sound to release prints. Great strides are being made in this area. In addition to the goal of using less water, less harsh chemicals, and increasing worker safety, these new methods will simplify the application process, provide better stereo sounds overall, and help extend the life of the sound track readers on the theatre projectors.

As a digital process, sound has already seen improvements in the capture and manipulation of production sound. In addition, the advances in image scanning have recently been adapted to audio. Sound engineers can now scan optical sound tracks into a computer and reduce hiss, crackle, and background noise by literally "cleaning up" the dirt and imperfections on the physical element (just like paintbox fixes to video). This clean up can be performed while enhancing, remixing, and balancing the track. Once these fixes have been completed, a new sound element can be output into any desired format. And, as with film, these sound elements can be saved to data or other high speed, large storage tape formats for future use.

This is still a burgeoning field in relationship to sound. So, even though the number of facilities that have the newest optical sound track cleanup capabilities is somewhat limited, they will grow quickly as the demand for the work starts to justify the equipment expenses.

These new tools will greatly enhance the levels of improvements achievable in sound restoration. This is good news for an industry that has re-dedicated itself to saving our classic films that have been damaged by years of improper handling, poor storage, and loss.

A Small Summary

What we do know is that if all this stuff comes to fruition, the future of our industry should be really cool.

A Bigger Summary

By taking a look at the current technology and what is possible right now it isn't hard to take that leap into the future and get an idea of what's in store for us. For the entertainment industry sending, receiving, and storing information will be a major focus and concern. It has already become evident that videotape formats have to continually stretch to new heights and recreate themselves to meet growing needs. The storage capacity and quality of video needs to improve each time technology advances, and even that may still not be enough.

In order for the digital world to continue to close the gap in resolution and clarity between film and video, we have to continue to search for better answers and processes. We must unite and become one with the computer "nerds," expanding our comprehension of *data*. How data is configured and stored is pivotal to the new digital world. A universal standard for storage and compression is a key factor in world acceptance (although we have lived a long time with various videotape standards worldwide, so maybe this is a wish instead of a must). While high definition is struggling to find a standard in all aspects of production, post, and distribution—data has an advantage. The disk or tape that data is stored on may improve and change often however, the method in which we store, write, and configure this data should change very little over time.

With the help of SMPTE the groundwork for storing content as data has already been laid. Using a file format called DPX, or digital moving picture exchange, each film frame can be stored individually with less compression and less chance of artifacts than the current tape format. Now, with a way to store content in a digital format with computer access that should be universally acceptable for many years, you can begin to imagine that there are endless possibilities and no limit to sending, receiving, and storing. These are exceptional advantages, with less capital expense and more power to reach the consumer. Pretty soon when you look down at your cell phone, you'll be accessing satellited information. How long before the world of advertisements creeps into your cell world? Probably not long. And then the fun stuff, music videos, TV shows, and even live broadcasts will be viewable in the palm of your hand. Cool . . . yes, it will be a cool world and post; well it will be technically a lot different.

In Summary

Congratulations. You made it to the end of the book. Hopefully, this means that you have successfully completed your project and have delivered a wonderfully creative and technically accurate program for distribution.

As you may have discovered while working on your project, experience is the best teacher, but having a place to look up some of the answers doesn't hurt.

Here is a summary of some of the highlights from the book that we feel warrant reemphasis.

Scheduling is the cornerstone of your project. Your schedule, as you may now know, is the key to staying organized. And organization is the key to success. (Sometimes a really expensive car works too, but that's another Hollywood story.) Your schedule will be fluid throughout postproduction, constantly changing to accommodate the project being created. Your schedule must always be up-to-date and available to everyone on the project—including your editors, your sound facility, your postproduction facility, and all of the other people who make up the postproduction team.

Understanding how the budget is created and what must be included will help you with the people who control the money. Sometimes the people most concerned with the "bottom line" do not understand all the necessary nuances of movie making. It is then incumbent on the postproduction management to explain and defend the steps necessary to completing a project. The ability to make sense of the spending can be very valuable, and that only comes with a clear understanding of the entire process.

Try to make good choices. There are a lot of new and exciting technologies out there. You can't be an expert in everything, and quite frankly, you don't have to be (even we need help from time to time). The key is to surround yourself with knowledgeable people (kind of like being president). Be meticulous and tenacious when looking for these people and you'll find them. Their purpose is to help you avoid making the really big mistakes.

The final piece is understanding your delivery requirements. The schedule and budget are based on what you must create to meet these requirements. These terms can be confusing and very costly when you have to go back after the fact and recreate elements. Ask a lot of questions when it comes to understanding the terms. Don't worry about feeling embarrassed. Embarrassed is much better than unemployed.

While you can do your postproduction job without an extensive technical background, you do need to understand enough about the process and the terminology to do your job correctly. You have to be able to communicate to the film laboratory if you are shooting film. You must be able to give your transfer house accurate telecine specifications for your dailies transfers. Understanding timecode is important so that you know what you are asking for when creating work cassettes and even masters. A technical understanding will also help you avoid problems and traps. You will know if specifications make sense and if each item is necessary. If your elements are rejected, being involved in finding solutions will help you resolve issues and communicate with the facility to order fixes and correct errors.

You will find that all of your facilities will want to help you. Draw from their knowledge and their experience. Let them help you if you need it. It is in their best interest to guide you rather than constantly redo jobs because you provided inaccurate information.

Also remember your place in the food chain. Your job is to manage postproduction. Your job is not to judge the producer's decisions or second-guess your distributor. Be politically savvy and professional. Use your legal department if there are any questions about credits, contracts, release agreements, or union rules. Cover your bases and you won't spend a lot of time covering your . . . derrière.

There should be joy and excitement during postproduction and satisfaction upon delivery. You are working in the entertainment industry. Chances are your name will appear in the credits throughout the living rooms of America. Take pride in a job well done.

Glossary

Aaton Motion picture camera with in-camera Keykode/timecode reader.

A/B Roll Technique of placing alternating scenes on two rolls of film and then playing them together to build fades and dissolves.

A-Frame Edit This video edit refers to the first frame of a 3:2 pulldown sequence. The A frame is the only frame in the sequence where a film frame is reproduced as one complete video frame.

Acquisition A feature film, TV show, or documentary created by one company or in joint production with a set of companies that is purchased by a studio, network, or combination of companies who thereby become the distributor.

Action Safe Area The area of a television picture that is visible on consumer television sets.

Address Track Timecode See LTC (Longitudinal Timecode).

ADR (Automatic Dialogue Replacement) Recording new dialogue or re-recording dialogue where the production sound is unusable or obscured.

AFM (Audio Frequency Modulation) Hi fi sound invisibly imbedded in the picture. Used in some cassette videotape formats.

Aliasing Visual effect lacking picture detail/resolution caused by an ineffective sampling technique.

Ambient Sounds/Effects Sounds recorded as part of the dialogue track.

Analog A continuously variable electrical signal.

Answer Print The first print struck from a finished cut negative.

Application Method of developing an optical sound track area on a composite film print.

Application Splash When the chemical used to develop the sound track area on film spills over onto the picture area, damaging the silver in the print stock. Often appears as a purplish-black area on the screen.

Artifacts Refers to video blemishes, noise, trails, etc. Any physical interruption of the video image is called an artifact and is usually introduced electronically.

Aspect Ratio The ratio of the picture width to picture height. The standard U.S. television aspect ratio is 4:3—four units wide to three units high (1.1:33). Other ratios used will include 1.66:1, 1.85:1, and 2.35:1. If these alternate ratios are preserved in the film-to-tape transfer, you have an option to put a solid black bar at the top and bottom of the TV screen. Some companies shoot for 16:9 in the event the material is used for high-definition TV transmission, ensuring that there is usable negative for the wider aspect ratio.

ATSC (Advanced Television Systems Committee) A group formed to study and make recommendations to the FCC regarding digital television.

Audio Hiss Over accentuated high frequency noise heard in audio.

Audio Hum Low frequency noise heard in audio.

Audio Limiter Automatic control on a recorder that lowers volume during recoding if the sound becomes too loud.

Audio Mute Loss of sound information causing silence.

Authoring Process of organizing materials and putting them into computer language for use with an interactive disc (such as DVD).

Auto Assembly Automatic combining of edits on videotape conforming to a prepared edit decision list (EDL) with little or no human involvement.

B Negative Film term referring to takes not originally slated to be printed from dailies but later called for to be printed. Has carried over into videotape and refers to noncircled takes that are later transferred as alternative takes.

Balancing Reels Building reels to assure that music cues don't overlap reel changes. Done by the film editor or assistant editor.

Banding A visual artifact whereby brightness or color gradients appear to be made up of bands of brightness or color. Often the result of not enough bits to represent each sample of a picture.

Bearding Highlights on one side which are obviously not part of background.

Betacam SP This is a composite analog 1/2″ videotape. There are two channels of analog audio and two channels of discreet or AFM channels. The analog audio channels are normal audio tracks. The AFM channels are actually recorded in the video portion of the tape. Therefore, they can be laid down simultaneous with laying down picture. But, if you lay down audio on channels 3 and 4 after the picture has been laid down, you will record over the picture. Conversely, if you insert the picture after recording on audio channel 3 or 4, you will erase the audio in that portion.

Betacam SX 1/2″ cassette with 10:1 compression ratio. Machine plays analog Betacam tapes.

Black Level The level of the television picture signal corresponding to the maximum limit of black peaks.

Blanking The point in the video signal where a horizontal scan line or vertical field that makes up one-half of a video picture is completed and another one starts. There is no picture information at this point in this signal.

Bleed-Through When audio or timecode information from one track can be heard, however faintly, on another audio track. Common in the VHS format.

Breathing Amplitude variations in a video signal at a slow regular rate.

Camera Report The form filled in for every camera roll exposed to explain what is on the roll and any special printing or transfer instructions.

Capstan A rotating wheel that pulls material along and maintains proper speed. Inside a VCR it pulls the tape along. On a telecine it keeps the film moving at a steady speed.

Chapter Stop A code embedded in a videodisc which identifies each new chapter or section beginning. Speeds up the process of locating specific segments on a disc.

Check Print First film print used to check color corrections.

Chroma Key Superimposing or combining of two video images to create one composite effect. One of the video sources must be a saturated color, such as blue or green.

Chrominance The color portion of a video signal. Also called chroma.

Chyron A company that manufactures special effects and titling equipment used in on-line edit suites. Also used as a common name for this type of equipment.

Clipping When a signal is stronger than the circuits can handle, the excess is clipped off. In video this can cause a milky appearance while in audio the sound can become distorted.

Clone A digital exact copy of a video image or audio track. Analog elements cannot be cloned; they can only be duplicated.

Closed-Captioning Signal that contains text information incorporated into video that can be viewed on your television when run through a decoder.

Coding Stamping or burning numbers into the edges of work print and work track to mark sync points. Done with a coding machine.

Color Bars Test pattern used to determine if a video signal is calibrated correctly.

Color Burst The color reference signal that establishes the reference for the color portion of a video signal.

Color Correction Color grading process that adjusts the picture color, tint, hue, etc., on either film or videotape. Also referred to as color balance from scene to scene.

Colorist A telecine operator who corrects the color and light balance while transferring film to videotape or videotape to videotape.

Component Video A signal with separate chrominance and luminance components. By retaining maximum bandwidth, the loss of quality is reduced.

Composite Audio A fully mixed audio track with dialogue, music, and effects married together. May be stereo or mono.

Composite Film Print A 16 mm or 35 mm film print that contains a sound track on the film element.

Composite Video A single signal made up of active video, horizontal and vertical sync, horizontal and vertical blanking, and color burst. NTSC, PAL, and SECAM are examples of composite signals. Basically a form of analog video compression allowing for economical broadcasting, the complete video signal.

Compression Process for squeezing digital data into a smaller space than it would normally fit. A 2 : 1 compression makes the data half its original size.

Conforming A variation of a layback. Instead of recording the audio directly to the videotape master, you record to a second audiotape machine allowing you to create a multitrack audio element that can hold several different languages. Also involves matching or syncing a sound track to match an existing picture element.

Continuity Script (Dialogue Continuity Script) The actual dialogue from the final version of a project.

Contrast The range between light and dark values in a video signal.

Control Track A guide recorded onto videotape that stabilizes tape movement during playback.

Conversion Lag Error as a result of standards conversion. Most noticeable in horizontal movement, image "trails."

Converter Electronic device which translates one frequency into another. Also called decoder device.

Credits Titles in a program naming the stars and others involved in creating a project. On film credits are created optically. On videotape they are created electronically.

Cross Color In video, an undesired signal interfering with the desired signal. Can be caused when an analog signal is introduced into a digital format (for example, using an analog captioner to caption a digital master). Looks a little like moire.

Crosstalk Bleeding of sound from one channel or track to another.

Crushed Blacks Lack of detail in the black areas in picture. Caused either in photography or transfer. If a result of photography style, it cannot be fixed.

Cue Sheets Spreadsheet or road maps of audio cues so sound recordists can locate specific tracks.

Cyan Sound Track A sound track used for making sounded prints that utilizes the cyan layer of the film.

D1 A component digital videotape. There are four channels of audio. This format displays no generation loss on multilayering work. A single D1 videotape machine can play back or record in either NTSC or PAL. The longer the tape run time, the thinner the stock. Stocks over 120 minutes are not generally recommended, as they may shred and break due to thinness.

D2 A composite digital video format. There are four channels of audio. Picture and audio quality are superior to 1″ and Betacam SP.

D3 A 1/2″ composite video format. There are four channels of audio.

D4 Considered bad luck in Japanese, a D4 videotape format does not exist.

D5 A 1/2″ component video format. It records standard definition and HDTV recording by use of about 5:1 compression. It has 8 audio channels.

D6 A 1/2″ high definition component video format. It's uncompressed and has eight channels of audio.

D9 (Digital S) Digital component format, low-end professional or semiprofessional format with four channels of audio, and replays S-VHS.

DA88 Audiotape The audio is recorded on hi-8 mm metal particle tape stock and provides up to eight channels of audio recording. The standard sampling rate is 48 Hz when referencing to video. DA88 tapes must be preformatted at a 48 kHz sampling rate referenced to video. At the film shoot, the DA88 will be connected to a 60 Hz reference. The tape will thus be pulled up when recording the production audio track. This method allows you to get a pull-down effect when working with the tapes in telecine, videotape editing, and sound editorial.

Dailies Footage that is shot in a day; called "rushes" in England.

DAT (Digital Audiotape) This is a two-channel digital audiotape format with a separate channel for recording timecode. Because it is digital instead of analog, the sound quality is considered superior to 1/4″. Converts analog audio to digital and records it. Then plays it back converting the digital data to analog audio.

Daylight Develop Rush film processing through a lab within a few hours instead of overnight.

D-Cinema Digital cinema, a.k.a. E-Cinema. Projection of content through computerized electronic projection system, utilizing data or video elements.

DCT A digital tape recorder using the DCT method to compress the signal before recording it to tape. A widely used method of compression.

Decibel (dB) A unit of measurement indicating ratios of currents, voltages, or power and used to represent audio transmission levels, gains, and losses. A decibel describes the smallest perceptible change in audio level.

Decode Reprocessing of a signal to get the desired part. In audio a signal is encoded when recorded and in playback it is decoded so that it sounds normal, but the noise is reduced.

DEFT A device for converting NTSC video signals into PAL video signals. This is a high-quality standards conversion generally accepted by countries around the world.

Degauss (Demagnetize) Used to erase recording on video and audio tapes so they can be reused.

DEVA Disk Is a disk format that is computer controlled and used for production sound recording.

DFTC (Drop-Frame Timecode) SMPTE timecode created to match run time, or clock time, exactly. Two frames of timecode are dropped every minute, except every tenth minute. Because it gives exact run time, broadcasters require masters to be delivered with DFTC.

Digital A signal made of two discrete levels—on and off—as opposed to signals that vary continuously between high, medium, and low levels.

Digital Betacam This is a 1/2″ digital metal tape format. There are four channels of audio. Some models will play back both analog and digital Betacam cassettes.

Digitize Process of loading video and audio into an off-line editing system. Quality of digitized material (number of frames captured) depends on the amount of storage space on the system.

Digitizer Person who digitizes material into the off-line system.

Director's Cut Rough cut created by the director once the editor's cut is completed. Usually followed by the producer's cut and picture lock.

Dissolve When picture or audio melds into another picture or audio. In film these are opticals. In on-line these are created electronically.

Distortion Poor quality sound often caused by an audio signal that is too strong.

Dolby 5.1 Describes a digital sound format that is separated into five discrete channels, left, center, right, left surround and right surround, and a low frequency effects channel which plays back on a subwoofer.

Dolby AC-3 Method of compressing five audio channels for use in DTV and DVDs.

Drift When an element does not keep a steady speed during playback. This is usually caused when there is not timecode to lock to or when the record machine power source was faulty, causing the recording to vary in speed. This term is also used when speaking about color-correction settings on a telecine that appear to have changed over time due to light-tube burn.

Drop-Out Temporary signal loss on a videotape or audiotape. Shows up randomly as white spots or thin horizontal lines on video and silence on audio.

DTV Digital television.

Dubbing (Audio) Also known as mixing. Combining of all sound tracks (dialogue, music, and effects) onto a single master source.

Duplicate Negative (Dupe Neg). Backup or safety copy of a cut negative, used for creating prints, thus preserving your original negative.

Duplication (Video Dub) Making videotape copies.

DV, DVC (Digital Video) Audio and video converted to ones and zeros for digital recording and playback. It also stands for a digital VCR format that uses 5 to 1 compression recorded onto a 1/4″ cassette.

DVC Pro Panasonic professional format based on the DVC but with less compression than the consumer DVC.

DVD (Digital Video Disk or Digital Versatile Disk) Cutting edge technology for recording on a 5″ CD using compression for picture and sound quality superior to VHS.

Dynamic Range The range between the lowest level of sound and the highest level without distortion.

EBU (European Broadcast Union) PAL timecode, it's nondrop frame.

E-Cinema Electronic cinema, a.k.a. D-Cinema. Projection of content through computerized electronic projection system, utilizing data or video elements.

Edge Damage Physical damage on one or both edges of videotape. Usually affects audio tracks, but severe damage will also cause picture breakup.

Edge Numbers Numbers printed on one edge of motion-picture film, allowing frames to be easily identified in an edit list. Human- and machine-readable. Keykode is the trademark name for Kodak edge numbers. The combination of letters and numbers identifies specific information about a particular roll of film, such as place of manufacture.

Editing Assembling a program by combining sound and images from various master sources, either film or tape.

Editor's Cut First cut of a picture. Usually followed by the director's cut.

Editor's Off-Line or Work Cassette Small-format videotape created from videotape master for use in off-line editing. Timecode matches the master tape and could include visible windows containing the Keykode information, audio timecode information, etc.

EDL (Edit Decision List) List of edits created during off-line or film editorial.

Effects When working with picture this refers to visual effects. In audio this refers to sound effects.

Electronic Pin Register Stabilizes the film's ride through the telecine. Reduces vertical movement and weave. Operates in real time.

Encoder A circuit that combines separate component signals into a composite video signal.

Episodic A television show with multiple episodes. Often used to refer to a one-hour program, but technically applies to half-hour programs such as talk shows and sitcoms.

Exabyte Data archive storage on an 8 mm cassette.

Fades When picture or audio slowly disappears. In film these are created as opticals. In on-line they are done electronically.

Field One-half of a video frame. Made up of either the odd or the even scanning lines of a picture.

Field Dominance Which field (odd or even) is the first field at the start of a new video frame.

Film Bounce An unnatural variation in the brightness of a picture.

Film-Out (Film Output) Process of creating a film interpositive or dupe from a digital image.

Film Perforation Also called "perf." The sprocket holes along the edge(s) of film.

Film Processing Exposed negative is treated and stabilized so it can be exposed to light without damage to images on the film.

Film Splice Place where two pieces of film are joined by either glue or tape.

Flash Frames In a film element these are white frames between frames with image on them. In video, these are mistimings in the EDL or editing that leave empty frames between cuts.

Flatbed Can be a Kem, Steinbeck, or other brand of film editing system for viewing picture and track together.

FLEx File Disk 3.5″ floppy computer disk that contains all of the telecine information gathered during a telecine transfer. Can include Keykode numbers, camera-roll identifiers, sound-roll timecode, tape timecode, and text comments.

Flutter Rapid fluctuations in the pitch of recorded sound. Also called "wow."

Foley Sounds added during audio sweetening to enhance ambient sounds, such as footsteps, door closing, and breathing.

Font The lettering style used in character generators.

Formatted Dupe A duplicate negative that has been made from a full frame or anamorphic image that has been formatted to make room for a sound track.

4:2:2 Original digital picture standard.

4:4:4 Twice as much color resolution as 4:2:2, resulting in sharper images and superior multilayering.

480i 480 lines interlaced scanning, is a standard definition television format. About the same resolution as NTSC.

480p 480 lines progressive scanning, is a standard definition television format. About the same resolution as NTSC.

4-Perf Motion picture film that has four perfs or sprockets per film frame.

Frame A compete video image made up of two or three video fields. Also a single film frame.

Frames-per-Second (fps) The speed that film or videotape is running.

Frequency Modulated (FM) A video or audio signal combined with a high frequency signal, encoding two signals into one.

Gain The amplification of a signal to increase its output.

Gigabit One billion bytes.

Gray Scale (Chip Chart) A standard graphic made up of two opposed horizontal nine-step tonal monotone scales (from 3% to 60% reflectance).

Half-Inch Four-Track Analog audiotape with three channels available for sound recording and one channel designated for the timecode channel. Older 1/2″ four-track formats were recorded with sync pulse tone or ranger tone and will have to be transferred to a 35mm mag or a timecoded source in order to play back without drift.

Hazeltine Machine sometimes used to color-correct film prints.

HDTV (High Definition Television) TV signal with extra lines and bandwidths broadcast with a higher resolution than currently used. Aspect ratio is 16:9 with 1125 scan lines.

Head Clog Loss of radio frequency resulting in a loss of a portion of the picture. Occurs when dust, dirt, or other debris passes over the video head during recording.

Heads-Out When the beginning of the material is left on the outside of the reel (as opposed to tails-out).

High Band High resolution VCR format.

High 8MM Semiprofessional analog videotape format. 2-PCM audio channels and 2-linear audio channels. Tapes also used as DA88s.

Horizontal Blanking The blanking signal at the end of each scanning line. The edge stopping point as each line of video is drawn.

Hum Bar A low frequency interference, appearing as a narrow horizontal bar moving vertically through the picture.

Image Enhancement Improvement of video signals through electronic correction using a video processor. Correction can be achieved to increase edge sharpness, noise reduction, and decrease edge "ringing."

IN (Internegative) A duplicating film stock that turns into a negative when printed from a positive print. Used to make opticals, titles, and as a source for making interpositive prints. Can be cut into the original cut negative. Also called dupe negative.

Insert Shots Additional footage often shot during postproduction to create an effect, cutaway shot, or add information.

Interlace Method The making of a TV picture by filling in all odd lines from top to bottom and then going back and filling in all of the even lines. The process is repeated about every 1/30 second.

Interlock Projecting picture and sound track elements together.

IP (Interpositive) A positive print made from an internegative on special film stock. Often preferred for telecine mastering and as a protection element so original negatives can be stored and not used.

IPS (Inches per Second) Refers to the speed at which audio reel-to-reel 1/2″ formats are recorded. Either 7 1/2 or 15 IPS is standard.

IRE The Institute of Radio Engineers, now known as The Institute of Electrical and Electronic Engineers.

IRE Scale A waveform monitor used to measure video signals.

ISO Camera (Isolated Camera) During a tape shoot, shots from the ISO camera are edited "on the fly" by the main production switcher and recorded onto the main VTR. The camera designated as the ISO camera can be varied at any time.

Jam (Jam Sync) Reading existing timecode, then generating a new element with timecode matching exactly to the original element's timecode.

Jitter A momentary loss of synchronization of a video signal. Can affect an individual line of picture or the whole picture.

K Kilo.

Keykode Trademark of Kodak edge numbers. See Edge Numbers.

Keykode Reader Device that reads the bar code along the edge of motion picture film. Attaches to either the telecine or a bench logger. The edge numbers are logged automatically without human error in about 10% of the time it would take for manual entry.

Keylog Disk See FLEx File Disk.

Lab Roll A roll of motion picture film made up of more than one camera roll spliced together. Labs create these rolls for film that will go through telecine so the operator is not constantly changing reels. These rolls are usually built in either 1000 foot or 2000 foot lengths for 35 mm film and 1200 foot lengths for 16 mm film.

Laugh Tracks Audience reactions. Added or enhanced during the dubbing stage. Primarily used for situation comedies.

Layback Laying the completed sweetened audio back to a videotape master.

Laydown Recording sound from an audio source or video element to another audio element. During this process timecode can be added or altered, channel configurations rearranged, or audio levels compressed.

Leader Opaque or clear film attached to the head and tail of film rolls.

Letterbox When a wide-screen image is projected onto a standard television screen, a space is left at the top and the bottom of the screen. Traditionally, this is filled in with black bars.

Lexicon Electronic pitch stabilizer used when speeding up or slowing down sound that you want to sound "normal."

Linear Audio Track Audio recorded along the edge of a videotape.

Locked Cut/Locked Picture Final version of a show after all the changes have been incorporated.

Locon A motion picture print made on low-contrast stock.

LokBox Synchronizing mechanism that locks film and videotape to run backwards or forwards together. Used for negative cutting.

Looping See ADR (Automatic Dialogue Replacement).

LTC (Longitudinal Timecode) Timecode that is recorded on a videotape, audio, or address-track channel. Also called linear or address-track timecode. Can be thought of as video sprocket holes.

Luminance The brightness or contrast of the video signal.

Magenta Track A sound track that utilizes the magenta layer on the film print and redevelopment process. Used for making composite sound prints.

Matrix An encoding device that can mix four sound channels into two stereo channels, which will then be restored to four channels upon playback. The four channels are LCRS or left, center, right and mono surround.

Matte The black bars found at the top and bottom of the picture when a wide screen format is projected on a television set. Or blocking out or cutting around an image in visual effects and graphics.

Megahertz One million cycles per second, represented by 1 MHz.

Microsecond One millionth of a second.

Mixer Sound recordist on a dub or mix stage.

Mixing Also known as audio dubbing. Combining of all sound tracks (dialogue, music, and effects) onto a single master source.

MO Disk (Magneto-Optical Disk) It holds 4.6 gigabytes of information.

Moire Video artifact seen in NTSC pictures along the edges of brightly colored objects, patterns, and graphics. Looks like colored dots or saw-teeth.

Monochrome Black and white.

MOS Term for picture without sound. Acronym used to represent the German slang "mit out sprechen."

Moviola American-made film editing machine.

MOW (Movie of the Week) A two-hour television movie.

Music and Effects (M&E) The sound track that contains just music, and/or sound but no speech or dialogue. Foreign-fill or augmentation is when the music and effects from the domestic stereo track are supplemented to create a track that can be used without the domestic dialogue track.

Nagra Professional 1/4″ audiotape recorder.

Nanosecond One billionth of a second.

Negative The original motion picture film that is bought raw and exposed during shooting and then processed at a film laboratory. Also referred to as original color negative (OCN).

Negative Assembly Film is spliced to create lab rolls, or negative is spliced to create a cut picture. Also referred to as negative cutting.

Negative Dirt Dirt on the film negative element. Can appear white. In some cases it will appear as sparkles across the screen caused by negative dust. Because the film emulsion is very soft, dirt can become embedded into the film stock and can only be removed by being washed by the laboratory (this is called a rewash).

Negative Scratch A scratch in the camera negative or dupe negative. Usually appears white, unless it has penetrated through the yellow, cyan, or magenta layers, in which case it may appear to have a slight tint of color.

Noise Interference in audio or video signals. Audio noise might be a hum or hiss. Video noise might be snow, streaks in picture.

Noise Reduction Electronic reduction of observable grain in the picture. While noise-reduction devices can provide a method of minimizing the discernible grain structure of film, extreme caution should be observed when using them. Unwanted side effects can include strobing and trailing images, reduction in picture resolution, and ringing effects.

Nondrop-Frame Timecode SMPTE timecode that counts continuously 30 frames per second. Does not match exactly to real time.

Nonlinear Editing Assembling video sequences in random order. Shots can be moved, deleted, copied, or changed electronically before being copied to videotape.

NTSC (National Television Standards Committee) The committee that established the color transmission system used in the United States, Canada, Mexico, and Japan. Also refers to the system of 525 lines of information, scanned at approximately 30 frames per second. The broadcast standard for North America.

Off-Line Editing Editing done prior to on-line to create an edit decision list to be used in the final assembly of a program. Applies to video only and can be done electronically or manually.

One-Inch (1″) Reel to reel analog videotape format.

1080i 1080 lines interlaced scanning. A high definition TV format. About twice the vertical resolution and more than twice the horizontal resolution of standard TV. Displayed in the 16 : 9 format.

1080p 1080 lines progressive scanning. A high definition TV format. About twice the vertical resolution and more than twice the horizontal resolution of standard TV. Displayed in the 16 : 9 format.

One-to-One (1 : 1) Transfer of one mag track to another mag track. Also called dupes.

On-Line Editing Final assembly or editing utilizing master tape sources. Usually done on high-quality computer editing system with computer-generated effects.

Opticals Refers to film effects, film titles, and film dissolves and fades. Term has carried over into videotape and is sometimes used to indicate video special effects.

Overdub Adding an audio track over an existing track. Often used in foreign language dubbing where one language track is lowered whenever the new track is being heard.

Overmodulating Too many video signals used when making a radio frequency signal. Results in a buzzing sound from the TV speaker when white lettering appears on the screen.

Overscan Image outside the normal TV viewing area.

Paintbox Digital graphics generator made by Quantel. Paint, pen, and airbrush are available electronically to the graphic artist. A generic term used to describe electronic picture fixes to individual video frames to mask dirt, scratches, and other blemishes.

PAL (Phase Alternating Line) 625 lines of information, 25 frames per second. The broadcast standard for many countries throughout the world.

PAL-M A version of PAL that is 525 lines, 30 frames per second. Used only in South America.

Pan and Scan Selecting parts of each frame from a CinemaScope or widescreen picture for projection on television. Changing the aspect ratio by only projection portions of the picture.

Phase The relationship between two identical sound waves. Proper phasing necessary for combining of mono audio channels without echoing.

Picture Safe Area See Action Safe Area.

Pillar Box Black bars on the sides of the picture. When a 4:3 image is put into a 16:9 aspect ratio, the sides don't fill all the way in without manipulation, so black bars may be placed to fill in the spaces.

Pixels Tiny dots that make up a picture.

Positive Dirt Often built in during printing, this appears black on the screen.

Positive Scratch A scratch in a film print element. Usually appears black on the screen.

Posterization Picture brightness levels reduced giving it a flat poster or cartoon-like look.

Preroll In video editing, it is the amount the videotape machine rolls back so that it will be running at the proper speed when it reaches the edit point. In telecine, it is the amount the telecine, videotape machines, and audio play back machines roll back so they will all be running at the proper speed when the record point is reached. When recording production sound it is vital to provide enough timecoded tape rolling prior to starting to record audio. For example, 1/4″ should have at least 5 seconds of timecoded preroll. DAT requires at least 10 seconds of preroll for use later in telecine.

Prestripe Record timecode onto a tape before recording or editing any audio or video onto it.

Printmaster A stereo mix master audio element consisting of two or four channels of audio.

Producer's Cut Often the final cut prior to picture lock.

Production Sound Audio recorded during principle photography on location.

Progressive Scan Making a computer or TV picture by filling in all of the scan lines sequentially from top to bottom.

QC (Quality Control) The act of scrutinizing audio, video, or film elements for technical specifications and visual/audio defects.

Quarter-Inch (1/4″) Audiotape This is a two-track analog audio recording magnetic tape. There is also a separate center channel for recording timecode or some other sync pulse generated tone.

Raw Stock Unexposed film or audio stock.

Regen (Regenerating) Creating new timecode by use of a timecode generator on an audio or video element.

Release Print A composite theatrical print.

Rendering The filling-in of a computer graphic frame.

Resolution Picture sharpness, usually measured in lines. The greater the number of lines, the sharper the image. Vertical resolution is basically limited by the number of horizontal scanning lines per frame.

Resolve Forcing an audio element to play at a certain speed.

RF (Radio Frequency) A combined audio/video signal that is broadcast through the air from a TV antenna.

RGB (Red, Green, Blue) Primary television colors.

Room Tone The "sound" of a particular room caused by echoes and background noises in the room.

Rough Cut Assembly of edited shots prior to picture lock.

Safe Title Area Center area of a TV screen or monitor that can be seen on any size monitor. Titles are placed there because you know they should show on all size monitors.

SAP (Supplemental Audio Program) Method for broadcasting a third audio channel along with the stereo channels. Often used for Spanish language or video descriptions.

Saturation The vividness of color.

Scoring Refers to the session in which live music is performed and recorded to match an existing picture.

Script Notes A copy of the shooting script prepared by the script supervisor noting camera angles, what lines were recorded by which camera, and the shooting order. Also notes shot lengths and circled takes.

SDTV Standard definition television.

SECAM (Sequential Color and Memory) 625 lines of information, 25 frames per second. The broadcast standard for France, Eastern Europe, and the former Soviet Union.

720p 720 lines progressive scanning. A high definition TV format. Displayed in the 16:9 aspect ratio.

SGI (Silicon Graphics, Inc) A computer manufacturer.

Simo Recording An additional video or audiotape that is recorded along with the master recording. Often used to make production sound backup recording or a small-format work cassette while recording to a master format.

Sitcom (Situation Comedy) Slang that describes a half-hour television comedy.

625 United Kingdom standard specifying the number of horizontal lines used to create a TV picture.

16mm Mag Magnetic 16mm audiotape which can hold up to two separate channels of audio. Contains sprocket holes, so there is no need for timecode for editing.

16mm Optical Track Mono only. Read by a light on a projector or telecine. Contains sprocket holes so there is no need for timecode for editing. For playback only.

16:9 A widescreen television format in which the image is long and narrow compared to today's nearly square television image. The ratio is 16 units wide by 9 units high. Normal television is 4:3.

Skew The control that adjusts the videotape tension in playback. When there is a skew error, the top of the picture flutters or pulls to the side.

SmartSlate Production clapper that includes a lighted readout of the timecode being recorded onto the production sound audiotape.

SMPTE (Society of Motion Picture and Television Engineers) The committee of engineers that set the rules for use of timecode and other technical procedures in the United States and various other countries.

Sound Mix The process of mixing all the sounds that will go into the final form of a movie or other project.

Sound Report Form filled in for each audiotape recorded that describes what is on the tape and any technical instructions for proper playback.

Specifications Usually shortened to "specs." This is a complete list of all the technical and layperson instructions for creating an element.

Splice Joining of two film or audio pieces. Usually done with splicing tape, but can also be "hot waxed."

Spotting Determining where either visual effects or sound and music effects are to be placed.

Standards Converter A device that coverts one standard of video into another (for example, NTSC to PAL).

Steady Gate Transferring film through a pin-registered device to provide a more stable image. Used for green-screen and blue-screen transfers where the separate elements must be steady for accurate compositing. Does not happen in real time.

Stereo Playing or recording two separate audio channels at once. One channel represents what the left ear would hear, the other represents what the right ear would hear. Requires two audio channels.

Stripe Record timecode onto a tape.

Super VHS (S-VHS) VHS format using special tape and yielding 400 lines of resolution.

Sweetening Enhancing sound or video that already exists. Video sweetening is also referred to as color correction.

Sync (Synchronous) Lining up proper picture with its matching sound. In dailies, when you hear the clapper close and see it at the same moment, it is considered "in sync."

Sync Sound Sound that is recorded with the intention of being married to a picture at an exact point.

SYQUEST A removable computer hard disk that is popular for moving graphics files between locations.

Tails-Out When the end of the material is left on the outside of the reel.

Tearing Displacement of a group of horizontal video lines from their normal position.

Telecine Equipment for transferring film to videotape. The equipment used is a movie projector/TV camera combination.

Telecine Floppy Disk See FLEx File Disk.

Temp Dub Temporary music and effects added to a rough cut version of a project for network or studio screening.

35MM Mag Magnetic audiotape that can hold up to six tracks of audio. Contains sprocket holes, so there is no need for timecode for editing.

35MM Optical Track Two-track (mono or stereo) audio format. Contains sprocket holes, so there is no need for timecode for editing.

Three-Perf Motion picture film that has three perforations or sprocket holes per film frame. Allows one to photograph 25% more image than the same amount of four-perf film. Requires a special telecine gate and edgecode reading software.

Three-Quarter-Inch (3/4″) Videotape Magnetic tape stock for playback and record. Contains two channels of audio and a separate timecode channel. Most commonly used for off-line editing and viewing cassettes.

3:2 Pulldown The formula used to convert 24 frames per second of film to 30 frames per second of video.

Time Base Corrector Electronic device to remove jitter and other timing abnormalities from a video signal.

Timecode The numbering system adopted by SMPTE that assigns a number to each video frame indicating hours, minutes, seconds, and frames.

Timecode Generator An electronic device that outputs timecode.

TK3:2 A high-quality device that converts NTSC to PAL. A few facilities have a reverse TK3:2 that will convert from PAL to NTSC.

Transfer A general term for recording from one source to another element.

Tri-Standard Monitor A TV that will display NTSC, PAL, or SECAM pictures.

Two-Inch (2″) 24-Track Analog magnetic tape with 22 channels of audio and two channels available for timecode and sync pulse. Very popular in feature audio mixing and dubbing and in the professional audio arena.

Underscan Altering the height and width of the image on a video monitor so the edges of the signal and blanking can be seen.

User Bits Areas in the vertical interval where various information, such as Keykode and various timecodes can be recorded. User bits have eight digits.

Varispeed Changing the frame rate of the playback of either film or videotape to lengthen or shorten the duration.

Vertical Blanking The blanking signal which occurs at the end of each field.

Vertical Interval Area in a video signal where nonvideo information such as time-code and captioning are stored. This information cannot be seen without the signal running through a decoder. For example, traditionally, closed-captioning information is placed on line 21, but you cannot see closed captioning on your TV set unless you are running your signal through a box that decodes the information and puts it in a window on your screen. Similarly, such information as linear timecode (VITC), audio timecode, Keykode, foot and frame, camera roll, scene, and take information can be encoded into this area. This needs to be done at the point when the information can be accessed. For example, if you will need Keykode information down the line you will need to make sure the Keykode information is gathered when the film is being laid down during the film-to-tape session.

VHS Tape Video home system 1/2″ videotape. This is a consumer format and can record two channels of analog plus two channels of high fidelity (hi-fi) audio. Used primarily for viewing cassettes and occasionally for off-line editing. A very unreliable tape stock in which playback can vary from machine to machine, making picture tracking an issue when used by music composers and off-line editing.

Video Level How strong a video level is.

Visible Timecode Timecode burned into a video picture so it can be seen when viewing the picture.

VITC (Vertical Interval Timecode) is timecode stored in the vertical interval signal of the video. Professional videotape machines can read VITC in either the play or the jog (manual) mode, making it ideal for editing.

VO (Voice Over) Ancillary dialogue, separate from the dialogue track and recorded separately on a sound stage.

VU Meter Measures the strength of a video signal. A 0 VU level is considered the optimum sound level and is usually used as tone reference.

Wetgate Print A print created using a chemical process that coats the print, hopefully filling in digs and scratches or imperfections that occur in the negative to help restore the image.

White Balance The mix of primary colors that equal pure white light. An adjustment in a camera that assures no color overpowers the others and the whites are not tinted.

Wild Sound Audio recorded without a sync relationship to specific picture.

Work Print Positive print of original negative used in a film cutting room. Print dailies are called work print.

Zip Drive A removable computer hard disk that is useful for moving graphics files between locations.

Index